"A cards-on-the-table binge-read.... ___ ... +o ɦours. Couldn't put it down."   —Lauren Daley, *Boston Globe*

"Andre Dubus III's idea of an essay is tantalizingly simple: tell something important that happened to him—suddenly having big money and not knowing quite how to cope with that, loving his long-divorced parents, growing up poor and outlasting it, not loving his dog as much as he worries he should. Here is human life often cloaked in transporting mystery. Dubus possesses a rare and empathetic brilliance."   —Richard Ford, author of
Independence Day and *Canada*

"Andre Dubus III is a literary treasure. These tender, elegant essays come to us directly from his battered heart, his noble soul, his powerful reckoning with the legacy of his childhood. To read this book is to touch the pulsing core of what it is to be human."
                    —Dani Shapiro, author of *Signal Fires*

"Andre Dubus III is a poet of masculinity. In the lyrical autobiographical essays of *Ghost Dogs*, he limns not toxic masculinity but its opposite: a masculinity rooted in family life, love, and hope. . . . In carefully crafted words, Dubus III both records and enacts his transcendence of the often brutal facts of his upbringing and our time."   —Elissa Greenwald, *New York Journal of Books*

"Dubus's sentences glide on a level pitch before seamlessly dovetailing into the poetically poignant. Within Dubus's vast heart lies a pugilist intent on defeating his own demons."
                    —*Booklist*, starred review

GHOST DOGS

GHOST
DOGS

ON KILLERS
AND KIN

ANDRE DUBUS III

W. W. NORTON & COMPANY
Independent Publishers Since 1923

Ghost Dogs is a work of nonfiction. Individual names and potentially identifying details have been altered in certain cases.

Copyright © 2024 by Andre Dubus III

Since this page cannot legibly accommodate all the copyright notices, pages 276–77 constitute an extension of the copyright page.

For information about permission to reproduce selections from this book, write to Permissions, W. W. Norton & Company, Inc., 500 Fifth Avenue, New York, NY 10110

For information about special discounts for bulk purchases, please contact W. W. Norton Special Sales at specialsales@wwnorton.com or 800-233-4830

Manufacturing by Lakeside Book Company
Design by Daniel Lagin
Production manager: Louise Mattarelliano

Library of Congress Control Number: 2024947716

ISBN 978-1-324-10504-6 pbk.

W. W. Norton & Company, Inc., 500 Fifth Avenue, New York, N.Y. 10110
www.wwnorton.com

W. W. Norton & Company Ltd., 15 Carlisle Street, London W1D 3BS

1 0 9 8 7 6 5 4 3 2 1

For Fontaine, Austin, Ariadne, and Elias

*And in memory of Fern and Elmer Lowe, Jeannie Owens,
Mary and George Dollas, and my father, Andre Dubus*

CONTENTS

FENCES AND FIELDS

—⸎—

t was a dry summer, and so hot it was a mistake to go barefoot on the sidewalk. When a rare breeze blew off the ocean one
or two miles east, we could hear the rattle of leaves in the tree
branches, smell the soft rubber and hot metal of cars in the street
and driveway. Every Saturday I would drive to my father's house
to cut his grass, but that summer I could wait three weeks or more
before the yellowed lawn needed a trim. Joggers exercised only after
dark. Dogs slept all day in the shade of maples and beech, or under
parked cars I'd worry would drive over them the way I drove over
my own dog, Dodo, when I was nineteen. At night we kept all our
windows open and I put two fans in my son's room, one to suck
hot air out the screen, the other directed at his crib, where he slept
in only a diaper, his curly hair matted in wet ringlets to his temples
and neck. In the other bedroom I lay alongside my wife and waited
for sleep with my hand on her swollen belly, the olive skin there
stretched tight. Our second child's due date had come and gone two

weeks earlier; my wife's mother and aunt had stayed with us then, but no contractions came, and my mother-in-law had to go back to work. So now we waited.

Those days I was doing carpentry work just two blocks from our house, building a gate and fence in a treeless yard. Between postholes, I had to dig a trench a foot deep, and by midmorning I'd be wearing only shorts and boots, headband and bug spray, my torso slick with sweat, my hair as wet as if I'd just gotten cool. Every time I heard the ring of a phone coming from someone's house, I would pause in my work and look up, and whenever a car drove slowly by, I'd wait for it to stop, expecting to see my lovely pregnant wife, her belly a full curved promise, come to tell me it was time.

One morning, as I was setting in my second post, holding my level to it, poised to kick more dirt into the hole once I'd found plumb, I heard breathing that wasn't my own and turned to see a little girl squinting at me in the sunlight. She was thin, her pale arms and legs poking out of clothes that didn't match: a sleeveless green and yellow flowered shirt, faded pink shorts with white ruffles on the hem, red sneakers with no socks, and white ankles coated with dust from the street and dry backyards. Her hair was dusty too, and so straight and fine that her normal ears stuck out. I think I blurted out a startled hello but she just pointed to the four-foot level I was still holding to the post: "So what are you doing with *that?*"

"Trying to make the post straight up and down."

"I'll help you," she said, and kicked in some dirt before I was ready. It was after coffee break, the morning shade from the house gone now, and the cool dark soil I'd shoveled earlier was already dry and cracked and flaking under my boots. My headband was saturated, the sweat beginning to burn my eyes, and this trench was taking longer than I'd estimated; I was beginning to fear I'd given too low a price for the work. At home there was a whole new cycle of bills coming in and I still didn't have another job lined up after this one and I felt sure our new baby would come any minute. I wanted to get this fence done as soon as I could; I wanted this little girl to go play somewhere else.

I asked her not to kick in any dirt until I said to. She stood quickly, looked over the job site, then picked up the spade shovel, its handle twice as long as she was.

"Now?"

I found myself nodding and she squatted and scraped a small mound of dirt into the hole, the shovel knocking against the post. I pushed in more and tamped it with my boot. She dropped the shovel and began to stomp around the base of the four-by-four, her thin leg fitting all the way into the hole, her red sneaker leaving nothing more than light prints in the soil. But we got into a rhythm. We set that post, then another, and I knew the job wasn't going any faster with her, but not slower, either, and as we worked I asked her name and told her mine. I asked if she lived in one of the houses nearby, and did her parents know where she was.

"My mom thinks I'm at my friend's. I don't have a father, just a stepfather. Well, he's not really my stepfather, just my mother's boyfriend. They're gonna get married when they save enough money."

A jug of spring water sat near my tool bag and she walked over, uncapped it, and drank. The jug was half empty but she had to hold it with two hands and she spilled some water onto her flowered shirt. She put the cap back on, then left it leaning against the tools and hurried back to the new posthole. "I was *thirsty*."

I was holding the level to the four-by-four. I considered telling her it's polite to ask someone for a sip of their water before drinking it, but I was glad I'd had the water when she needed it so let it go. "Do you ever see your father?"

"He died when I was little." She looked up at me and made a

sad face, as if she were no longer sad but felt that she still should be, that it wouldn't be right to say her father was dead without showing me her downturned lips.

"Do you remember him?"

Now she did look sad, her gray-blue eyes looking off into the dry brush at the yard's edge. "Know what I wish?"

"What?"

"That he was here and my mom was with *him* and she didn't even *know* her *boyfriend.*"

Something fell away inside me. I began to get an image I didn't want of this tiny girl lost under some man. I said her name and she looked at me, her eyes not quite seeing me.

"Does your mother's boyfriend treat you okay? Is he good to you?"

She shrugged. "Nah, he doesn't even look at us." She began to kick more dirt into the posthole and I let out a breath.

"He doesn't?"

"He hardly remembers our *names.*"

A breeze picked up. It blew a feathering of sawdust into the trench. It cooled my back and legs. The girl's fine hair blew sideways in her face, and as she worked she reached up with her finger and stuck a loose strand behind one ear. I guessed her to be eight or nine years old, but at that moment, pulling the hair from her face so she could keep working and not stop, her eyes on what she was doing but not really, she looked for a moment like every hard-time girl and woman I'd ever worked with in halfway houses and group homes and pre-parole. They were either lean and scrappy or else obese and resilient; they moved with intent or didn't move much at all, but smoked cigarette after cigarette, drank too much coffee or Diet Coke, talked too loud or kept silent—all of them, it seemed, doing essentially this: stomping dirt into a hole with a tiny red shoe, trying to cover and bury and hide their solitary hearts.

I called her name.

"What?" She pulled her leg out of the hole, picked up the too-long shovel, and began to push in more soil.

"Your dad will always be with you, you know."

She straightened and looked at me, the shovel hanging in her hands; her mouth hung partly open and in her eyes was a tentative light. I'd seen that look on my two-and-a-half-year-old son whenever I would try to explain away something common that frightened him, like a balloon or a clown's face; when each word I spoke was a step on the high wire over the valley of his normal fears and terrors. She blinked and looked at me harder, and for a second I was afraid my choice of words would be wrong, that I'd stumble and drop her into a worse place than she'd been before. But this doubt faded quickly; I began to imagine being dead, with my young child still on earth, and I felt sure I was telling her the absolute truth.

"Your father loves you too much to leave you alone. He'll watch over you your whole life."

"He will?" Now her eyes were bright and alert.

"Of course he will. He's probably watching over you right now."

"Can I *see* him?"

"Probably not."

She looked down at the shovel in her hands.

"But you might be able to feel him, sometimes." The breeze picked up again. It blew through the brush and high grass at the yard's edge. It began to dry the sweat on my neck and upper back. "Feel this wind? That could be him trying to cool you off."

She cocked her head at me, skeptical, standing as still as if her very body was in danger of plummeting into deep disappointment.

5

I began to wish I'd kept quiet, once again in my life wrestling with the question of what true helping really was.

We continued working, the sun directly over us. The breeze died down, then blew in one last time. I felt a chill and knew it was sunburn. My post was leaning out of plumb and I put the level to it, then tamped the dirt at the base. She dropped the shovel for me to pick up and use, I thought, but as I reached for it I glanced at her and saw her standing there in the hot breeze, her eyes closed, her chin raised slightly, a solitary strand of hair quivering against her cheek, her small dirty hands held up close to her chest.

We worked together until almost lunchtime. She abandoned the shovel and began to pull the dirt into the hole with her hands. The air was heavy and so hot my lungs felt tender. The girl's mother called her from the front stoop three doors down and out of sight. Her voice was shrill and coarse. From too much daily yelling, I imagined, too much alcohol and cigarette smoke, too much of one thing and not enough of another, and I wanted to protect my young helper from it. She jerked at the sound, dropped the shovel, and without a word cut through the backyard the way she'd come, wiping her hands off on her pink shorts, leaving light footprints in the sawdust and dirt.

Soon after, I covered my tools with a tarp and walked home for lunch, and I think I knew then our second child would be a girl, that I would be the father of a son and a daughter. I think I made yet another silent prayer for our baby to be born safely, for my wife to come through it well, and that if the baby was a *boy* to please not be hurt that I'd had the premonition of a girl. But as I walked down the shaded street, I began to sense deeply we *would* have a girl and that loving a daughter would be different from loving a son.

And then she was born; early on an August afternoon when it was almost a hundred degrees and there was a full moon we couldn't see in the cloudless sky, she came. After twenty hours of labor there was the blinding light of the operating room, my exhausted wife's bright blood, our daughter coming headfirst out of the incision, her hazel eyes wide open and a nurse almost jumping back from the table. I held my tiny daughter and she cried and I cried and her valiant mother cried, lying on the table, the surgeons still working on her behind a raised blue sheet.

Later, as my wife began to recover in her room and our son played with his grandmother and aunts and our baby girl slept in the hospital nursery, a pink name tag attached to her clear plastic bassinet, I went outside into the heat with my brother and father. We drove to a package store, then to the river two blocks from the hospital, its banks thick with trees. We sat in the shade at the edge of a jogging path, my father in his wheelchair, my brother and I sitting on a railroad tie. It was late afternoon and we were sweating under our clothes. A hundred yards away on the other side of the jogging path was a softball field, and people were playing, men and women, I think, though it could have been teenagers, their voices high with a winded purpose that sometimes sounded cruel to me. Already I wanted to keep that sound from ever entering my tiny daughter's ears, and her older brother's too. We could see the sunlight on the water through the trees, and we drank beer and smoked our cigars. I began to speak, though I could not do it without crying, for the word *daughter* was ringing through my blood, her name already deep in my heart with her brother's, as if both had been there since my own delivery nearly thirty-six years earlier. With my son's birth, a love had opened up in me that forever left my small heart behind the way a flood scatters sandbags. And now the walls of my heart seemed to fall away completely and become a green field inside me. Through tears I told my father and brother how much I felt, and that even that faithless corner of my heart that worried about money, worried that once this fence job was through nothing would follow—even that part of me was assuaged. Because how can there be green fields inside us and no food on our tables?

My brother had a disposable camera and he was taking pictures of me, but I was seeing a picture of him, twenty-three years old, holding his blue-eyed baby boy, whispering to him, a mischievous and delighted smile on his son's face, playing imaginary games on the floor with him, eating cheese and crackers at the table, painting pictures, laughing, all before he had to drive him back home to his mother. I told my brother I loved him and grieved for his truncated fatherhood. I told him I knew his son would be in his life more fully one day, a presumptuous thing to say, and again I found myself on the verbal high wire over the depths of another's pain. But I was certain what I said was true, and as my brother, father, and I wept, I knew I would feel none of this certainty without my baby daughter and lovely son, without the horizonless love and attendant faith and hope that opens up in us when we are given the gift of children.

A woman jogged by, my age or older. Her T-shirt was wet with sweat, the wires of her bra were easy to see, and her hips wide beneath jogging shorts. I think she glanced in our direction as she passed, her flushed face a mask she'd chosen to give us—three men drinking and smoking in the mottled heat. It said: *I can take care of myself and I can outrun you, and I will if I have to.* And I felt so keenly then that my new child was a female and not a male, and I wanted to shield my daughter from all the forces that had ever put that look on that woman's face. I wanted to stand and say: "It's okay, we're *fathers*. We're *fathers*!" But I of course knew better; she could not see the green fields inside us—and how many fathers had torched their own fields and burned their children, leaving their own hearts nothing but ashen caves they continued to poke around in as if they were still living?

My beer can was empty. The sting of sweat was in my eyes, and I squinted out at the sun on the river through the tree trunks. I remembered last winter at a restaurant in Boston, a friend in his forties saying over a Thai dinner that he would never bring children into such a violent and ugly world. My wife was sitting pregnant beside me and he apologized, and his girlfriend, who was the mother of a twenty-year-old daughter, turned to him and said, "But you can't have a child without having hope, too. It comes with the birth."

I glanced over at my father. I am his second child of six, and he looked broad and handsome in the wheelchair that would be his legs for the rest of his life. His forehead was beaded with sweat, his eyes ringed and moist. I saw pride and love in his eyes, pride and love from his two weeping sons. I believe he still grieved the three broken marriages behind him and knew the pain it caused us, his children, and he knew all too well the challenges facing our own young marriages. But sitting there then, his beard gray and white, I saw only hope in his eyes, hope for all of us.

But hope is one-dimensional without resolve, and in the last few moments I'd been picturing my baby girl still alone in the hospital nursery, swaddled in her clear plastic bassinet, her mother recovering from surgery while her father smoked and drank down by the river. Yet, I knew I was doing far more than that: I was communing with my father and only brother; I was sinking back into the arms of all the manhood I would need and more; I was celebrating the historic and ephemeral moment of my daughter's birth, which was already fading away and becoming something else, the first hours of her infancy.

I stood, and as we drove the two blocks back to the hospital, our windows open, the hot August air blowing in our faces, I thought of that fatherless girl who started coming daily to the job site to work with me, her dirty ankles thin and bony, her fine hair clinging to her skull, her small face already beginning to take on the same mask as that woman jogger. And I imagined her father's spirit fighting deep sky and rains and wind to be her breeze in the heat of a small dirty yard, to hold her upturned face in his airy hands, to gently thumb a strand of her hair from her eye, her face—in that moment, as open and vulnerable as a newborn's; and I could hardly sit still. I wanted to be in the hospital nursery cradling my baby daughter in my arms, her entire body fitting from elbow to palm; I wanted to smell her new skin and hair; I wanted to kiss her sleeping eyes and rock her and hold her to my chest, her tiny ear and cheek pressed to where she could feel the beating of her father's heart—my grateful, hopeful heart.

THE GOLDEN ZONE

— ‹‹•›› —

We were hunting a man who got paid to kill people. He was bisexual, and his preferred weapon was an Uzi submachine gun that left its victims nearly unidentifiable. He was employed by a powerful organization with a lot of money to spend and more to lose, and somehow, at age twenty-three, I found myself in Denver in my beat-up Subaru doing surveillance on the apartment of the killer's girlfriend, hoping he'd show up, hoping he wouldn't.

Her apartment was on the first floor of a complex on the edge of the city. Beyond it the plains stretched to the mountains, soft with smog, and every afternoon I'd park my car in the space facing her unit. Up in Boulder, my girlfriend had left me months earlier, and I lived in a motel room in the shadows of the Flatirons where I wrote fiction every morning, an act that was making me less of a participant and more of a witness, but if I considered the risk I was now taking, I would probably do it anyway. I was a young and reckless recorder of others, traits my boss must've seen immediately as fitting the kind of work he did on the side and sometimes needed help with; Christof and I worked together in a halfway house for convicted adult felons out of Cañon City Penitentiary, and he also owned a bounty hunting business that specialized in going after people who'd done terrible things. This one had a $250,000 price on his head.

His girlfriend was ten years older than I was. She wore Nike sweat suits and had dark hair she kept in a braid down her back. From where I parked every afternoon, I had a direct view of her profile as she sat on the couch and watched television. Sometimes she'd be reading something at the same time, a book or a magazine in her lap, and every few seconds she'd glance up at the screen I couldn't see. Because of the time of day, I assumed she watched soap operas. She talked on the phone a lot, too. Every hour or so, she'd go to the kitchen and come back with what looked like a yogurt or a plate of crackers or a glass of something to sip. Most of the time she'd be watching TV, talking on the phone, and reading all at once. Sometimes she'd hang up, set the magazine down, and walk to the bathroom. I'd watch her turn on a bright fluorescent light, a red shower curtain hanging there, then she'd close the door.

I'd stare and I'd wait. It was something I was used to now. But it wasn't me waiting, it was the other me, Christof's associate with the fake name, that's what it felt like, as if I were watching myself the way I was now watching characters come and go on the page, a dangerous thing to do, for these were real people with real guns, people who would not tolerate being watched.

———

A HALF-MOON SHONE WEAKLY OVER OLAS ALTAS BAY. I WAS LEANing on a concrete seawall peering down into the pale darkness at rats on the beach. They were shadows of movement below, scurrying from the cracked shells of coconuts, an empty Pacifico bottle, a withered palm frond, and the carcasses of roosterfish and dorado thrown off a boat when the sun still shone over Sinaloa and the Sierra Madre and this port of Old Mazatlán.

Christof stood beside me in his white linen suit. He was over six feet and two hundred and thirty pounds and wore a straw cowboy hat tilted back on his head. In the darkness his handlebar mustache looked blacker than it was. He was reciting a Neruda poem in Spanish. The air smelled like dead fish and crumbling concrete and the sea.

It would have been easier if we'd found our killer in Denver, but the word from the US Marshals was that he'd been seen in Mazatlán, a place outside of their jurisdiction but not ours. The plan was to find him, then give the location to Christof's Mexican friends, who would then capture him, tie him up, throw him on a boat, and sail up the coast to the waters off San Diego where the US Marshals and DEA would pick him up, that promised six-figure bounty so unreal to me I didn't even think about it. Now I was leaning on the seawall along Avenida del Mar in the moonlight, listening to Neruda and the scurry of rats, the lapping of the water along the sand. Christof and I had just come from a gay bar called Caballo Loco, a place our killer had been many times before. It was a small one-story building set into a hillside of mimosa and morning glory trees. Christof told me the Mazatlecos called them *palos del muerto*, sticks of the dead. Drink from the waters near it, and you'd go crazy. Maybe I was already crazy.

The bar was warm and dim, its window shutters open to the salt air. The floor and walls were tiled with brown porcelain, blue flowers and vines painted along the edges, and a jukebox in the corner was playing Julio Iglesias, the room crowded with men, some standing at the bar, others sitting in twos at small wooden tables that held a burning lantern and their glasses of beer or jiggers of tequila or snifters of brandy. Some were smoking, others were kissing or holding hands, and I didn't like how a muscular man at the bar kept looking me up and down, his eyes lingering on my ass as Christof and I found a table and sat down.

Christof wore leather sandals, that white linen suit, and an open-collared silk shirt. In the low flickering light of the table, he looked healthy and gay. Which is what I was supposed to be, too. Just a gay tourist with my boyfriend in a bar on the water. Again, this weakening boundary between my imaginary world on the page and what I was now doing in this bar in Sinaloa, simply allowing myself to drift into the skin of another, this time a gay man with a name that wasn't my own nor even the one the federal and state agents knew me by. Just before we flew to Mazatlán, Christof sent me to Denver to pick up the latest mug shots of our killer. I stood in an office on the thirty-seventh floor of a skyscraper overlooking downtown Denver and the plains. The agent was in his fifties and wore a pink shirt and gray tie, the handle of his gun an oiled walnut. He was standing behind a counter. He slid the sheet of photos over to me. "Be careful down there. These aren't nice people."

I thanked him and left. In the elevator I studied the killer's face. I'd seen his picture before, but these were clear close-ups and it was like seeing the face of a cousin who'd died before you were born, the awakening sense of being connected somehow, sharing something you barely knew you had. He was twenty-nine years old, half Italian, half Irish, a kid of the streets who had turned his rage into a job, and he was handsome the way mill town brawlers I'd grown up with were handsome, something cut or chipped or broken off his face, this breaking worn as defiantly as a family name.

A shirtless teenage boy came to our table. He held an empty tray at his side, and Christof ordered a brandy for him and a soda water for me. For this trip I wasn't drinking. It was a decision that seemed to rise out of the Mexican earth soon after we landed. It hadn't been a long flight, but how could we have arrived so soon at a world so far from our own? We sat in the back of a white shuttle van, and I stared out at the glare of sun on scrub and mesquite among the low rolling hills. Off in the distance was a brown ridge, at its base a grove of thorn trees, Christof told me. Then he pointed out a tall strangler fig, and in its shadow a jackrabbit raised its nose and disappeared.

Then came the homes of the poor. Tiny shacks made from discarded or stolen street signs, sections of billboard advertising Carta Blanca or Coca-Cola, corrugated tin for the walls or half a roof, the other half open or covered by a ripped tarp or construction plastic or canvas. Beside one was a rusted-out Datsun pickup truck, two boys squatting in its shade in the dirt. They were barefoot and shirtless, their black hair dusty, and they were playing some kind of game at their feet with rocks or rusted bolts. Then we were in the narrow streets of Mazatlán, the stone and plaster walls of shops and houses, many with enclosed courtyards in the shade of coconut palms, flowers snaking along the tops of walls and spilling over: cardinal sage and spider lily, pink trumpet and *mata ratón*. Again, words Christof gave me, and I was learning this about words: once you knew the names of things, you saw them clearly for the first time.

The driver's window was down now. I could smell car exhaust and frying tortillas from the marketplace, El Mercado in the Centro Histórico. Even these words from a language I did not speak, they too had the power to make me more here in Mazatlán, and so when Christof asked if I wanted a cold *cerveza*, I heard myself saying, "No, I want to stay awake."

Now the moon was low, and Christof and I were walking away from the rats on the beach back to the hotel. We'd stayed at the Caballo Loco for that one drink, long enough to see that our killer was not there. Two tables over sat the only other white man in the place. He was small with gray hair he'd combed to the side, his lavender button-down shirt pressed, his hand in the hand of a Mazatleco my age. He had long black hair cut unevenly, and he wore a dirty T-shirt, ripped jeans, and sandals. On the way out, Christof stopped and said hello to the American, who was drunk and began to talk openly about himself, as if our very presence demanded that he confess he was a retired professor from Minnesota here on vacation. The Mazatleco beside him wasn't smiling. He looked up at us as if we were interrupting him in his work and didn't like it. Outside, we waited for our *pulmonía*, one of the open-topped taxis that ran day and night from Old Mazatlán to Zona Dorada. Christof said, "That young man with the professor?"

"Yeah?"

"He probably has a wife and kids."

"And he's gay?"

"No, he's poor. He does what he has to do."

———

WE STEPPED OUT OF THE *PULMONÍA* AND INTO THE HOTEL BELMAR, its plaster façade pink and white, its arched entrance open to the sea air. During a Carnival ball in 1944, the governor of Sinaloa was shot to death in the lobby. His murderer had used a .45-caliber pistol, its bullets still sunk in the tiled column after having passed through the governor's torso. Now, as I got closer to that column, I stopped and looked again at those nickel-sized holes. I pushed my fingertips into them, felt cool mortar and wood, a tiny fragment of

lead; there was so much to know and to have known, so much to
do and have done, and one life was just not enough to live it all.

The next morning I sat in the shade of a fan palm in the Mercado Pino Suárez. I was sipping hot coffee and watching Christof
pass out gifts to *los mutados*, the deaf-mutes of Mazatlán. They
were boys who lived in the street, the oldest maybe eighteen, the
youngest nine or ten, and because Christof had been coming here
for years and was fluent in sign language as well as Spanish, he'd
befriended them, would bring them new Converse and Nike sneakers, T-shirts and shorts and socks. They were crowded around him
in the morning sun, a dozen or more thin brown boys laughing and
speaking with their hands and faces, two or three of them peering
over Christof's shoulder to see what else he'd pull from his plastic
trash bag. Christof was clearly happy doing this. He was sitting on
a bench, his face shadowed beneath his straw cowboy hat, laughing, speaking slowly in Spanish for the lip readers, handing out box
after box to boys whose feet might not even fit into shoes they were
already pulling on without socks.

There was a breeze from the water. I could smell frying tortillas and coffee, dead fish and cigar smoke and sweet *mata ratón*.
The marketplace was filled with men and women and kids, most
of them working their vendor carts, one heavy with raw cuts of
beef and pork on ice, others stacked with papayas, mangoes, and
bananas. From where I sat I watched a tall tourist buy a coconut
from a Mazatleco who then cut it in half and squeezed lime juice
onto it and sprinkled it with salt and chile powder and handed it to
him on a paper sack. There were carts of woven sombreros hanging on hooks, folded shawls striped orange and yellow and the
dulled red of sunset. There were beaded necklaces and crucifixes
and carved figurines of Jesus next to a rack of black T-shirts with

hot pink lettering: *Mazatlán*. In the shade behind me, old men sat on a short stone wall talking and smoking cigars and spitting at their feet. At their backs was a stand of banyan trees, their gray roots clawing up their own trunks like the ghosts of ancestors refusing to leave, and high in the branches was a parrot, its squawk lost in the voices below, the honking *pulmonías* in the street, a guitar strumming Spanish chords, and was that really an iguana walking languidly under the sun not far from my feet? Was Christof really showing the mutes photos of our killer? Yes, he was, for nobody paid attention to these homeless deaf boys, he'd told me. People said and did anything in front of them because they didn't see them as full human beings. But give *los mutados* a day and a night, and if our man is still here, they'll know where.

———

TWELVE HOURS LATER, WE WERE IN THE BACK OF A COVERED TAXI driving down a rutted country road. The driver took it slowly, his car bouncing in and out of dips in the packed dirt, and Christof was drunk and singing a love song in Spanish. The driver ignored him. In the months I'd known Christof, I'd never seen him drunk. It seemed a strange thing to be under the circumstances. We had just eaten marlin tacos at an open-air restaurant in the Plazuela Machado, and while Christof drank margaritas, I'd kept to soda water. My abstinence was beginning to feel like a pose of some kind, but there was an easy clarity that came with it, a constant alertness, and now that I knew we would be hunting our killer out in the country, I'd gotten nervous and wanted to stay as ready as I could. I told Christof I'd feel better if we had guns.

"Why?"

"Because he does, doesn't he?"

Christof narrowed his eyes at me, pursed his lips beneath his mustache. At another restaurant across the plazuela, a mariachi band was moving from table to table, their black sombreros tilted way back on their heads as they played.

"Gun energy invites gun energy."

"What?"

"I've been doing this a long time. I've never needed a gun."

"What if we see him at this place in the country?"

"We call my friend."

"Does *he* have guns?"

"Oh yes, many."

At the next table, an American woman laughed and leaned in close to her date. She kept one finger on the rim of her wineglass, and she was speaking softly to him, smiling, and I heard myself say to Christof, "I'm curious what it's like."

"*Qué?*"

"To pay for it. To drive someplace and pay a stranger for it."

———

AFTER DINNER CHRISTOF HIRED A TAXI. ON THE WAY OUT OF Mazatlán, as we moved farther from the water and deeper into the side streets, there were the homes of the working poor, one-story, two-room shanties of bleached wood timbers and cracked plaster, of scrap and stone behind fences of rusted wire or battered planks, fan palms leaning over them like sullen teenage boys. Some didn't have electricity or running water, and dogs lay in cool dirt near the stoops, and it was like being on my hometown streets again, the gut-sick giddiness that only trouble can be found here. And then eight or nine young men were piling into the bed of a pickup truck, each of them carrying a rifle or shotgun or pistol. One had a red bandanna tied loosely around his throat. We could see them in the shine of the taxi's lights as they sped off, two or three glancing back at us like we were a half-forgotten memory, the wind blowing the hair around their young faces.

"The fuck is *that* about?"

Christof took in my question. He was in his white linen jacket again, and he turned and asked the driver something in Spanish. The answer was only two or three words.

"*Sí, sí.*" Christof looked back at me. "Drugs. One gang going off to fight another."

Then we were driving through low dry hills in the moonlight, moving in and out of ruts in the road. Christof was singing "Cucurrucucú." Somewhere behind us to the west, away from the tourist hotels of the Golden Zone, those boys could already be shooting at other boys, and if I'd been raised here with nothing, what could have kept me from doing the same thing? Was aiming your shotgun at another's chest, then pulling the trigger, that much different from punching and kicking him in the head?

Yes, I thought, and no, but they were on the same continuum you fall into after breaking through that part of you that once broken stays broken; what I'd known, though, felt small compared to what these boys knew and when the driver stopped in front of a half-abandoned motel in the darkness, I felt young and vulnerable and now too reckless for my own good, especially when the driver turned the taxi around and drove away, his headlights jerking up and down through our dust that hadn't even settled yet.

We stood in front of a cinder-block compound. At the far corner, bugs flew at an exterior light shining onto weeds and a steel barrel cut in two. Beyond that lay the sign for this place, its letters too rusted to read. A soft blue light glowed on the other side of the open doorway. Freddy Fender was singing on the jukebox, and Christof and I stepped inside.

The blue light came from a neon sign for a tequila I hadn't

heard of. It hung over the bar to our right, the bartender nodding at us as we came in, the stools empty. Scattered throughout
the room were small folding tables and mismatched chairs, and it
was so dark I didn't at first see the women sitting along the wall,
twelve or thirteen of them. Some were smoking and talking over
Freddy Fender's song, which ended, and I could hear their voices,
the everyday sound of women chatting in a hair salon, and now
more music began to play, something with more brass, the singer's
Spanish tiredly festive.

Christof and I sat down at a table in the center of the empty
room. A woman walked over in a loose T-shirt and jeans, and in
the bar's blue light I could see she was older, in her fifties or sixties,
her lipstick black in that blue. She was explaining something to us
in Spanish.

"*Sí, sí*," Christof said to her. He nodded and said something
else and the woman turned and went to the bar. I asked him what
she'd told him.

"The house rules."

I looked back at the women. Some were sitting, others standing. Most were in short skirts or tight dresses, and even in that blue
shadow I could see the dark smear of their lipstick and eyeliner.
Every one of them was staring back at us.

"What *are* the house rules?"

"We have to pick who we want. It cuts down on infighting
amongst the señoras and señoritas."

The older woman set a brandy in front of Christof and an iced
drink in front of me. I told her *gracias* and sipped soda water and
lime juice, and now I wasn't as curious as I'd been back in Mazatlán. Choosing one would be like picking a cut of meat from a vendor in El Mercado. Choosing one would be not choosing another.
And how could I even be doing this? This would only help to enrich

the son of a bitch they worked for; this could only help run the machine that exploited them. I wasn't even aroused at the thought of being with one of them, there was only my desire to know what it felt like to be doing this, to stand and walk through the blue darkness to a line of women against the wall, to move quickly for the one with short hair and a pretty face who smiled at me and dropped her cigarette on the floor, stubbing it out with her high heel as she stood and took my hand and led me back to our table.

I'd done it before my adrenaline could back up on me, before I could think much more about it. There was another woman beside Christof. She was plump, her shoulders bare, her cleavage pushing up out of her dress. She was speaking Spanish loudly over the music, her hand on his, and I hadn't seen him choose her. Later I would learn he'd told the older woman that only I was here for the girls, and so she'd sent another one to drink with him, to run up his tab on booze.

The woman I'd chosen was sitting close to me. She smelled like nicotine and lipstick, and she was speaking Spanish into my ear. She rested her hand on my thigh and sipped from a drink she'd ordered as soon as she sat down. The woman next to Christof was speaking more softly, smiling, Christof shaking his head and smiling back. He looked close to nodding off, and I remembered his girlfriend in Denver, a woman who owned a clothing shop that catered to the rich. Was he staying at this table because of her? Or was he hoping our killer would stumble in? Or was he morally opposed to what I was doing? Or was he just too drunk?

"Fuck and suck?" The woman squeezed my leg. I looked at her directly for the first time, saw that her front tooth was chipped and she was much older than I was, thirty-five, forty. "Fuck and suck, sí?"

"*Sí.*"

We stood, and I followed her through the cigarette smoke of the other women I didn't look at. We stepped outside through an open doorway, ahead of us a long row of motel rooms, a red or white bulb glowing over half the doors. The tiles under my feet were loose, and off to the right was a rectangular hole in the ground, weeds sprouting out of it like hair. At the end of the diving board someone had set a cane chair upside down, its four legs poking up at the stars, and on the other side were more rooms, their windows dark. A few of them were cracked or shattered. She stopped and unlocked a door and I followed her inside.

———

CHRISTOF HAD SWITCHED TO COKE AND WASN'T AS DRUNK NOW. On the cab ride back he was talking about our killer, how he might have been there earlier or would be there later or maybe *los mutados* had the wrong place. I nodded. The driver's face was lit from below by a battery-powered lamp on the seat beside him. There was a day of whisker growth along his chin and throat, a white stubble, and on the radio was a Top 40 song from the States that made me think of polyester shirts and barrooms and waking up hungover beside a naked woman I did not know.

I'd learned nothing from doing what I'd just done. It felt no different from any other loveless act. There was the momentary sweetness of release, then a hollow emptiness, the body taking the soul to a place where there were only echoes. Everything that happened there I could have imagined. Not to have done so instead had diminished me somehow.

This driver was taking it faster than the first one, and we were bouncing in and out of the ruts in the road, the light of his headlamps jerking ahead of us. Off to my right lay a field of brush and mesquite under the moonlight, my shoulder pressing hard against the door.

Soon we were once again passing the homes of the poor. A new song was on the radio now, Christof quiet and pensive. I thought again of the young men my age in the bed of that pickup, and I pictured two or three of them lying dead under the moon, their blood leaking into the dust.

Over the one-story shacks and through the *matapalo* branches came the white and yellow lights of the Golden Zone. Then we were in it, a wash of neon and palms, and off to our right was the moonlit expanse of Puerto Viejo Bay. I began to feel afraid—the woman I'd just been with; the killer we were looking for; the deaf-mutes we'd publicly bribed with kindness to get information; Christof getting recklessly drunk—all of this began to feel like some cosmic debt I was going to have to pay, and pay soon.

I rolled down my window to the smells of dead fish and wet sand. Lined along the beaches were wooden fishing boats, many of them on plank frames with an axle and two bicycle wheels so the fishermen could pull them into the water without help.

Soon we were in the darker streets of the Centro Histórico, the driver pulling up to the pink and white entrance of our hotel. Christof gave him what looked like many pesos, and the driver thanked him three times, then Christof and I were passing through the lobby and its massive potted palms and tiled columns. This time I ignored the one with the commemorative bullet holes, and I followed Christof down the long tiled corridor to our room. But something was different, a square of light where there shouldn't be any, and it was coming from the left, the door to our room wide open, a sliver of wood from the casing lying across the threshold.

Christof stopped and stood still and held up his hand. Now was the time for a gun. Now was the time for a knife or a baseball bat or a tire iron. My tongue was thick in my mouth and then I was stepping into the room behind him.

What little we'd brought to Mexico with us was scattered across the floor—shirts, shorts, underwear, a novel I'd been reading. Both mattresses had been upended and one lay sideways across its frame, the sheet torn off. Christof moved quickly toward the bathroom, pushed open the door, and stepped inside.

"We're alone."

I was staring at the pesos I'd left beside my notebook on the small desk. Christof had told me not to carry too much with me at one time, so I'd left it behind. I could hear him step out of the bathroom behind me. I pointed to my money. "Why didn't they take *that*?"

Christof's linen suit was wrinkled, and his eyes had a dark cast to them I'd never quite seen before. He lifted up what he was holding at his side. It was our killer's mug shot, the one I'd gotten from the US marshal in Denver.

"Where was it?"

"Someone's told him about us. We'll have to leave in the morning."

Who? I wondered, but of course: Why wouldn't a professional killer—someone always looking over his shoulder—have people he paid to look, too? Christof was gathering up clothes with cool efficiency, but my legs became cold water and I pulled the cane chair from under the desk and sat down. I was looking at our open door, its casing splintered, and what would keep him from stepping inside with his weapon of choice and spraying us dead?

I swung the door shut and wedged the chair snug beneath the porcelain knob. I felt young and stupid. I squatted and began to pick up my scattered clothes and stuffed them into my backpack. I set the novel on the table beside my bed.

That night there was little sleep. We closed and bolted the shutters against the sea air, and now the air in the room had grown thick and close. Christof snored on his mattress a few feet away, and I could smell the tequila he'd drunk earlier, our sweat, the thin cotton of our sheets. Why wouldn't our killer decide to just get rid of us? We were in Mexico, beyond the protection of the law enforcers who'd sent us. My heart had become an electronic thumping behind my eyes, and while I had never done anything like this before, the black dread opening up in my chest and gut was nothing new.

I was the son of a single mother who, when we were kids, moved us from one rented house or apartment to another, one year three times, always for cheaper rents. I was the constant new boy who got beat up in the schoolyard or the street simply because I was new. Then, at fourteen, I snapped and began to fight back with my fists and feet till that's all I ever seemed to do anymore. Then I was a grown man, writing daily, trying to become other people with words, an act of sustained empathy that had made it difficult for me to view people as good or bad. I could see only the gray, that dark tangle of human desire and motivation and hurt and action and apathy that made a life. And that prostitute who was probably the age of my own mother, the dim yellow bulb hanging over her head, how she'd said something to me in Spanish and pointed to a wooden bench against the wall, a place for me to leave my clothes, but underneath it was a pair of white baby shoes. And after, the way she'd looked at me like she would never think of me even for one moment ever again.

Lying half naked in the boxed heat of that room at the Hotel Belmar, waiting for our killer and his submachine gun, my only weapon my fists, I kept asking myself why I'd come to Mexico. And I knew it wasn't just for the money; it was for this: to be tossed into the dark heart of danger, to then emerge stronger, bigger, and more fully myself.

But I already knew what it was to walk onto an asphalt lot crowded with running, shouting boys, many of whom would turn on me because I was new and did not belong there with them. I knew the violence that would follow, and while it was only insults and a slap or a punch and some kicks to the ribs and back, I knew the quiet after, the fear of more of the same, and once, after knocking out the front teeth of a local thug, I knew the carload of young men who cruised slowly by the gas station where I worked, the promise of revenge in their stubbled faces. And now this, the possibility not of being beaten up, but of getting shot to death. Strange how similar it all felt, how greater danger did not bring greater learning with it.

Deep in the night, sleep came against my better judgment and against my will. Then Christof was rousing me awake. He was already dressed, then so was I, and it was a long walk down that sunlit corridor, the hotel's shutters open to the sea, the naked sense that we were easy targets now.

On the shuttle ride out of the city, Christof and I were the only passengers. The windows were open and the driver was smoking a cigarette, its smoke blowing back into our faces, the scent of the flowers snaking up along the stucco walls we passed, the dust rising alongside us. Christof was back in his linen suit, and he sat quiet and hungover beside me, his eyes seemingly on the meeting with the federal agents, who would not be pleased.

But I didn't care about that. There was the drafty, light-skinned feeling we were narrowly escaping something catastrophic. We drove deeper into the country, and I stared out at the shacks made from half-built concrete block walls and billboards and sheets of tin. There was the rusted-out Datsun, the morning sun glinting off its cracked side mirror, and as we passed I turned in my seat to look for the two young boys who just yesterday had been squatting and playing in the dirt. There was only the Datsun and the shack, the frayed corner of a tarp hanging over the Coca-Cola sign that served as a wall. I turned back around in my seat. Christof asked me what I'd been looking at.

"Nothing."

But I thought of the boys in five or ten years armed in the back of a speeding pickup, their hair blowing back from their faces as they drove into lethal danger, not as an adventure or an experience, but as a way of life that would be far too short. I had told myself I'd come here for a job, but I began to feel like a thief, like a white bird of prey.

Up ahead was the small airport, the narrow control tower, a plane taking off from the tarmac into the air. Soon we would be on one just like it, and I vowed I would not be coming back here, not like this, a tourist of other people's misery, a consumer of it.

When the driver pulled the shuttle van to the curb, I leaned forward and handed him all my pesos. He held it as if it might explode, his eyes careful and still. I told Christof to tell him to keep it.

"That's a month's pay. You may insult him with that."

"Tell him I mean no disrespect. Just, tell him that."

As I stepped out of the van and hauled my backpack onto my shoulder, the concrete sidewalk felt too bright and open and exposed. I hurried inside the terminal to wait for my boss and my translator, the glass door closing behind me, this rising desire to get back to the empty page, but this time with more faith that I might be able to find something true there without having lived it myself.

I turned and began walking toward a line of men and women, some American, others Mexican or European, but I was looking for the face that had been left on the toilet of our hotel back in Old Mazatlán, a face I hoped never to see again, a face not so different from my own.

THE LAND OF NO

—◁•▷—

Jessica was twenty-three years old and had a $2 million trust fund. She also had a warm smile, spoke kindly to everyone she met, and was blond and beautiful, with the erect posture of the ballet dancer she'd once been. We lived together in Manhattan in a tiny first-floor apartment. Six shifts a week, I tended bar at a chophouse down in the Garment District.

Jessica didn't have to work, but while she was looking for an internship at a TV studio, she found a job in a bookstore. She said she was grateful for her inherited wealth but did not earn it so would not use it. Sometimes, though, she'd dip into it to buy me things she thought I needed: a new leather jacket, hand-stitched cowboy boots, a wool sweater from Ireland. I was grateful for these things but felt undeserving. I'd never been around anyone with money before—someone who could just buy whatever she wanted whenever she wanted it.

This was in the 1980s, a decade when there were five thousand homeless families in New York City and what seemed like a millionaire on every block. The homeless would be huddled in the concrete corner of a subway station or curled up under dirty blankets on a grate outside a hotel or apartment building, the smaller children tucked between a mother or father and the granite wall. I found myself giving a lot of my tips to them, more than I could afford, though in some shadowed sliver of my psyche I knew I had Jessica and what was given to her: a soft, deep place to fall, something my family had never known.

———

IT WAS THE SUMMER OF 1970, I WAS ELEVEN YEARS OLD, AND IN OUR small rented house there was no escape. They got under your clothes, under your shirt and pants and underwear, an itch you could never quite reach—between your shoulder blades, up your neck, behind your knees, and in your hair. If you took a shower and stood wet and naked in front of a window fan, it helped, but only until you were dry again. Then they seemed to rise up out of your own skin: fleas, gnats, bedbugs, lice—whatever they were exactly we didn't know, only that we were besieged by them, and no matter how many times our mother called the landlord, he never sent anyone to fix the problem.

We were living in northern Massachusetts then, in an old shipbuilding town on the Merrimack River three miles from the Atlantic. Its downtown was an abandoned cluster of mill buildings with no glass in their windows; the sidewalks buckled and were littered with trash. Dry weeds sprouted in cracks down the center of the asphalt streets, and the only working businesses were a diner, a newsstand, and a barroom, its dim interior filled with the shadows of men and women drinking.

But it was a place of cheap rents, and it was the first town to which our young mother moved her four kids after the divorce from our father. Twenty-eight years old, she got jobs as a nurse's aide and a waitress, then earned her way through school till she was out and working in social services, helping poor families like us.

We moved often, one year three times, always for a cheaper rent. We kids spent too much time watching television, roaming the streets, getting high on stoops waiting for the school bus. Children got pregnant at fourteen, boys went off to reform school and later prison, my best friend to an early grave, his own knife stuck into his liver by the girlfriend he'd tormented far too long.

As predictably as leaves dropping from their branches in the fall, the landlord would be at our door asking for the rent check our mother just did not have, and we'd be moving again, loading up a U-Haul truck with what little we owned, our clothes tossed into plastic trash bags, my mother's boyfriend driving the truck while the rest of us piled into whatever Mom drove at the time—usually Japanese cars that still lived after 200,000 miles and once a '67 Cadillac that ran on only three of its eight cylinders. Our mother called it "the pig."

———

SOME SUMMERS, WE ESCAPED ALL THIS BY HEADING TWO THOUsand miles south to Louisiana, where our maternal grandparents lived. We never owned a car that could make that trip, so the five of us would take a bus into Boston, to a squat concrete building behind chain-link and barbed wire, its oil-spotted yard crowded with new-looking cars. Our mother would sign some papers, then we'd be climbing into a VW van, or a four-door Buick, or once a black Trans Am with leather seats, air-conditioning, and an eight-track player with quadraphonic sound. These were repo cars, and our mother would be paid to drive them to New Orleans. It gave her enough money for gas and two rooms at a motel with a pool, then five Greyhound tickets from New Orleans to Fishville, Louisiana.

Swimming in a Holiday Inn pool somewhere south of Knoxville, I could see the last of the sun glinting off our black Trans Am in the parking lot, and I knew that after we'd all cooled off there'd be enough money for burgers and Cokes, and later we'd all be lying on our hotel beds watching a color television in air-conditioned rooms. *This is what it's like to be rich*, I remember thinking. *This must be it.*

———

ONE NIGHT, CROSSING THIRD AVENUE FOR THE BAR ON THE CORner, Jessica and I were talking about an old friend of mine, a woman who'd gotten pregnant in high school, dropped out, then had two more kids with the same man—someone who beat her up regularly, who had knocked out some of her teeth and put her in the hospital. After years of this, she left him, went back to school, and became a registered nurse. Jessica had met her once. She liked and admired her. As we crossed Third Avenue she said, "You know the first thing I'd do if I were her?"

"What?"

"I'd get my teeth fixed."

Weeks before this, she and I had spent the night at her family's home. It was one of five they owned; her parents were away that weekend at their ranch in the Southwest. I'd never been in a house like this. It had rooms off of rooms, and in each of them were deep sofas and chairs, woven carpet over polished hardwood floors, tasteful paintings on the walls. She asked if I was hungry, and she opened the fridge and it was stuffed with food—cold cuts and cheeses, fresh vegetables and fruit and imported condiments, milk and orange juice and European beer. Jessica was the youngest of five, all of them grown and out of the house. How was it possible for a refrigerator to hold so much? Especially in a home of only two?

She was surprised at my surprise. I tried to tell her how little my mother had been able to give us, how one night a friend came over with a case of beer and I just opened the fridge, and he put it on one of three empty shelves beside a jar of mustard. She looked at me as if I were exaggerating. How could I tell her how differently we'd been raised? In the circular driveway in front of her house were five Porsches her father had shipped over from England to sell here for a profit, something she told me was called the "gray market." In my family, the market was where we went for food, if there was enough money to buy some.

I did not feel sorry for myself; I felt the superior pain of the inferior, the pride of the sufferer, the shame of the poor. I could also see that my dark mood was pulling her down and that she was beginning to feel guilty for something that had little to do with her. I kept quiet and felt far away from this kind young woman who seemed to love me just the way I was, this woman I judged when she was doing no such thing to me.

But now, stepping onto the sidewalk on the other side of Third Avenue, I heard myself yelling: "You don't think she'd like to have new *teeth*? Of course she would, Jessica, but she doesn't have that kind of *money*, and if she did, it would mean no oil in the burner that month, no food in the fridge. It would mean being late with the fucking rent. But you can't even think those things because you're from the Land of Yes when the rest of us are from the Land of No. We don't even *think* we can have these things you take for granted, like new fucking *teeth*."

It wasn't the first time I'd done this to her, and it wouldn't be the last. She stood there staring at me. In her eyes were hurt and a resigned sadness, then the hard light of resentment as she turned and walked down Third Avenue, lengthening her stride, getting as far away from me as fast as she could.

———

TWO WEEKS LATER, BUSINESS AT THE CHOPHOUSE HAVING BEEN slow for months, I got laid off. I spent the next month walking from one restaurant to another looking for work, but there was none. Rent was past due, and I had no money in the bank.

Maybe because of our fights over her privileged life, Jessica told me she would not even consider dipping into her trust fund, though she did not make enough at the bookstore to support us both. I could see she was beginning to worry.

In the fourth week, I stopped looking for bartending work and got a job cleaning apartments and offices, but I earned half what I'd made serving drinks. Any day now, the landlord would stand at our door the way he'd always stood at my mother's, his hand out for the check that would not be coming. Jessica and I would have to move, but where? I saw us huddled together on a grate, or curled under blankets beneath hedges in Central Park, and I remembered one night when those bugs had gotten so bad my mother and I had slept in the pig parked out in the street. It was a humid July night, my sisters and brother miraculously asleep inside. My mother took the front, and I lay in the back. The bars had closed hours ago so we weren't worried about the drunks; we opened our windows all the way. For a long while, I stared at the ripped fabric of the ceiling. I could hear the fan in my sister's window, then the even breaths of my sleeping mother. She worked so hard and always fell asleep so fast.

———

NOW IT WAS DUSK IN MANHATTAN, AND I WAS WALKING UPTOWN from my new cleaning job, preparing myself to tell Jessica it was time for us to start packing. But when I walked into our tiny place, she was pulling roasted chicken from the oven, her hair pulled up and back, and she kissed me and handed me a cold European beer.

"I paid our rent."

"How?"

"How do you think?" She smiled recklessly, as if she were flirting with a stranger and knew she probably shouldn't but would anyway. She seemed a little drunk.

"I thought you weren't going to do that."

"We're paid up for six months." She grabbed her glass of wine and moved past me and sat on the couch. She snatched up the remote and flicked on our color television.

I couldn't deny the relief I felt. Like standing naked and wet in front of that window fan, all the itching gone. And it was clear she did not want to discuss it. I sat next to her on the couch. I sipped the beer she'd paid for. I watched whatever it was she was watching. Her hand rested in her lap, and I wanted to reach over and hold it. It was only inches away, but it may as well have been in another country, another land, one we both knew we would never be living in together.

BLOOD, ROOT, KNIT, PURL

— ‹‹•›› —

It was December 1986, and I had less than three weeks to make my aunt Jeannie a Christmas present. She was eight years older than my mother, had lost her husband in her forties, was done raising my two older cousins, Micky and Eddie, and at fifty-six was going blind. She'd always been a large woman, and lovely, with long graying hair she held back with silk scarves or pinned up with tortoiseshell combs. She preferred silver earrings and bracelets, wore minimal makeup, and had a much stronger Louisiana accent than my mother, who'd fled the Deep South when she eloped with my father in 1958. They ended up in New England, and their marriage lasted less than ten years.

That winter I was twenty-seven years old, living with my girlfriend on the Upper East Side of New York City in an eight-by-thirteen-foot room. It had a kitchenette and a tiny bathroom, the ceiling high enough I built a loft for us to sleep in. Beneath that was my desk looking out the barred first-floor window to 82nd Street, and every morning before going to work as a bartender down in the Garment District, I would work on the novel I was writing.

My girlfriend was two years younger and had found a job working in a bookstore on Second Avenue. She was kind, charming, and athletic, and she had also grown up rich while I'd grown up poor. This created a chasm between us we tried to pretend wasn't there, but daily I was writing myself backwards into the ugly mill town I'd been raised in by my own overworked and underpaid single mother, and at night, sharing a meal on the new sofa my girlfriend had bought us, wearing the Irish wool sweater and cowboy boots she'd bought me, too, her five-speed convertible parked in a garage not far away, her $2 million trust fund in a bank downtown, her sweet disposition and good skin and straight teeth, her perfect grammar from private schools, her family's five homes here and abroad, it would all become too much. I would accuse her of not knowing what the real world was really like. She would deny this, and I would start yelling. I would yell that she was from the Land of Yes while the rest of us were from the Land of No.

"Do you understand what I'm saying to you?!"

"Yes! I fucking *understand*!"

She'd be crying, and I'd feel like a bully, for she'd always been loving and generous to me. If I could summon the nerve and the will, I'd apologize. But more times than not, I wouldn't, even though I knew I should. And because our apartment was so small, there was no place for either of us to retreat to except the mattress up in the loft or the new sofa below.

That night in December, Christmas looming, I lay up there feeling small. How was it her fault she'd been born into wealth and privilege? How was it her problem that I saw the world as hard and unjust, and anyone who did not was naïve?

Outside it was snowing. I could hear it ticking against the window glass, the taxicabs and delivery trucks passing by in the street. Down on the sofa my girlfriend flicked on the TV and picked up her knitting. Her fucking *knitting*. It was another thing that made me feel far away from her. Who knitted but sweetly oblivious old ladies? To me, it seemed the busywork of people who were happy to *watch* life, not take part in it. But more than this, it was a domestic art from before the freedoms of feminism; my girlfriend was twenty-five years old, her adult life just beginning, and here she sat with her legs curled under her, her eyes on the TV, her fingers working the needles and yarn without having to peek. She looked like some young wife and mother from a hundred years ago; she looked to me like a woman who relied on her man to take care of everything.

But there was something deeply comforting about this image of her. I did not know what it was, but I also could not deny it. Nor could I deny that I was drawn to that comfort. A few months earlier my father had been run over by a car and crippled for the rest of his life. Every other weekend, if I could get time off at the bar, I'd take a bus up to Massachusetts to see him. He was no longer broad-chested and robust, his beard neatly trimmed, his cheeks pink. Instead, he was a one-legged man I didn't recognize. He lay in great pain on his living room couch, and his beard was long and bushy, his cheeks pale, his chest narrow, his arms withered. When I bent down to hug him, he smelled like old bandages and dead skin and dried blood.

He was fifty, but his third wife was pregnant with their second child, their five-year-old daughter, my half-sister, running around the house nearly crazy with all these changes. And more changes were coming. Just weeks after her mother would give birth to her sister, they'd move away from my father, and he would be divorced for the third time.

As I watched my girlfriend knitting from up in the loft, I don't know if I was thinking about any of this, though it was probably the deeper root of my distance from her, not some working-class outrage, but envy that she was the youngest of five children to a mother and father who clearly still loved one another and who would stay married for the rest of their lives. I did not believe lasting love was possible. My girlfriend did.

But I craved the warm solidity of family, something I was not conscious of until I was among my own—not my mother and brother and two sisters, not during those years anyway—but the larger clan our parents came from down in the Deep South.

Fishville, Louisiana, was no more than a break on Highway 8 in the pines of Grant Parish in the heart of the state. It was little more than two Texaco gas pumps in the gravel lot of a roller-skating rink, and across the highway, a narrow two-lane of cracked asphalt, lay Big Dean's Creek, a watering hole locals would swim in, the teenagers swinging off a tree rope into the warm murky water, its banks slippery red clay. It was fed by streams running into it from the woods where men fished and caught gar and crayfish and trapped loggerhead turtles, and half a mile up the road lay the camp built by my mother's father.

His name was Elmer Lamar Lowe and, like every one of my blood relatives on both sides of the family, he was raised in Louisiana. He was the son of a mule skinner, and after the third grade he never went back to school. At ages nine and ten he was working alongside his old man, tying thick rope to barge cleats, cinching it around the leather harnesses of mules who'd then pull the loaded barges alongside the banks of shallow muddy rivers and bayous. There'd be cottonmouths coiled in the trunks of cypresses and live oaks, Spanish moss hanging so low my grandfather probably had to brush it away from his young face. By age sixteen he was the foreman for a gang of gandy dancers, grown men laying miles of railroad tracks under the blistering Louisiana sun. By the time Elmer Lowe became the father of my mother and her older sister Jeannie, he'd established himself as a pipe fitter who helped build power plants that brought electricity throughout the South and Southwest.

But this was a man I barely knew. Not until my parents' marriage ended and our mother, Elmer's youngest daughter, began what turned into the next decade of raising us four kids alone along the Massachusetts–New Hampshire border. Many of these houses were in poor, tough parts of town, and with my small body, my glasses, and long hair, I quickly became a target for cruel and angry boys, many of whom would grow into self-destructive men, just about all of whom are dead as I write this now: one to a stabbing, two to drug overdoses, another to cirrhosis of the liver, another to a car accident. That second summer after my parents' divorce, I spent a lot of time hiding inside our small, hot rented house, my younger brother and two sisters there, too, and all we did was watch hours and hours of whatever was on TV.

When our mother eloped with our father, Elmer told her, "If you get divorced, don't bother coming home. There's been no damn divorces in our family."

But that was ten years earlier and maybe that summer she called or wrote her parents. Maybe she told them her kids needed something to do or somewhere to go, or that she wanted her mother and father to know her kids, I don't know, but soon we were speeding down the highway in a black Trans Am, a repo car my mother was being paid to drive to New Orleans, where we hopped a bus north to Fishville and what would become for me the place I'd grow to call home.

It wasn't the camp itself, the outbuildings Elmer—we called

him Pappy—had sided with riveted sheet metal. And it wasn't the ten acres of tall jack pine or our grandmother Fern's chicken, sausage, and okra gumbo, or Big Dean's Creek, or Pappy's pickup we got to ride in the bed of up and down Highway 8. It was being in one place where people we were actually related to had lived for many years.

Since our parents' divorce in 1970, my sisters and brother and mother and I moved nearly once a year, sometimes more, from one cheap rented house or half-house to another. Just as we seemed to settle into one, we packed up and moved to another. Friends were hard to come by. Then, just as I was about to enter high school, our mother found a large house to rent in Haverhill, Massachusetts, a half-dead mill town, and we lived there for six years. I eventually became friends with a boy from a big Irish Catholic family, nearly all of whom had raised their families there. On his father's side alone, my friend had nine uncles and nine aunts and dozens of cousins. Up the Merrimack River in Lowell, he had about as many from his mother's side. On Sundays, my new friend spent the afternoons at a relative's house eating homemade dinners, throwing a football or baseball around with uncles and cousins, swimming in his aunt's backyard pool. For me and my siblings, Sunday was the day our father drove to our house to take us to a movie or out to eat, our mother home alone, the six of us the only family we knew, every one of our blood relatives sixteen hundred miles away in Louisiana.

But every summer after that first trip in the repossessed Trans Am, our mother would drive us down during her two-week vacations. Some years we drove other repo cars—once a VW van, a Chrysler sedan with air-conditioning, a yellow Dodge Charger. But as we got older and could help with the driving, we drove our old red Toyota, and we took turns driving straight through so we could skip having to pay for rooms at a Howard Johnson's or Holiday Inn.

Then we four kids were all in our twenties with jobs of our own and summers were hard to take off. Pappy and Fern's fiftieth wedding anniversary fell in January, and we threw them a big party, and it was good being in Louisiana in the winter: the frost on the pine needles; the bare magnolia branches scraping the camp during a cold wind; the scrap fire we'd burn outside and stand around while Pappy smoked a brisket over hickory coals in his cast-iron smoker. Somebody, probably my mother, suggested we start coming down every Christmas. To save money for travel, there came the No Presents rule: Too expensive. Too hard to carry. Let's just each draw a name. One name, one gift, and you can't buy it; you have to make it yourself.

One year I got a short blue candle poured in a mold for me by cousin Micky's seven-year-old son. The next year I got a case of mayhaw jelly from Micky himself. Another year, because he'd heard I'd started writing fiction, Micky's older brother Eddie, a carpenter, sanded a four-inch length of alder branch into which he drilled two holes to hold two pencils. One Christmas, I drew my sister Suzanne's name and baked her sour cream enchiladas I then froze and wrapped and tied with a bow. The following Christmas, I drew my cousin Micky's wife, Sue, and I bought wire and beads and bent her a pair of earrings. The year after that, I drew Pappy's name and didn't know what to make him so cheated and bought him some cologne and two Louis L'Amour novels.

Every year, at least one of us would cheat and go to a store and buy our one present we were supposed to make. That December night in 1986, I was tempted to do that for Jeannie, but I couldn't. I loved her too much. Whenever I saw her briefly during those summers or for a few days every Christmas, she seemed to *see* me, whoever the hell I was, even when she was going blind. She'd sit me down and ask me questions about my life: Are you in love? Are you taking care of yourself? Are you drinking too much? Do you know how you're going to make a living and be an artist?

Two short years earlier I'd published my first short story in a magazine. She read it and called me on the phone. "Andre, I'm just so happy you're not squandering your youth."

I felt loved by this woman, my mother's big sister, and I wanted to show her that I loved *her* too.

Down below, just a few feet from my knitting girlfriend, TV men and women fought and made up or did other happy or melodramatic things I did not believe, but now I was looking closer at what was in my girlfriend's lap. It appeared to be a small blue blanket.

"What're you knitting?"

At first she didn't answer. I asked her again, and she reached for the remote and muted the TV. "A sweater."

"Who for?"

"My sister's new baby."

Her second or third, I knew that. But I hadn't seen the obvious, that my young, rich girlfriend was somebody's aunt, too. I may have told her that was nice of her. I hope I did, but maybe I didn't.

The previous Christmas, Jeannie had drawn my name. With her fading eyes she'd painted me a portrait of Pappy and his twin sister Tootsie. It came from a black-and-white photograph taken in 1915, when they were ten years old. They're both on a log in the woods. She's leaning on it in a dress, a bow in her hair, and Pappy, in knickers, is squatting on it and whittling a stick with a knife. Jeannie had this painting framed under glass, and when I unwrapped it, sitting on the couch beside her down in Fishville, she said she could hardly see it anymore but she hoped I liked it. I hugged her and told her I did, though I more than liked it; somehow she knew how much having family meant to me; somehow she knew I needed tangible evidence of my own roots.

And what *Jeannie* needed was something she didn't need to see to appreciate. She needed something she could *touch*.

"You think you could teach me to do that?"

My girlfriend's needles stopped clicking against one another. She looked up at me, her expression cautious but hopeful. "If you really want to."

"I want to knit my aunt a scarf."

In seconds I was sitting on the couch beside my girlfriend choosing a roll of gray yarn to work with because that's what she had the most of. She put aside her nephew's sweater and handed me two knitting needles. "Number 10's," she said.

They were a little heavier than I'd imagined they'd be. I liked how smooth they were, but holding them, I couldn't help feeling emasculated till I remembered Rosey Grier, that big football player, knitting on some TV talk show, and I felt better, but I also felt shallow that I'd needed to feel better.

My girlfriend showed me how to "cast on," a process so complicated I gave up and asked if she could do that part, then hand it over to me once the actual knitting would begin. I watched as she rolled out the yarn and about two feet down tied a slipknot she cinched onto one of my needles. Then she took the other one, her thumb and index finger working the yarn into loops and more knots. It was like watching a spider spin a web as naturally as breathing, and soon she was handing me both needles and telling me I should probably just knit Jeannie's scarf in a simple knit-purl pattern, whatever that meant. She placed both her hands lightly over mine. She showed me how to first make a knit stitch. These details are foggy now, but I remember pushing the point of my right needle into her slipknot and wrapping the yarn from the back to the front of the needle before pushing it back under another knot, which left the yarn somehow at the rear of my right needle, then I was pulling yarn to the front, sticking my needle under a new knot I'd made, then doing it all over again, looping from the back, sticking in the needle, looping from the front and sticking, looping and sticking.

My girlfriend went back to her own knitting, and she left the TV muted and all I heard was the clicking of her needles and the much slower click and slide of my own, the snow blowing harder at our window, the street muffled and quiet.

Every night after dinner, the two of us would sit on our couch in front of whatever was on TV and we'd knit. After a few sittings, I had what was beginning to look like the first five or six inches of a real scarf, and while my girlfriend told me that this was a simple pattern, it looked wonderfully intricate to me, its raised ribs and soft valleys precisely one-quarter inch apart. It made me think of snakeskins and Native Americans, and I felt joined to all the men and women across cultures down through the ages who'd done something useful with their hands, who'd made essential things from whatever was in front of them.

And I was looking forward to wrapping it and giving it Christmas morning to my aunt Jeannie down in Fishville, Louisiana. But this feeling of joyful anticipation rarely came while I was actually knitting, for the act itself was too calming for that, the constant sticking and looping and light cinching and more sticking and looping, my fingers moving in a rhythm they'd never known before. It required me to focus and it allowed me to drift too, the way running a long distance required my feet and legs to do one thing while my mind could do another. I recall thinking a lot about my father, his new life to be lived in a wheelchair; I thought of the novel I was writing, of how most days I was convinced it just was not working because I was still too angry about the childhood I was trying to capture; I thought of my mother, how she'd raised us as best she could and now she was free of it all, living with her boyfriend on an island in the Caribbean delivering food and liquor to restaurants and hotels; I thought of my brother and two sisters, those years we huddled around the TV in our small rented houses, how I was looking forward to seeing them again; I thought of Jeannie going blind, this woman who loved sculpture and paintings and books so much. I pictured her pulling this homemade scarf from its box, the way she'd squint at it, run her fingers over it, maybe smell it before I leaned over and kissed her; and I thought of my considerate privileged girlfriend knitting beside me, how we probably wouldn't make it. We wouldn't. But I loved her anyway. I also wished her and her family well, rich or not.

In the lamplight, her blond hair down around her shoulders, her eyes on the TV while her needles clicked away, she looked content and beautiful. She turned and smiled at me. Except for meals and sex and drinking in bars, there was very little we'd ever done together—but now she'd helped me to create something I couldn't have without her. Between us on that sofa her money had bought us was something warm and palpable and vaguely parental. I felt shy in the face of it. I smiled back and returned to my knitting, to my looping and sticking and cinching in snugly before looping again, for this had become the conversation between us, the clicking of our needles, this soft woolen truce.

CARVER AND DUBUS, NEW YORK CITY, 1988

—‹‹•››—

I t was 1988, the year we would lose Raymond Carver, and I was
in a crowded room in New York City making my way to where
he stood up against a wall. He wore a jacket and tie and held a
glass of water close to his chest. He looked like he was trying to lie
low, though he was at the height of his fame in a room full of writers, so this was hard to do.

This was in Washington Heights at the awards ceremony for
the American Academy of Arts and Letters. I was there with my
sister Suzanne and a few close friends, and we'd all driven down
in a convoy from north of Boston with my father, the short story
master Andre Dubus, who'd just won the Jean Stein Award for his
volume of selected stories published that year. Less than two years
earlier, our father had stopped his car on the highway to help two
young people who'd been in an accident, and he was run over at 58
miles an hour, suffering thirty-four broken bones and two pulver-
ized legs, one of which had to be amputated below the knee. Not

long after this, his third marriage ended and his wife left him and took their two young daughters, my half-sisters, with her, so now my father lived alone in his small house on a hill of poplar trees in the rural part of Haverhill, Massachusetts, and we all did what we could to help out: my brother Jeb and I built wheelchair ramps and installed wall railings and made his bathroom accessible for a wheelchair; my sisters brought meals and encouragement; three times a week I drove over to his house to help him get his strength back with the weight training he used to love; and on Thursday nights, ten to fifteen writer friends would gather in his living room for a workshop he taught free of charge. It began as a way to bolster his spirits, to bring him back into the warm folds of community, but it quickly became a master class taught by my father. It had been a hard and dark time for him, and so when he learned of this new accolade for his work, this piece of good news gave birth to a much-needed road trip for us all.

We drove down in two cars, my father behind the wheel of his handicapped-accessible Toyota, his wheelchair stowed in the compartment installed on the roof of his car. My sister Suzanne and her husband rode with him, as did our father's loyal friend Jack Herlihy. Jack was a writer and a self-employed carpenter, and not long after my father's wife left, Jack moved in to do whatever needed to get done. I rode with an old friend of mine in his car, a dancer and poet who had been one of my father's students ten years earlier. He was looking forward to watching his friend and former professor receive his award down in the big city, as was I, but we were also looking forward to seeing and maybe even meeting some of the major American writers we knew would be there, men and women whose work had reached in and done something to us.

This was before the internet and Google, but I knew from the invitation back at my father's house that literary giants had been invited: E. L. Doctorow and Joyce Carol Oates, Saul Bellow and Norman Mailer, Susan Sontag and William Styron and Allen Ginsberg and the great short story writer, Raymond Carver.

Before hitting the road, as my father transferred himself from his wheelchair to his driver's seat, hooking the chain that would then hoist his chair up into its container on the roof, I told him I was looking forward to seeing all those writers.

"Yeah," he said. "I just want to meet Carver."

We all knew he was to be inducted that day into the academy itself, that he was sick with brain cancer and had been sober for the last ten years when he had written and published some of his finest work, that he, too, had a volume of stories come out that year, *Where I'm Calling From: New and Selected Stories*. As Jack Herlihy got into my father's car, I saw that he had that thick volume in his hands.

I was twenty-eight years old then and had been writing fiction daily for nearly seven years. I had published three short stories and, after nearly forty rejections, my first book, a story collection, had been accepted by a New York publisher and was coming out in hardcover in early 1989. I wrote every morning and tended bar at an Irish pub at night. I lived in a rusted-out trailer across from a row of weathered beach houses on the Atlantic, and I spent a lot of time reading and studying what made great writing great. All I wanted to do other than pay my bills and work out daily was to learn to write as well as I possibly could, yet I was still surprised I was doing this at all, that a handful of people, like my dancer-poet friend in that car driving behind my father's, were beginning to think of me as a writer when I never would have called myself that.

I have written about this in other places and won't go into it here, but writing came to me unbidden, and it had gotten me off a violent and self-destructive path, the kind a few other young men

I'd known growing up had not gotten off of, and they had gone to prison or died young or both. I had a book coming out, yes, but my father was the writer, not me. I was just his oldest son with the same name who loved to write. I felt sure that any day now my real life would present itself, and I would go on to do something else, even though I knew I would no longer be me if I stopped writing.

Though I was also keenly aware, as were many others, that as accomplished an artist as my father was, his work was not read by nearly enough people. His book advances had always been low, as had the sales of his books. The overwhelming majority of the stories he'd published had come out in literary journals with small circulations, yet he was a writer's writer, a man who had worked diligently his whole life on the form that he found in his late twenties when he discovered the short stories of Anton Chekhov. My father's first book, *The Lieutenant*, published in 1966, was a novel, a far more commercial form in the United States, yet he would never write another and was happy to devote his life to an art form many considered obsolete.

But then in the late seventies came the stories of John Cheever and now Raymond Carver, and this view of the short story began to change. Their stories were published widely, and their books sold well and won big prizes (*The Stories of John Cheever*, published in 1979, won the Pulitzer Prize, the National Book Critics Circle Award, and the National Book Award). These developments my father celebrated, not so much because he had hopes more cultural light would shine on his own work, but because he deeply admired the art these two writers made, for if my father was anything in this life, he was generous and he was humble.

The first Carver story I'd read was "What We Talk About When We Talk About Love." I was dating one of my father's students, and she'd handed it to me and said, "Now, *this* is good writing." I read it right away and thought it was even better than that; I was immediately struck by the narrator's voice, its vaguely blue-collar, this-is-how-it-is tone. And I liked how Carver began in the middle of the story: "My friend Mel McGinnis was talking. Mel McGinnis is a cardiologist, and sometimes that gives him the right." I liked how Carver then takes us and the narrator, Nick, immediately into this conversation between two couples drinking before dinner, and I found myself marveling at how spare the sentences were and how that magnified the physical gestures of the characters, like Nick touching the back of Laura's hand, or Mel emptying one bottle of "cut-rate, lousy gin" only to open another. And I, whose own early stories had a lot of action in them, much of it violent, was so impressed with all that was being captured solely through authentic dialogue between these very real men and women on the page, all of whom were being painted without any authorial judgment whatsoever.

When I finished reading that story's final line—"I could hear the human noise we sat there making, not one of us moving, not even when the room went dark"—I felt that *I* was sitting alone in that dark room, drunk with my friends and my girlfriend Laura, dumbfounded by the true nature of love. Years later, I would read this definition of art from Leo Tolstoy: "Art is transferring feeling from one heart to another." With every Carver story I read, that was happening: from the grief-stricken parents in "A Small, Good Thing"; to the aggrieved wife in "So Much Water So Close to Home"; to the revelation of the stoned and jealous husband in "Cathedral," Carver's art was going inside me and doing something substantial.

My father's stories, also deeply realist yet suffused with his Christian faith, were equally powerful, each of his characters rendered with the same sort of compassionate tone and nonjudgmental hand, one I knew Carver admired, for my father had heard from several writer friends that Carver would consistently teach my father's stories in writing classes, and my father did the same with his. Now the two would meet for the first time, Raymond Carver fighting a terminal disease, my father without the use of his legs and still in quite a bit of pain but driving cheerfully ahead of us down the highway for New York City, the midmorning sun shining on his wheelchair roof box, a USMC decal on his back bumper.

PEOPLE WHO LIVE IN WHEELCHAIRS HAVE TO PUT UP WITH INDIG-nities the rest of us never even have to think about: where to park if there's no handicapped parking space; how to maneuver your wheelchair between cars and up and down ramps, if there are ramps, and if there are only stairs, is there an elevator too? And if not, what then? What about when you make it out of the garage? How do you make it down a sidewalk and off its curb without falling over in the street? How do you get up over another curb, then another and another? And if you get to the building you're hoping to enter, is there a ramp or will you have to be carried up steps just to get inside? And once inside, are there stairs to face before you get to the room where you need to go? Or is there an elevator, and if so, is it wide and deep enough to accommodate a wheelchair that needs to turn 180 degrees so the man or woman or child sitting in it isn't facing the back wall? And what about bathrooms? Or that people who sit in wheelchairs in crowded rooms are stuck looking at other people at waist level, and when these people finally take the time to look down and address this man or woman in the chair, they tend to speak louder and more slowly, as if whatever has put this fellow human being in a wheel-chair has also robbed them of their faculties.

In the last twelve and a half years of my father's life, I watched

him have to live through all this again and again. When we got
to the neighborhood of the academy, the nearest parking garage
had no handicapped space and no elevator, so Jack Herlihy and
my friend and I carried my father in his chair down two flights of
concrete steps, and we took turns lifting my father up and down
curbs along crowded sidewalks. When we got to the grand building that housed the American Academy of Arts and Letters, there
was no wheelchair ramp, so we had to carry him in his chair up
three flights of stairs to a room crowded with well-dressed men
and women, some of whom I recognized right away from their dust
jacket photographs.

There was William Styron talking to an older man and a much
younger woman. There was Joyce Carol Oates with her curly hair
and famous round glasses. Over in the corner I saw E. L. Doctorow
in a dark suit, his beard graying, his eyes bright with intelligence
and a kind of mischievous good cheer. The room was packed with
writers and editors and literary agents, most of them holding a
drink or a glass of wine, the din of their voices rising all the way
to the vaulted ceiling and back. A few glanced over at us coming
in, their eyes on us briefly before dropping to the man in the chair.
Some nodded respectfully, but most went back to their conversations, and my sister and I had to do what the loved ones of people in
wheelchairs nearly always have to do in crowded places: we had to
move ahead of him in his chair to clear an opening that our father
could roll through.

My father stayed cheerful for this. He was dressed in a short-
waisted white suit jacket and an open-collared maroon silk shirt,
his thick gray beard neatly trimmed, his chest hair curling over
his top button. As we pushed him through, he said hello to a few
people, and a beautiful woman in black leaned down and hugged
and congratulated him, and he thanked her and hugged her back.

We were making our way to a side table beneath a window, late afternoon light streaming in. Suzanne pulled away a chair and Jack rolled my father into place. My dad fixed his wheel brakes and wiped sweat from his forehead and smiled widely at me. I asked him if he wanted a drink, and he said, "Just some water, man," and I was off.

I walked through the crowd and got in line at the bar. While waiting there, I recognized Calvin Trillin talking to a tall man who looked very much like Arthur Miller. I saw others I vaguely recognized too, and I became aware of all the hard-earned accomplishment in that room, of all the sentences that had become paragraphs that had become long passages and chapters in fine books all written by these men and women. I was a grown man, but I felt like a child.

I ordered a beer and a glass of water. As soon as I got back to my father's table, he thanked me and said, "I can't move in this room. Go find Carver for me, man."

Me? That would mean I would have to talk to Raymond Carver myself, that I'd have to ask him to follow me. I felt instantly shy but said, "All right." I set my beer on the table and stepped back into the crowd.

It didn't take me long to find him. He was the man standing alone against the wall with his glass of water, and his face looked just like his face in his books, long and clean-shaven, his hair short, his eyes lit with an earnest sincerity. I walked up to him, my mouth suddenly dry, and said, "Mr. Carver?"

"Yeah." He did not smile, but he did *not* not smile either.

"My name's Andre Dubus."

He looked confused.

"Same name as my dad, the writer. He wants to meet you, but he can't get over here in his wheelchair."

"He's *here*?"

"Yeah, follow me."

Then I was leading Raymond Carver through the crowd. Quite a few people looked over at us, and I could see they knew very well who was following me, though they did not know me but now thought perhaps they should. I began to feel I was being thrust into the light of some positive attention I had not earned, and I wanted to get Carver quickly to my father, then recede into the shadows.

When my father saw us emerge, he smiled and opened his arms for Carver as if he were a friend he hadn't seen in years. "There he is," my old man said. "There he is."

Carver leaned down and hugged him, and my father held him tight, patting his back and telling him to have a seat. My sister and her husband stood behind my dad holding drinks, and they introduced themselves, as did Jack Herlihy, who sat in the chair against the window, Carver's new hardcover on the table in front of him.

Raymond Carver glanced at it and sat in the only other chair at the table. It was directly across from my father, and instead of disappearing, I knelt on the floor between the two men, my back to the talking, laughing crowd. I had the sense that something truly momentous was happening, and I was getting to see it. Raymond Carver and my father both leaned forward and began to speak quietly. It was as if they were picking up a conversation they'd had long ago somewhere else, that they did this every time they met, though they never had. My father pointed to his own forehead and said, "How is it?"

"They've got me on steroids." Carver said a few other things about his cancer treatment, but then his eyes dropped to my father's wheelchair. He nodded and said, "You? How're you getting along?"

My dad spoke very briefly about living in a wheelchair, and it was clear he saw the other man's plight as so much tougher than his own and did not want to talk about himself at all. He seemed grateful to be interrupted when Jack Herlihy held up *Where I'm Calling From*, and asked Raymond Carver if he'd be willing to sign it.

The room had gotten louder somehow, and the crowd seemed to be moving, the awards ceremony starting soon. I couldn't hear what Jack was saying to Raymond Carver, though twice Carver glanced down at me and nodded with a kind of respect I did not understand or feel even remotely worthy of. My father began to tell Carver how much he loved his work, and Carver said he loved his, too, and now a handsome red-haired woman with a name tag pinned to her blouse came up to Carver to whisk him along, and he put his head down and signed Jack's book. He reached out and grasped my father's hand. My father said, "I love you, man."

"I love you, too."

And Raymond Carver stood and followed the woman into the streaming crowd and was gone.

––––

THERE WAS MORE TO THAT AFTERNOON, OF COURSE. THERE WAS the moment Raymond Carver was inducted into the academy. He was sitting onstage with all the other academy members, dozens of the most celebrated and revered writers of our time, and when his name was called he'd stood slowly, shyly, it seemed, his sports jacket bunched at the shoulders, as he was given a standing ovation. There was being in the audience as my father's award citation was read, and those of us who had driven down with him all hooted and hollered out our love and pride. There was the party after the ceremony and my friend meeting William Styron and telling him how much he loved *Lie Down in Darkness* and Styron thanking him sincerely. There was sitting at a table next to Allen Ginsberg and having him introduce my friend and me to his Indian publisher.

Ginsberg asked what I did, and I did not tell him I was a writer. I told him I was a bartender.

"You like it?"

"Yeah."

"That's good, right?"

"Yes."

I never saw Raymond Carver again that afternoon and early evening, nor did my father. But it was a joyous day, and we all got joyously drunk and stayed in some hotel none of us could afford, then drove north the next day cheerfully hungover.

When we finally drove up the hill of my father's driveway at dusk, the sun behind the ridge of maples on the other side of the road, my father tired but looking happy as he pressed the button that began to lower his wheelchair down from its roof box, Jack handed me his copy of *Where I'm Calling From*. He opened it to its title page, and there, in small, careful penmanship, Raymond Carver had written:

For Andre III,

With my congratulations—

Ray Carver

"Jesus, Jack."

"Congratulations, brother." He hugged me, and I thanked him for what I thought was too generous a gift. I said goodbye to my father and sister and brother-in-law. I dropped off my buddy and headed back to my trailer near the beach. I lay on my mattress and opened Jack's gift and began to read all the Carver stories I had not yet read, and I reread the ones I already knew and loved. I did this till I'd read every page, and every now and then I'd turn to the title page and read what he wrote to me, and again, I'd feel unworthy of his congratulations, for I had such a long, long way to go.

———

TWENTY-FOUR YEARS LATER I STOOD IN THAT SAME GRAND BUILD-ing, this time to receive an award for one of my books. It was a warm afternoon in late May, and I found myself standing in that same crowded, sunlit room, and many of those same literary lumi-naries were there too. I met and spoke with Joyce Carol Oates and Calvin Trillin, with E. L. Doctorow and Jhumpa Lahiri and others whose work had moved me, had made me want to write better than perhaps I ever could.

The actress Meryl Streep was there, as was ninety-three-year-old Pete Seeger. Everywhere I looked there was a face that belonged to a name that belonged to a body of work that had contributed to our culture, that had somehow illuminated truths that make the rest of us more awake and realized and alive.

Soon it was time for the awards ceremony, and as the room began to clear I kept glancing back at that same window where in 1988 there'd been a small table, and where two great American short story writers had finally met. Raymond Carver would die months later, my father eleven years after that. Pete Seeger has now joined them, as has William Styron, and Allen Ginsberg and E. L. Doctorow, and as I write these words now I think of how death is forever stalking the creative writer to get his or her work done, no matter how he or she feels about it, and how grateful I and so many readers are that Raymond Carver, in his short time here, made it to his desk each day, as did my father, setting the brakes of his wheel-chair before picking up his pen. And I keep thinking how these two men both professed their love for one another that afternoon when each had only known the other for his work, for his stories.

FALLING

— ‹‹•›› —

I t was after midnight, and we were standing on the flat tar roof of the Marriott Marquis in Times Square, fifty-six stories above the street. The light cast from below was the color of embers. We were so high just a few other buildings rose above us, and we couldn't hear the taxicabs moving through the square below, but from the short knee wall we could see them, small as dried kidney beans, though she had only glanced down for a second before pulling back.

Her hair was long, brown, and curly. She wore gold earrings, and it was late spring and chilly so she must have been wearing a jacket. She was twenty-six, and I was twenty-eight, and twelve hours earlier in Massachusetts she'd sat next to me in the backseat of my friend's car, and now we had known each other for less than one day. We'd been walking through the Lower East Side looking for a place to dance, but we got lost and ended up in a dark neighborhood, empty crack vials crunching under our feet. She had to stop to bend down and adjust the strap on one of her shoes, and she reached out her hand to me and I took it, telling myself I shouldn't, but I did anyway.

We continued walking. I kept her hand in mine, and we held hands all the way to Times Square and its unapologetic assault of neon, where she needed to find a bathroom, and so we found ourselves in the grand lobby of the Marriott Marquis, where I waited for her, staring at the glass elevators sitting in the center of the carpeted lobby. Then she came out of the bathroom and looked so beautiful, walking with the straight-backed poise of the dancer she was, and I took her hand again and said, "Let's go *up*."

The elevator rose fast, and we could look out and see each floor of the hotel fall away beneath us. She stepped closer to me, close enough that I could smell her hair, and that did something to me, and when I stepped out onto the carpet of the fifty-sixth floor, I took her hand again, and said, "Let's go to the roof."

What I did not know is that she was afraid of heights, and what she did not know is that for months I had been trying to get over a longtime girlfriend by seeing more than one woman at the same time, trying to feel something substantial for each and failing, and so just a day earlier I'd cut it off with all three of them. I vowed to spend the next year alone, and so why was I holding the hand of this woman less than one day after leaving the others? Why was I pulling her up to the unlocked rooftop of the Marriott Marquis in Times Square?

Because hours earlier, sitting in the backseat of my friend's car, she told me that all she wanted to do was what she was already doing, which was to dance and to draw, and I wanted to look away from her dark eyes looking directly into mine, but I could not, for I had known this woman before, maybe many times, before my births and after my deaths, and now I wanted her to feel how high we were; I wanted her to see those tiny taxicabs of New York City. I could feel the knee wall pressing against my shins. I could feel the lighted city far below, faint car horns rising like wisps of smoke.

She stepped back quickly. A small voice inside me said, *You're supposed to be alone now. It's time for you to be alone.* But when I turned away from the roof's low wall, she hugged me, and I could feel how afraid she'd been of falling, and then we were drawing closer and then we were kissing. It was soft and warm and lasted longer than I knew it should, for this wasn't my plan at all, it just was not. But I kissed her again, and I kissed her last night and this morning too, twenty-nine years fallen away behind us, our three children grown and living elsewhere now, doing their own falling, one ride and climb and fateful kiss at a time.

THE DOOR

— ‹‹•›› —

This was our first night home from the hospital, my wife recovering from her C-section, and something was wrong. Our baby cried right till dawn, only taking a breath to be fed when I carried him to his mother's breast in the darkness. Then I'd hold him to my shoulder and pat his tiny back, though he never burped or spit up. Instead, a labored grunting noise would come from his small mouth near my ear, and then he'd start crying again. What was strange was how he felt against me. I'd held babies before, most recently my youngest half-sister, and in my arms she felt soft and pliant, too pliant, and I was always careful to cradle her head and neck against my palm. I did the same with our newborn son, too, except there was something about his torso: it was his stomach; it felt as hard and bloated as a wineskin about to burst.

Early the next morning I called my brother Jeb and told him I wouldn't be in till the afternoon. We were remodeling a house in

Charlestown. My younger brother, a far more skilled and experienced carpenter, was my boss.

"Everything all right?"

"Our baby needs a checkup."

"Already?"

I did not want to tell him that we feared something was wrong with our son. To say this would make it true.

Later that morning, his pediatrician examined him and told us he just needed to "pass gas."

I said: "Then why won't he?"

Our doctor shrugged. "Give him some time."

We took her at her word.

When my wife, Fontaine, got pregnant, we'd been married nearly three years. She's a modern dancer and choreographer, and those years she also worked as a part-time dance instructor and self-employed upholsterer of furniture. We lived north of Boston in a small apartment in the house of her former high school art teacher. In the basement, Fontaine had a workbench and a sewing machine, and some nights when I came home from my own jobs as a carpenter and adjunct writing teacher, I'd find her down there tying down the springs of a wingback chair, or pulling buttons back through a frame to create diamond tufts in a brocaded fabric that often cost more per yard than we'd let ourselves spend on gas for our one car, an old VW. We never made much money, but it was enough.

It was a life of making things: a dance performance, a short story or novel, a chair, a deck, a new kitchen or bathroom, which sometimes paid me a bonus that Fontaine and I would then blow at a restaurant with friends, many of whom spent their days making things, too. She and I made love quite often and we ended up making this baby, Austin Christopher Dubus. The afternoon she told me she was pregnant, I was lying on the couch in our small living room trying to summon the will to get to my writing desk. It was early spring, a cold rain falling outside, and I'd already spent over eight hours demolishing a bathroom, hauling out the old sink, toilet, and bath, ripping horsehair plaster and lathe down to the studs, clearing between the bays the shredded newspapers used for insulation a hundred years ago. I wore a mask over my face for the lime dust, and I'd taken my flat bar and yanked every square-cut nail from each stud before ripping up the half-rotted floor planks over the joists, exposing ancient pipes for the plumber coming first thing in the morning.

That winter and spring I worked for Yaron. He was an Israeli who'd been in the army when the Egyptians bombed them in the desert. He had deep eyes, long black hair, and a mustache, and he would've been handsome if not for his shoulders, which were forever hunched as if he was still bracing himself to be blown to bits. He had a heavy accent, and his constant answer to any question about work or life was: "Why? It's not worth it. It's just not worth it."

Yaron was married and lived with his wife and two young daughters in a cul-de-sac in the north end of town, an antiseptic neighborhood of nearly identical houses with matching two-car garages. Every morning at six forty-five he would pick me up in his Taurus (No truck. "It's not worth it," he'd say. "My materials are delivered"), and we'd ride to the job site together. I was thirty-two years old and he was ten years older than that. One gray morning, both of us sipping from Styrofoam cups of hot coffee, he told me about the black-and-white photographs he used to take in Europe, how he had an exhibition of them once in London, how that's what he'd thought his life would be, a life of art.

"What happened?"

"I fucked my wife and had two kids."

He shrugged and changed the subject. I couldn't imagine using that word when it came to making love with my wife, and he may have started talking about the job, about strapping and Sheetrock and electrical outlets, things that honestly bored me. I'd been doing construction work off and on since leaving college, but I never felt called to do it. Those years I wasn't even that good at it. When I began writing fiction in my early twenties, I made the decision to avoid jobs where there was room for advancement up some invisible ladder to greater responsibilities and more money. I was afraid they would define me and my life and would rob me of the time and energy I'd need to teach myself to write. Also, I preferred to write in the mornings, so I often took night jobs, working as a halfway house counselor, an office cleaner, a bartender, and for six months when I was twenty-two, I worked for a private investigator and bounty hunter.

The last job I'd had before I got married was as head bartender at an Irish pub in our small town on the Merrimack River. I worked four nights a week and had seven mornings to myself, but Fontaine's life happened during the day, and I did not want us to be on two different schedules, never seeing much of each other. I'd also just published my first book. It was a collection of short stories that very few people bought or read, though this did not surprise me or even disappoint me much; that manuscript had been rejected by more than thirty publishers, and I was happy just to hold that book in my hands. I was also happy trying to write the novel my agent was in his second year of sending around. And now I was trying to write another one, a better one, though lying on that couch after another day with unhappy Yaron doing unhappy work, my body tired and heavy, I was beginning to feel my work life had taken a wrong turn. Soon it would be dark, a time I associated with going to a job after I'd spent the day writing, but now I was giving the best part of each day to ripping out toilets or hauling away old kitchen cabinets or nailing roof shingles on the gable of some lawyer's guesthouse in a misty rain. There were far worse problems to have, I knew, but I could feel the novel I was working on begin to slip away like a boat whose bowline I no longer had the strength to hold with both hands. And that's the moment my wife walked into the living room from the bathroom, smiling, her long curly black hair pulled back into a loose ponytail, a turquoise scarf around her neck. She looked so beautiful to me then that I did not at first take in what she had just said.

"What?"

Her eyes filled. She held up something short and white. "You're a daddy."

My body seemed to move on its own. I was up off the couch, holding her and kissing her and telling her positive words I do not now remember, though I know I felt like a liar saying them; in no time I'd be Yaron, my life of art forever behind me as I drove slope-shouldered from one job site to another, sipping bad coffee, telling the young man beside me that nothing good is worth doing, "Believe me, it's just not worth it."

———

I WAS WRONG, OF COURSE. IF I'VE EVER BEEN MORE WRONG ABOUT anything in my life, I do not know what it is. Almost immediately within minutes of her telling me, it seemed, I could only see this big, new thing in our lives as good; I loved my wife, she loved me, and we would find a way to make room for this baby we'd made. I brewed coffee and opened my notebook and got to work.

Daddy. It's not something I ever thought of being. I had a hunch not many other men gave it much thought either. You fall in love, you make love, and one day or night your wife turns to you in bed and says, "I want a baby."

"You do?"

"Don't *you?*"

"If you do."

"But don't you?"

"It's just not something I've ever thought much about."

But in one way I had. Like too many people, I come from a broken family. When I met Fontaine (and the first time I saw her she was performing onstage), I knew I would marry her. This was not so much a wish of mine as a knowledge, as if what I felt for her was music and the only dance for it was marriage, an institution that pulled me back to a dark time, my mother and father yelling at each other, throwing pots and pans, swearing, crying, this going on for months and months till that early Sunday morning in November when we four kids in pajamas followed our father out to his car before he drove away. When I heard the word *marriage*, yes, I thought of kids—hurt kids, lost kids, kids believing if they'd only been better kids their mother and father would still be together, kids who pretended it wasn't their fault.

"I really want a baby, honey. I want to go off the pill, okay?"

"Okay."

A few days after she told me this, I drove to my father's place nine miles east. He lived alone in a small house on a hill overlooking a two-lane road and the rise of a grassy slope, its ridge a thick stand of maple trees. It was late afternoon, and I knew he'd be finished with his day's writing and working out, exercises he did with dumbbells from his wheelchair.

He met me at the door. His hair was wet and he was naked, a towel draped over his crotch and right stump. He was fifty-six years old and had wide shoulders and a deep chest, and he was smiling, his eyes lit with love for me. "Hey, man." He held up his arms. I leaned down and hugged him. He smelled like soap, clean hair, and skin.

Soon he was dressed, and we were out on his back deck. The sun was low over the ridge of maples, their branches still bare. It was cold and I was wearing my leather jacket, but my father sat there in a short-sleeved shirt and sweatpants, the empty right leg of which he'd tied around his stump with a red bandanna. He was lighting a cigarette with his Zippo, one hand cupped around the flame. The night before, I'd called him and asked if I could stop by just before supper; I had to ask him a question. He said, "Yeah, man. I'm here."

This was new, my going to him to ask for any advice. It was my mother who raised us four kids, moving us from one cheap rented house in one mill town after another. When we saw our father, it was for two hours on a Sunday when he'd pick us up and drive us to church or take us out to a movie or restaurant he could barely afford. There was the feeling he was relaxing with us, that we, his kids, were part of his recreation, and there was also the feeling that he was doing the best he could, and if we were to ask for any more than that, he wouldn't be happy.

But that was years ago. Since then, he'd married and divorced two more times, and now he had two daughters with his third wife, who was a year older than I was. She and my half-sisters lived ten miles south, and he primarily saw them on weekends, the way he used to see us. Ever since I was old enough to sit in a bar with him, my father and I had had the easy rapport of drinking buddies; we sipped and talked about whatever came up: lifting weights, a good book, politics and women, and we might tell each other a few dirty jokes. But I don't remember him ever asking me what I might want to do with my time on this planet. Once, at a party at his house when he still had legs, I overheard him tell a friend of his, "I never tell my kids what to do with their lives." This, in many ways, was fine with me. I seemed to prefer to learn everything on my own the hard way anyway. And I rarely, if ever, sought out teachers.

"What's on your mind, man?"

"Fontaine wants a baby."

"Of course she does."

"But isn't it irresponsible to have one when you're as broke as we are?"

My father was looking over the railing out at the trees and sky. He took a drag from his cigarette and shook his head. He told me that lack of money will always be a problem for most people, but that shouldn't stop anyone. "I just believe, son, when the woman wants a baby, then that's it. It's time to have that baby."

I found myself agreeing, nodding.

"Besides, all that shit work you have to do, when you know it's for diapers and food for your child, it makes all work holy."

Holy. This was one of my father's words. He was a Catholic, and I was not. He believed there was a God who loved him; I did not. He believed he was being watched over, while I felt strongly that I was entirely alone and the only good that would ever come to me would have to come from my own hard work and occasional good luck.

Still, driving away from my thrice-divorced father's house, I felt better, for I believed that if my wife wanted a baby, then that should be that. Women only had limited time to get this done, and who was I to say she could not?

———

THEN SHE WAS PREGNANT, HER BELLY GROWING BY THE WEEK. IT was a cold winter and it snowed a lot, and whenever we walked up the shoveled icy sidewalk to our apartment, I'd take Fontaine's arm and hold her close. I imagined her slipping and falling, she and the baby imperiled. I read books on nutrition for pregnant women and learned that if the fetus didn't get enough calcium, the mother's body would take it from her own bones. I made sure my wife ate yogurt and drank milk four to five times a day. When the baby began to kick, Fontaine would kneel in front of our record player, her curly black hair down and around her shoulders, her back straight, and she'd place our stereo headphones against her protruding belly and play Mozart, Motown, and Stevie Wonder. From the couch, I watched her do this. It was like watching a flower blossom into a shape you didn't see coming. We were beginning to feel less like two and more like three, and all I felt about this was joy.

Then there was the bright light of the operating room, a gloved nurse handing me our newborn son. His mother's labor had been hard and painful, more than twenty-eight hours long, her cervix never fully dilating, and now she lay conscious on the table with an oxygen mask over her nose and mouth, looking up at us, quietly weeping. Just below her breasts, there was a short curtain to keep her from seeing the surgeons sewing up her abdomen, but seconds earlier, the moment our son was born, I had looked over that curtain and watched him being lifted from the incision, his tiny face handsome and raging just before he blurred and my voice broke and I told Fontaine, "He's a boy. He's a *boy*." Wiping my eyes and staring at him, I thought, *It's you. It's you*, for I recognized him from some other time and place. How was this possible? But I did, I recognized him, and now I was carrying him behind the nurse to the warming table, his fine hair wet as he cried with all the air he could summon from his small, pink chest, the stub of his umbilical cord still attached to what would become his navel. I laid him under a warming lamp, and the nurse handed me a pair of shears. I opened the blades. I was afraid to get too close to his skin.

"A little more, honey," she said. "You won't hurt him."

Snipping my son's umbilical cord felt like cutting through coated wire, an act he didn't seem to notice. The nurse began to clean our baby with a warm sponge, and I couldn't stop staring at his eyes and nose and mouth and chin, his tiny chest and nipples, his rising and falling abdomen as he kept crying, his penis and thighs and ankles and feet. I couldn't stop crying either, and I leaned in and stroked the side of his head with my thumb. I told him I was his dad and everything was going to be all right. Everything. I promise.

——

I FIRST NOTICED THE BLOOD WHEN I WAS CHANGING HIS DIAPER on the apron of the stage. This was at the high school where Fontaine taught dance, and I was there to pick her up and drive her home. The rehearsal had just ended, and while Fontaine was talking to one of the dancers and the rest chatted gleefully while drifting up the aisles of the dark theater, it was clear our four-week-old son's diaper needed changing, so I laid him down on a blanket under the colored gel lights of the stage. Maybe if I had not done this in that hazy purple light I would not have seen what I saw, a thread of orange in our son's stool. I finished cleaning and dressing him, then carried him and his open diaper out to the lighted foyer. That thread of orange seemed to be gone, but then I looked closer and saw traces of what had to be only one thing.

When I showed Fontaine, she was concerned but calm. Like my father, she had a deep and private faith. But I was a boy again, living in a shabby house on a shabby street, getting chased by other boys out to get me, and now they were out to get my son, too, this sleeping infant against my shoulder I already somehow loved far more than I loved my own heartbeat, my own breaths that were shallow now as I rushed out of that theater to buckle him into his seat and drive him and Fontaine back home to where there was a phone.

Our doctor told us to bring him in first thing in the morning.

"But shouldn't we take him to the *emergency* room?"

"No, not yet."

Early the next morning, our doctor, a kind woman with six kids of her own, examined our infant son and said, "I still don't think this is serious, but we'll do a GI series to be sure."

I said: "Doesn't he have to drink *barium* for that?"

"Yes," she said. "He'll have to do it through his bottle."

Fontaine and I looked at each other. Her black hair was held back, and again, she looked calm. I picked up our nine-pound son. He grunted against me, his belly more distended than it had ever felt before.

The upper and lower GI series was scheduled for the following morning. That week Jeb and I were in his shop, close to finishing the construction of custom cabinets, and his deadline for delivery was just days away; I'd be hurting his business if I did not go into work that morning. Fontaine said she would call me just as soon as they had the results. She said this to me as we lay in bed, Austin swaddled and finally asleep in his baby basket on the floor beside us. I rose up on one elbow and peered down at him. His face was so small. On his head was the knit cap we put on him because we kept the heat low. Even in sleep, his expression was slightly strained, as if he was never quite comfortable, and when was someone going to *notice* this? I pictured being in Jeb's shop in Charlestown a few miles away from the Boston hospital where Fontaine and my son would be. It wasn't that far, but still, I imagined my wife having to feed our infant barium from a bottle by herself. This felt like abandonment to me; I was abandoning my family when they needed me most. But we also had to pay our bills, didn't we? I got paid by the hour—no work meant no money—and I couldn't let Jeb down either. Fontaine was beginning to drift off against me, but I climbed out of bed and wrote the phone number for Jeb's shop on a piece of paper. I placed it under her car keys on the kitchen table, then knelt at Austin's basket. I leaned down and kissed him lightly on his small forehead. He smelled like clean skin and wool and something sweet I couldn't name.

Minutes later, lying in the dark beside my wife, I prayed for the first time. If I'd prayed even once in my life before this moment, I do not recall doing so. But now I was silently asking God to help our son. *Please, let this not be serious, and if it is serious, please— whoever you are, whatever you are—please heal our baby of it.*

I felt like a hypocrite. But as I closed my eyes I also felt just a little bit better, even if I did not believe anyone or anything was truly listening or cared.

———

WHEN THE CALL CAME THE FOLLOWING AFTERNOON, I WAS STAND-ing at the drill press, drilling identical holes one after another into medium-density fiberboard. On the other side of the shop, Jeb was gluing and clamping together cabinet boxes, a smoking cigarette between his lips, and his partner Bob, a quiet man with two grown kids and an ex-wife, had just finished ripping maple stiles on the table saw and switching it off, and that's when he heard what I did not: the black phone on the wall ring.

My job was simple, but the holes had to be perfect, and even though I seemed to be boring into the center of each penciled X my brother had drawn for me, I kept seeing Fontaine holding our son in her arms, trying to get him to drink some chemical element that probably tasted terrible—and then what?—was our baby put into some kind of X-ray machine? I didn't know, and it felt irresponsible to me that I didn't know.

"Andre?" Bob's deep voice, his hand on my shoulder. "Your wife's on the phone."

The telephone was in a corner of the shop. Taped to the wall was a sheet of emergency numbers, a water-stained bank calendar from three years earlier, a pencil stub hanging by a string. It's the image that comes when I hear again my wife's voice in my head, high and nearly breathless, as if she's running in the dark away or toward something and there isn't much time—*birth defect, malrotated, life-threatening*.

"*What?* What do they fucking mean '*life*-threatening'?"

"Yes, they think—" She couldn't say the rest, and I couldn't hear anymore, and then I was out of the shop and driving too fast through the streets of Boston toward my wife and son and the doctors who'd just given her this news.

———

OUR FOUR-WEEK-OLD SON NEEDED EMERGENCY SURGERY TO CORrect something called a malrotated upper bowel. It happens in about one out of six thousand births, and it had happened to Austin. In his tenth week of embryonic development, Austin's organs had finished developing outside what would become his torso. His spleen, liver, kidneys, and appendix then had to do a 270-degree revolution into the cavity that would hold them, finding their rightful place, the small and large intestines fanning out in that shape most perfectly suited to easy digestion. But with Austin that revolution never occurred. The organs, while functional, went into the wrong places, and the intestines twisted and bunched and never fanned out the way they should have. Most babies who experience this die, or the diagnosis comes so late their intestines no longer work, and then these children are hooked up to medical machinery for as long as they live.

I no longer see the face of the surgeon who told us all this; I only see his assistant, a man my age then or younger, tall and pale-faced and wearing black-framed glasses. I stood there in my carpentry sweatshirt, jeans, and work boots, sawdust feathered across my chest, and he nodded at me and said, as if I needed the language made simpler: "It's life-threatening."

Fontaine was holding Austin to her shoulder, patting his back and bouncing slightly. She looked pale and focused but calm, her faith rising up from wherever faith lives. But I did not trust these men or this hospital. They were just other men who'd learned another trade, and what if they were wrong? But there was no time for a second opinion, and from whom would we get it? This was one of the best hospitals for children in the world. Wait any longer and our son might not make it, or his intestines might not, and he'd be attached to a machine for the rest of his life. What was there to do *but* trust these men? Trust them and let go and have faith they could save our son?

———

HOURS PASSED BEFORE THEY WERE READY TO OPERATE. THERE was a waiting room with a TV and magazines and deep chairs, black night outside the hospital windows. Austin kept crying and crying; because he was going into surgery, we were not allowed to feed him, and he hadn't eaten in hours. We took turns holding him, walking him back and forth. Sometimes he'd fall quiet, and then rage again, his piercing wail in my ear. He sounded betrayed, and I felt neglectful and cruel.

A nurse finally came in and told us they were ready. She pointed to a wing of the building where the operating rooms were, and Fontaine and I hurried in that direction, Austin against my chest and shoulder. This faster movement calmed him down, and he seemed to take in the swinging doors we passed through, then the empty, quiet corridor, only a third of its overhead lights on. Against the wall in the shadows were three or four gurneys. Their mattresses were stripped, and Austin stared at them. Fontaine and I just stood there. I heard the faint buzz of the fluorescent lights above, nothing else. Fontaine may have said something about us being in the wrong place, I'm not sure, but now there were voices, low and feminine and cheerful, then soft footsteps, two women in surgical blue coming around a corner toward us. They were smiling, and they both had their hair tucked up, cotton masks hanging beneath their chins.

They introduced themselves as our son's anesthesiologists. There was the shaking of hands, their eyes on Austin, and one of them took him from my arms while the other handed me a clipboard with a form on it.

"You just have to sign this, and we'll be off."

Fontaine and the doctors began to talk about Austin's curly hair, his handsome face, but I was reading the form as quickly as you'd run barefoot over smoking embers: *accidental death, not responsible, no liability*, etc. I signed and handed the clipboard to the one who wasn't holding Austin. Then they were walking away before I could kiss him or touch him, both women holding him between them, his small head erect on his neck, his tiny back straight as they carried him into deep shadows through another set of swinging doors that opened and closed swiftly behind them, Fontaine and I turned to each other, holding tight, our crying echoing down the hallway.

———

WHEN AUSTIN WAS TWO DAYS OLD, HIS TROUBLES UNDIAGNOSED, Fontaine slept all afternoon in the bedroom recovering, and I held him swaddled in my lap in a rocking chair I'd pulled over to the gable window. Outside it was snowing, the wind kicking up every few minutes and gusting against the glass. I'd turned the heat up, and now I was rocking gently back and forth, staring down at our son's small face and hands and fingers. Sometimes I'd look out the window at the snow, but not for long. I couldn't stop staring at the sleeping face of this child we'd made, this child I somehow already loved more deeply than anyone I'd ever known or loved before.

A phrase came to me, words, it seemed, for what was happening to me that afternoon when nothing felt more important or pressing or essential than what I was doing at that very moment, holding our child, keeping him safe and warm: *state of grace*. I don't know where these words came from, and I did not know what they meant, but they moved through me like notes from an old cello miles away.

Hours later, when Fontaine had woken and was breast-feeding Austin in bed beside her, I took down our dictionary and looked up that phrase. The first definition I read was this: "to be surrounded by God's love."

God. Part of me resisted this. And another part, well, it just did not.

———

FONTAINE AND I SAT IN THAT WAITING ROOM, AND WE WAITED. IF there were other people there, I do not remember them. If any of our families came, I can no longer summon who they were. But I see the flat light of that room, my reflection in the night windows of the hallways I'd pace every ten or fifteen minutes. It was long and empty, and as I walked it, there was the heavy-shouldered, hollow-chested feeling that I was being punished for that late afternoon nearly a year earlier when I lay on our couch and Fontaine came into the room looking so beautiful and happy to tell me of this unspeakable gift coming to us, and my very first response, before all that came after, was to reject it.

The sins of the fathers are visited upon the sons. The Bible now, a book I'd never read and had no intention of reading. But I had no words for the limitless love I felt for our son, or the shadow side of this love, and I needed some. I remembered Hemingway: "When you have a child, the world forever takes a hostage." And there was Rilke, too: "Beauty is the beginning of terror, which we are only just able to bear."

Through the waiting room window, I could see Fontaine sitting straight in her chair, her eyes closed, her lips moving almost imperceptibly.

―――

THE OPERATION TOOK HOURS. IN MY MEMORY, IT TOOK ALL NIGHT, because when the doctor called us out to that corridor, his eyes bloodshot but warm, the early sun was shining outside the windows behind him. A cotton surgical mask still hung beneath his chin, the stubble there beginning to show. *Successful.* That's the word that comes. And *surgery.* And *no complications.* And *congratulations.* Fontaine and I holding each other, the doctor's face blurring, his big hand in mine, my hand squeezing his shoulder. And it may have been then or hours later or maybe even the next day that we got the full details of how they opened up our infant's belly. How they took out his appendix because if, years later, he ever had appendicitis, the doctors would never know it because his appendix would be in the wrong place. How they could not move Austin's other organs, but they could and did save his intestines, which saved him, fanning them out the way they were supposed to be in the first place.

"And that's it?" I said. "He'll be all right?"

"He'll live a completely normal life."

Austin may have come home with us that day, or the next, I no longer know. All I know is that profound relief, joy, and gratitude were shooting heat through me like kisses from the gods, and I had to do something with it all: we had been given something so good, and I had to give something, too. I kissed Fontaine and told her I would be right back. I was half walking, half running down that hallway, looking for the first person who could tell me where I could give blood, anything. There were kind faces and helpful faces, men and women, fingers pointing to signs and elevators and closed rooms behind glass doors, all of this on a moving current of what I can only call love. Then I was sitting at a desk filling out a form, adding my name to all those willing to give the marrow of their bones to a stranger who one day might need it. A woman took a vial of my blood, but this did not feel like enough. I wanted to give something away right then, on the same day my son was spared. I kept looking for the blood bank but could not find it, and I wanted to get back to my wife and child. I wanted to hold him. I wanted to hold him close and never let go.

——

BUT WE HAVE TO LET GO, DON'T WE?

This was more than twenty years ago. Austin is now over six feet and two hundred and twenty pounds and wears a size 13 shoe. He lifts weights six days a week and reads and writes and loves serious films and good music and all sports with balls in them. When he was a baby, the scar on the right side of his abdomen was pale and an inch long. As he's grown, it's grown a bit longer and deeper, though now it's largely covered with dark hair. Every single time I see that scar, I feel only boundless gratitude.

Austin lives a thousand miles west of us, on his college campus in Ohio. He has an eighteen-year-old sister and a sixteen-year-old brother. With the birth of each, my capacity for love seemed to grow exponentially larger, opening up in me its attendant fear of loss, but a deep reservoir of joy, too. So much joy, as if my deepest, truest life could only begin once I became a father.

Soon our daughter, Ariadne, a dancer and artist like her mother, will be moving to another campus, and not long after Elias, an athlete and drummer, will want to do the same. Fontaine and I will be two again. Back to where we began, for we do not own these three people that came from us. We were simply given them to love and to guide and to set free. And even though I still do not believe in an all-powerful and loving God, I know I'll pray for my children's health and safety daily and nightly, as I do now, as I will until I am no longer on this earth, for *something* is here among us: something I cannot see but feel; something I cannot hear but sense; something I cannot smell but know; that one late afternoon, this life will bring you to a door your lover may walk through smiling, and just because you're tired and afraid and have little to no faith, you're supposed to lift your head and breathe and walk with joy and trembling right through it.

SHELTER

—◁◂•▸▷—

t was the coldest winter in New England in over a hundred years, and we were framing my house in the snow. For over thirty days straight the windchill was below zero, and most mornings my younger brother, Jeb, and I and our friend Jim would spend over an hour just shoveling off the job site so we could set up our cutting station, oil and load our nail guns, and light the propane heater to get the compressor warm enough to run. Most days I'd have to chisel off the decks just so we could snap a line for the toe plates of walls. I grew a beard to keep my face warm.

Why not wait till spring?

Because I'd bought these two acres of land over three years earlier, and it had taken us that long to get all the necessary permits in place; because for the past nine years my wife and I had been raising our three children in a vinyl-sided half-house that was small and dark and cluttered with toys and the secondhand furniture we owned; because since my birth forty-three years earlier I'd lived in over two dozen rented houses and apartments, had always had a landlord, some threatening my single mother with eviction, some threatening me, and now—for the very first time—I had money in the bank, a lot of it, all from a novel I'd written over four years in my parked car; and because, well, I just couldn't wait.

At first there was the desire to get the whole project started and done with. Like most writers, for years I'd been hoping for a time when I could give my entire day to writing and reading. Now, after over twenty years of daily labor, I could finally do just that. My agent kept calling to ask why I wasn't hiring somebody to build my house. "Don't you want to write another novel?" I did, of course. But for the kind of house we wanted to build—an in-law apartment for my wife's aging parents, a bedroom for each of our children and one for us—it would just be too expensive to hire a builder when I had the skills to do it myself.

I estimated I could cut costs in half, an accurate estimate, it turned out, but part of me didn't want to do it at all: Wasn't a house just another material object anyway? Did we really need to own one? Did anybody?

But this ambivalence began to dissipate the week after our permits were approved. It was a cold Sunday in November, the sky gray, the air heavy with future snow. Two days earlier my foundation contractor had poured our footings, and he told me they'd cure better if I kept them warm. So that morning I drove to a local farm in my pickup and bought a dozen hay bales, drove to my wooded lot, tossed them off, then used a pitchfork to spread hay over concrete, *my* concrete poured in the shape of *my* house, on *my* land.

It took us over two years. Every day I'd pull up to the site at 7 a.m., the smells of sawdust and pine pitch in the air, those lovely naked two-by-six walls standing plumb, level, and square, and I'd buckle on my leather carpentry belt of tools and work alongside my brother and my friend, and later, with a new carpenter I'd hired, too. That spring the snows melted, but it brought some of the heaviest rains in fifty years, and we hung massive tarps to work under. By early that summer, the four of us were roofing my house during a heat wave.

When it came time to cover the exterior walls with cedar shingles, my wife Fontaine, a modern dancer who used to make a living upholstering furniture, spent two months nailing up over half of them while I did the rest. I hired my sixty-seven-year-old mother to paint the corner boards, the soffits and fascia, the window and door casings. While my wife had a fear of heights, my mother had none. There were electricians and plumbers on the job now, and every hour or so I'd pause in my work and glance up to see my mother standing on the scaffolding forty feet in the air, squinting in the sun as she brushed paint onto the trim of my house. I remembered the doctor we rented a house from when I was twelve, a tall man with thick glasses who stood at our door in his coat and tie and asked that our mother leave and take us four kids to live in the projects. I remembered over the years all the scrappy places we'd lived in that somebody else had owned. Painting my big, new, homemade house, my mother looked so happy, and it made me happy seeing that.

The truth is, except for those moments of unspeakable grace holding our three newborn children, I've never been happier than when I was building for us this house. One late afternoon, a cold rain starting to fall, I stood on a plank outside my daughter's second-story bedroom, trying to finish the shingles around her window. The sun was down and the plank was getting slippery, and a small voice inside me said to quit now and head home. But I no longer felt that where we lived was home, and as I fit a shingle into place up against my daughter's window, this motion felt like something else, though I did not at first know what it was. Then

I did; it was just like pulling the covers up to my daughter's chin right after she fell asleep. It was like doing that with her two brothers, too. It was like closing their bedroom door and tiptoeing down the hall. It was like locking the front and back doors and checking the windows and turning off the lights; it was like holding them as babies and wanting my arms to be a shelter for them and never wanting to let go.

IF I OWNED A GUN

— ‹‹•›› —

I

The summer I turned seventeen, I nearly killed my younger brother with a 12-gauge shotgun. This was in Fishville, Louisiana, where my mother's parents lived on ten acres of pine trees alongside Highway 8. It was July, and my mother had two weeks off from work and she had driven us four kids down from Massachusetts for a rare visit. My grandfather was in his mid-sixties then but looked ten years older, his lined face clean-shaven and Scots-Irish handsome. His shoulders were still broad but slumped forward, and every time he raised his arm to push a wad of chew between his gum and cheeks, you could see his biceps bunch up under his sleeve. He was a retired pipe fitter who'd never gone beyond the third grade, but for years he worked as a foreman building power plants for big companies like Babcock & Wilcox and Brown & Root, their logos etched into hard hats hanging on nails in one of the two corrugated-steel shops he'd built with his own hands. He'd also built the larger of the two camp houses he and my grandmother lived in, and because he'd been a pipe fitter and not a carpenter, the exterior was sided with strips of riveted sheet metal that under the Louisiana sun would grow too hot to touch. At the time I knew nothing of these construction details, nor did I know much about what I saw as the manly world of woodshops and the many power tools and pine scraps and pipe fittings inside them. But a year or so earlier up north is when I'd cut off my two-foot ponytail and begun to lift weights and box and fight, and now that I was around my grandfather, a man who spoke very little but seemed to be constantly appraising my brother and me, all I wanted was to appear like a man. And what a man did, according to our grandfather, was *work*.

His name was Elmer Lamar Lowe, but we grandchildren called him Pappy. In his retirement, he'd cultivated a vegetable garden the size of a small farm, and every day he was out there not long after dawn picking peas and tomatoes, or starting up the rototiller to carve furrows into the ground for a late season planting of some kind, and if he wasn't doing that, he'd be taking his chain saw to a tall jack pine that was crowding other pines, or he'd be demolishing the back door's cracked brick steps he'd laid ten years earlier, swinging his sledgehammer down onto brick and mortar he'd dump into a wheelbarrow and haul off to a junk pile behind his biggest workshop.

Our first morning there, my grandmother cooked us a breakfast of smoked sausage and grits and eggs and homemade biscuits, and my brother Jeb and I made the mistake of sleeping in until we smelled that breakfast, Pappy already up and working for over three hours. When he walked into the kitchen carrying a basket of green beans and tomatoes, his face gleaming with sweat, his work shirt damp with it, he eyed my brother and me sitting beside our sisters like we'd not only disappointed him but that he could also already see what kind of lives we were going to have, and it was nearly too late to save us.

He set the basket down and sat at the table across from us. My grandmother Fern, the daughter of a rice farmer, a wry and small-boned woman who prized physical labor as much as he did, slid a full plate in front of him. He ate it slowly and quietly. Every now and then he'd swallow and glance over at one of my sisters and ask, "How's school?" He'd nod at whatever he heard, though his eyes were on me and my still long-haired younger brother. I ate my breakfast quickly, but I felt like the dog and Pappy was the collar.

My mother, still young and beautiful, a single mother since she was twenty-eight, was talking about taking us all down to the creek for a swim. But Pappy said, "Those boys are gonna work first."

And that was that. But I could feel my brother stiffen beside me. He was fifteen then and for the past two years he'd been teaching himself to play classical music on his guitar in his room eight to ten hours a day, sometimes longer. His long hair was frizzy and wild, and his cheeks and chin were covered with young whiskers he'd rarely shave. I still had not grown any myself, and I envied those whiskers. And I envied what my brother did and said next. "I can't. I have to practice." Then he stood and carried his empty plate to the sink and walked outside to the bunkhouse and his guitar and metronome and music books.

My face burned. I glanced over at Pappy and saw him shake his head once. Then he narrowed his eyes at me as if to say, *Well?* and I nodded and carried my plate to the sink and stepped out into the heat. I could smell the sunbaked concrete of the patio, the hot sheet metal siding behind me, pine bark, and my own rising sweat. Because my mother and father had eloped and left Louisiana, finally settling in Massachusetts, where my father had found a teaching job and where my parents' short marriage came to an end, I had spent very little time around my grandfather, nor had I known any of my uncles, and my father's father died when I was a small child. Being around a man related to me felt new, and so waiting for my grandfather out under the July Louisiana sun felt like far more than waiting for just him.

And I didn't have to wait long. Soon enough I was following him down the narrow path between the camp buildings and his two woodshops to his large garden in the sunlight. Standing on a patch of turned-over earth was a new-looking rototiller, and the rest of that week was an eye-stinging blur of endless work under a taunting sun, yanking on the rope of the tiller till it roared, then sliding it into gear and having to wrestle it through dry stony ground, breathing its exhaust, the unrelenting gas-moan of its guttural engine, Pappy showing me how to swing a sledge with my legs spread and my target—those back brick steps he would soon replace with new ones—just the right distance away so I didn't come up short and break the handle or else stand too far away and swing the hammer down onto my own foot or shinbone. He taught me how to hold and start a chain saw, its steel teeth spinning so fast along the cutting bar it was just a loud clacking hum, and when I touched it to the trunk of a tall pine, bits of bark and yellow pulp flew into the air and I nearly closed my eyes and I had to grip tighter or get jerked into the tree I was killing.

Those entire two weeks it seemed that all I did was till and cut and haul, my T-shirt and jeans heavy with sweat, my palms newly blistered along the calluses I already had from lifting weights back home. And sometime that first week, maybe even that first day, Jeb was working with me too, his hair pulled back in a ponytail, his drawn cheeks no longer pale for once but flushed with blood, and always there was Pappy standing off to the side watching us, his arms crossed over his chest, a wad of wintergreen chewing tobacco in his left cheek, and there was the feeling that I was competing against my own brother, even against myself, in a very important test, one that would determine something essential.

And then Pappy asked us to kill something.

Down Highway 8, past Big Dean's Creek and the gas station and roller rink across from it, was a back road that wound east through the pines, and on it lived Pappy's friend Howard Keyes. He was older than our grandfather, and he wore denim overalls with no shirt on underneath, his skin deeply tanned from working out in the vegetable garden that was his primary source of food. His chest and arm muscles, though slackened with age, were still defined and showed a lifetime of hard labor, and Howard had few teeth, but he shaved every morning, always missing a patch of white whiskers here and there. Today we might describe Howard as being on the autism spectrum, but Pappy just called him slow, his friend who every time he said goodbye would lift his hand and smile and say, "Hope y'all good luck."

But now Howard was not smiling, he was crying. This had to be Sunday, the only day Pappy did not work, because since early that morning our grandfather had been stoking the fire under his smoker, a big steel cylinder on trailer wheels he'd built for smoking the brisket and chicken and sausages he was slowly cooking now, its barbecue hickory smoke drifting over the patio where my brother and I sat in the shade of a pecan tree. Jeb was practicing chords on his guitar, and I was drinking a cold Falstaff from a can. From inside the house came the happy voices of my grandmother, mother, and sisters, the muffled snapping of peas, the drip of the air conditioner, and through the pines an occasional pickup or logging truck drove fast up Highway 8. My fingers and hands felt swollen from a week of nonstop physical work, but my muscles felt warm and ready for the next task, and there was the sweet contented feeling that I'd earned this chair I was sitting in, that I'd earned the beer I was drinking and all the good food that was soon coming, and Jeb had too. For while he still spent hours in the bunkhouse practicing his Bach preludes, words and sounds that were a foreign language to me, something had made him put his guitar down and join me and Pappy out in the heat, something that he did not seem to need to do as much as I did, for it appeared to have neither added to him nor taken anything away, but I could see the grudging respect Pappy was giving to my brother every time he reached for his guitar.

Because it was Sunday, Howard wore his newest denim overalls and a faded blue button-down shirt beneath it. His thinning white hair was combed back, and as he stood near Pappy's smoker shaking his head and crying—and I had no idea *why* he was crying—my grandfather just half nodded and turned over chicken breasts with a long fork, squinting into the heat and smoke.

By suppertime, Howard had stopped crying, and he ate quietly and reverently at the end of the kitchen table. I wanted to ask my grandfather what was troubling Howard so much, but then Pappy drove him home, and I sat with my mother, sisters, and grandmother getting ready to play Rook, a card game we only played when we came down to Fishville. Outside the windows the pine trunks looked copper in the last of the sun, and Jeb was back in his room playing old European music to his metronome, the kitchen smelling like coffee and blackberry cobbler. I had just finished a plate of it and was standing to serve myself some more when Pappy walked in and said, "Andre." He motioned me to follow him back to his bedroom, and I left the table and the card game and soon enough Pappy was reaching into his closet and pulling out a side-by-side 12-gauge shotgun.

He handed it to me along with a box of Winchester shells he pulled down from a shelf. I had never held a shotgun before, but I did not tell him this for he'd handed it to me the way a fellow worker would a sledgehammer or a chain saw, just another tool every man surely knew how to use.

"Armadillos are getting into Howard's garden. Y'all need to get down there tomorrow morning and shoot 'em."

I held the shotgun in one hand and the heavy box of shells in the other. I felt I'd just been given permission to do a bad thing for a good reason, and well, I had no choice, did I? Besides, armadillos were ugly and looked vaguely sinister too, with their long noses and tails and the leathery bony plates of their hides. They'd probably been on the earth since the dinosaurs, and wasn't that long enough?

Early the next morning, I laid the shotgun and box of shells in the backseat of my mother's faded red Toyota sedan, and Jeb and I drove down Highway 8 toward Howard's place. We had all four of our windows down, the road wind whipping Jeb's long hair in his face, something he ignored as he looked straight ahead. His mind seemed to be on other things, the great music of Johann Sebastian Bach most likely, but there was an almost erotic pulsing in my blood, and I could hardly wait to load both barrels of that shotgun and start killing the armadillos who were killing the garden that fed my grandfather's friend. It had been a long time since I'd shot a gun, and I was looking forward to it.

The first time was when I was six years old. This was in 1965 just outside Iowa City, my father and me standing on dried mud behind our rented farmhouse. It may have been summer or winter, I don't remember, only that the sun was high in the sky, and I could smell my father's cologne as he leaned close to me, his palm under the grip of his .22 Colt revolver I held with both hands as he told me to close one eye and line up the sights at the fence post I was aiming at, to hold my breath and squeeze the trigger, not to pull it.

But I did pull it and the pistol jerked in the loud bang that smelled like burnt metal, and my father was smiling down at me and taking his gun back.

He was twenty-nine years old then and still kept his hair as short as the ex-Marine captain he was, his brown mustache thick as a cowboy's. Later that afternoon or another afternoon, my father shot and killed a rabbit with that same pistol, and I held the rabbit's warm legs as my father cut and peeled its fur off, the skin underneath thin and wet and purple, the dead rabbit shitting pellets down my arms.

My father also owned a rifle, and when I was eight or nine and we'd moved to New England and lived in the woods, my mother and father only a year or two from breaking up, my father taught me how to press the rifle's stock into my shoulder and lean my cheek against it so that I could shut one eye and line up the sights on my target—a fat pine tree thirty yards away—and, again, hold my breath and squeeze the trigger.

I did squeeze it, and there was a crack in the air, the stock tapping into my shoulder as bark flew off that pine. My father praised that shot, but I didn't need any encouragement. I loved holding a loaded gun in my hands. I loved shooting things. I loved watching how just the twitch of my finger could change things permanently far away from where I stood.

When I wasn't watching *The Rifleman* on our black-and-white TV, I was watching soldiers in Vietnam getting zipped up into black bags, their eighteen- and nineteen-year-old bodies loaded onto helicopters to be flown back home. I watched Martin Luther King Jr. and Robert Kennedy shot months apart. And I watched my father drive away from us through the woods, his car loaded with his clothes and books and gun. But I had a gun of my own, a Daisy BB rifle, and for months after my father left I walked through the woods looking for birds or squirrels or chipmunks, and I would aim at them and squeeze the trigger and I tried to kill them all.

Now Jeb and I were pulling up in front of Howard's house. It had a front porch under a shingled roof, and the posts looked newly painted, the front and side yards freshly mowed. I left the shotgun in the car and knocked on Howard's front door. There was no answer so we walked around to his garden out back, but he wasn't there either. I assumed he was on one of his long walks somewhere, and I was glad he wasn't there; I couldn't wait to load that shotgun and do what we came here to do.

Standing beside our mother's car, I found the switch that opened the shotgun's barrels on a hinge so it could be loaded. I asked Jeb to hand me a shell. It was red, and I was surprised by how heavy it was. I pushed it into the right barrel, then took another, my fingers trembling slightly as I pushed it into the left. I swung the barrels back up and locked it into place and made sure to keep it aimed at the ground. Jeb started to walk to the side yard, and I said, "No, I go first, remember? The guy with the gun is always in front."

It was something our father had taught us, and walking ahead of my brother with that loaded shotgun into the rising heat of Howard's open yard, I felt like I was stepping into the tracks of men who had come hundreds of years before me, hard good men prepared to do a hard good thing.

It was still early, the sun on my face and neck as we crossed Howard's side yard to a split-rail fence overgrown with kudzu. Off to the right stretched Howard's vegetable garden, but something was drawing me to that fence, and when we got there Jeb whispered, "See it?"

"No." And then I did. On the other side of the fence was the biggest rabbit I'd ever seen, its fur brown and gray, its ears pricked at a danger he was beginning to sense too late, for I'd already raised the shotgun and pulled the butt of the stock to my shoulder, leaned my cheek against it and sighted down the barrels, my finger squeezing the trigger, a bomb going off against my shoulder, the shotgun jumping, then dropping onto the top rail of the fence. The air smelled like fireworks and good times, but lying in the grass twenty feet from where it had been sitting was the rabbit, a hole through its torso the size of a softball.

I have no memory of what my brother and I might have said to one another about this, though I knew we stood at that fence a while staring down at the awful power of what I still held in my hands. I began to feel sorry for that rabbit and remorseful for killing it, but then I recalled how big he'd been, which meant he was one of the raiders of Howard's garden, which meant that rabbit had deserved to die.

And now it was time to find what we came here for, those armadillos that had made old Howard cry. I cracked open the shotgun and pulled out the shell. I asked Jeb to hand me a new one from the box and he did, my fingers shaking now as I pushed the red slug into the right barrel. The sun was in my eyes and I was sweating, and we were already walking toward Howard's garden when I swung the long double barrel back into position and an explosion flung the shotgun backwards out of my hands. I looked down at my empty palms and fingers. I turned and looked at the smoking shotgun lying in the grass. Then I looked at my brother. He was standing six feet in front of me, his lips parted, his face pale, and just a foot to his left, half a fence post was gone, its splintered insides blond, nearly white.

My mouth filled with saliva and I had to bend over and rest my hands on my knees. I may have sworn at my brother then. I may have yelled at him for walking in front. But I knew it was my fault. Those two barrels should not have gone off, but it was an old gun, and dirty, and I was the man carrying it. I was the one who should have been paying more attention. But I hadn't. And I'd nearly blown a hole through my only brother's back.

I spat on the ground, then picked up Pappy's shotgun. It felt poisonous to me now. I carried it carefully and quickly back to our mother's car. Jeb followed with the box of shells, and we drove fast back up Highway 8. We'd killed a rabbit, I could tell Pappy that. I could tell him what else had happened, but I knew I could not and would not.

When we got back to our grandparents' place, I could see our grandfather out in the garden stooped over some plant, and I hurried inside with the shotgun and wedged it deep into the corner of the closet. I put the box of Winchester shells back on the shelf too, then I closed the door and I did not open it again.

II

Two years later, my older sister was raped at knifepoint by two men who were never caught, and my father began to buy and carry handguns. He and I and my brother would drive out to a sand quarry and shoot at empty bottles, shattering them into pieces we left on the ground behind us. Afterward we'd go to a bar and drink beer, and as I slowly got drunk I could still feel the kick of each handgun in my right palm and fingers, especially my father's high-caliber semiautomatics that could fire off rounds faster than any thought you could ever have. That's what scared me; it was too easy to use these weapons without thought. And during these years, changing my body from soft to hard, exorcising that frightened and hurt nonfighter boy inside of me, boxing in gyms and fighting in the street, a gun in my hands was a nuclear switch for a madman. And even though I enjoyed these rare outings with my father, once the shooting was through, I felt as if I'd stepped away from a field of half-buried mines.

Then for my nineteenth birthday my father bought me a rifle. It was a .22-caliber Weatherby made in Italy, and it had a lovely rosewood stock and a 24-inch barrel and a magazine that could hold enough rounds to do what had to be done. It also had a switch near the trigger so the shooter could decide if he wanted to make it a single-shot weapon or a semiautomatic, pulling the trigger until the magazine was smoking and empty and—and *what?*

It was a gift I did not want. Or need. Though that new rifle looked beautiful to me, the same way my father's handguns looked beautiful—the silver gleam of his .38 snub-nose, the flat checkered grip of his .380 semiautomatic, the square barrel and sure weight of the 9-millimeter, the Old West echo of his Colt six-shooter. And it was fun shooting at cans and bottles, deeply satisfying when I hit them, which was often, and so I thanked my father for this rifle but I only shot it a few times at that quarry, and when I left home for college in Texas, I asked my father to keep it in his house until I returned.

Those years he lived in campus housing at the liberal arts college where he'd been teaching ever since we'd moved east, and since my sister's rape, he'd set up a shooting target in his basement laundry room. The target was a red steel box, and he'd hang a paper target over its opening, one designed to absorb the shot and direct the bullet in a ricochet into the belly of the box. One day my father called me and asked me to come over. He was excited because he'd done a domestic chore with his hands, probably the first time he'd ever done such a thing, and he was proud, and we both laughed as he showed me the hook-and-eye lock he'd put on the inside door casing to the laundry room. There were three or four holes near the hook latch, his earlier attempts at lining it up with the eye, and I shook my head and asked him why he needed that lock in the first place? He stopped smiling and narrowed his eyes at me. He told me his wife Peggy had walked in with a basket of laundry just as he was getting ready to squeeze the trigger of one of his handguns. "And I almost shot her in the head."

———

A FEW YEARS PASSED, AND IT WAS EARLY FALL AND I WAS MOVING to New York City with my girlfriend, Jessica. She wanted to find work in the TV news business, and I had started to write and to act in local plays, so why not go see if I could do that where people did it seriously? Through a friend, we found an apartment to rent, and we loaded her car with our books and clothes and at the last minute I drove over to my father's house for my rifle. My girlfriend told me that it was illegal to bring a firearm into the city, that doing so could get me a year on Rikers Island, but this was New York in the 1980s. In the first year of that decade alone, there were 1,814 murders. In the subway tunnels every year, thousands of felonies were committed on passengers, over 14,000 in 1981. Forty-Second Street in Times Square was lined with peep shows, prostitutes, and drug dealers, and not long before learning all this, I'd read about a twenty-three-year-old actress who'd moved to New York City from Massachusetts. She was working and taking drama classes, and one night after she had come back to her apartment from a Broadway show, a man jumped her and dragged her to the roof of her building and began chasing her with a knife. The news article said that people who lived nearby could hear her screams, they could hear her pleading with the man, and they heard her shout her name and apartment number over and over, something she'd been taught to do in self-defense classes. The neighbors finally called the police, but they could still hear the screams of the young woman as she tried again and again to reason with this man, and then they heard the worst screams of them all, and then nothing.

I put down my newspaper and stared at the wall. Why hadn't they tried harder to help her? Why hadn't they *done* anything? And I pictured being at the window of an adjacent building on a floor higher than that flat roof where this woman was trying to reason with what could not be reasoned with; I could feel the rosewood stock of my rifle against my cheek, could see the man's shadowed face and head in the sights of my 24-inch barrel, could feel the squeeze of the trigger as the man dropped without a word, his knife harmless now, that desperate young woman free.

The apartment we were renting was on the Upper East Side on 82nd Street between Lexington and Third. It was on the first floor, but it wasn't a real apartment at all. It was the former building supervisor's office, and when we walked into that eight-by-thirteen-foot room, I couldn't believe the rent they were asking us to pay for this. There was one window and a kitchenette with a mini fridge, and just behind the door was another that held a tiny bathroom. My girlfriend and I both looked at each other, shrugged, and moved in.

The last thing I carried in was my rifle. It was night now, our short cross street well lighted, very few people on the sidewalks. I leaned into Jessica's car and grabbed the handle of the case that held my gun and bullets and hurried inside.

That first night we slept on the floor, but over the next few days we bought a couch and a mattress and I found a hardware/lumber store not far away where I bought two-by-fours and plywood. It took me three trips to carry it all down the sidewalks to our building, but I got to work and built us a sleeping loft above our only window. Screwed into the concrete wall outside that window were black iron bars that could be swung open on a hinge, and I bought a padlock and locked it shut, then Jessica and I managed to get that mattress up into our new loft that smelled like freshly cut plywood, the ceiling just two feet above us.

Beneath the loft I loaded books into our two bookcases, then made a desk out of a knobless interior door I'd found on a trash heap near the East River. I rested it on cinder blocks, then used more blocks to assemble shelves with pine boards across from our couch. We set our TV and stereo on those, wedged in our remaining books beside and around them, and Jessica wanted to lay a throw rug down but she couldn't find one narrow enough.

My rifle had been leaning in the corner of the room in its case near the barred window, but I began to imagine some man following my lovely girlfriend home from the bookstore where she'd found a job, and what if he was armed and I couldn't get to my rifle fast enough? I had found a job working as a bartender in a Midtown restaurant, and one afternoon before my night shift, I pulled my gun from its case, then carried it up into our loft. I loaded the magazine with hollow points, pushed it into my rifle, set the safety catch, then laid it between my side of the mattress and the wall, an act that made me feel safer but also somehow more imperiled. Like I was asking for trouble doing this, and one day it would surely come.

Then it was summer, and we kept our window open, the black iron bars snaked with green ivy I would often stare at while sitting at my writing desk each morning. We both worked night and day shifts, and on those I had off and Jessica did not I would walk the length of Manhattan. I'd cut west through Central Park and take one of its trails down to Central Park South and the Avenue of the Americas, the sidewalks always crowded with people, every day in this city like the Fourth of July anywhere else. I tried to avoid bumping into passing men in business suits, women in business skirts or shorts and halter tops, little kids holding the hands of their tourist parents, an old homeless woman pushing all of her belongings in her rusted luggage cart, and I'd pass Rockefeller Center, then head west for the towering neon madness of Times Square, men in red coats hawking theater tickets, a brown boy banging drumsticks on an upside-down plastic bucket, some drunk getting handcuffed by a young cop, prostitutes in net stockings and platform shoes on the stroll in front of triple-X movie houses, plastic crack vials snapping under my feet. I'd keep walking down the concrete canyon of Broadway past Herald Square, street musicians playing under the trees where I could smell pot smoke and truck exhaust and hot pretzels from a vendor's cart. I'd head south down Fifth Avenue past all of its expensive shops, their plate-glass display windows set back in granite and trimmed with gold, mannequins wearing suits and dresses and shoes that cost more than I made in months. I'd keep heading south, passing under the Washington Square Arch into the park where couples would be lying together on blankets in the grass, smoking, listening to a jazz quartet of young musicians my age or watching a shirtless man juggle bowling pins while riding a unicycle six feet tall. I'd pass through Greenwich Village and its open-air restaurants, their sidewalk tables full of men and women sipping wine and speaking languages from around the world. I'd walk by all the smoky jazz joints and Italian and French restaurants to Canal down through Chinatown, its streets crowded with people speaking Cantonese and Mandarin, a woman hawking potatoes and cabbage laid out in bins on long tables, a man sitting in a canvas kiosk selling Chinese newspapers and magazines, another man cleaving cooked ducks on a bench, then hooking their red carcasses on a rack alongside twenty or thirty others, the fresh stench of prawns in trays of crushed ice beside large white fish stacked on top of each other like firewood. And I'd keep moving south, past the New York Stock Exchange and into Battery Park. In the shade of its many trees were junkies passed out like the dead. There were homeless men and women and children. There were often men kissing one another, an old woman in four overcoats curled up against a maple. And I'd make my way to the steel railing overlooking New York Harbor, and for once there was wide-open space and I could smell salt water and feel the sun and I could breathe.

I'd look out over the bay to Ellis Island, then farther south to the Statue of Liberty, her arm raised in the air as if she'd like to make just one important point if only someone would listen. I'd stand there at the southernmost tip of Manhattan and look out at the water as long as I could. I already wanted to leave New York. I was happy to know that this wild tangle of living history and humanity existed, but I hated living in it. I hated how crowded it was and that this city never quieted down or stopped, that even at four or five in the morning there'd be bar customers making their loud way home past our window, taxicabs shooting by all night, car alarms going off. I hated how expensive it was to live in this place, and I especially hated seeing so many homeless people in this city with so many millionaires and billionaires. I did not know how much longer I would be here, and on one of these afternoons as I squinted out at the sun on the water I had to summon my will to walk back into the crowded human noise behind me, and then I was on Wall Street and I heard someone running behind me and a man shouting, "On the *ground*, motherfucker!"

Something slammed to the concrete and I turned and there, five feet in front of me, was a teenager on his chest and stomach, a big man with a short red beard straddling his back. The man was breathing hard and he was pressing a .38 revolver to the back of the kid's head. The sidewalk was crowded with men in ties and three-piece suits, many of them carrying slim briefcases as they walked right by what was happening at their feet. The man on the kid's back was in a denim jacket and jeans, his chest heaving, his finger curled against that trigger. I could see the brass rims of the bullets in the chamber, and it would be so easy for one of these stockbrokers to bump into this man and blow this kid's brains out.

Then one stepped over the kid's legs and kept walking, and for a flash of a second I pictured myself pushing the man off, but then I saw the silver handcuffs in a leather pouch on his belt. I saw the kid's outstretched arm on the sidewalk and the paper bag he still held, a dozen crack vials spilling out of it in the sunshine. The cop was sweating and he kept saying to the kid, the muzzle of his gun pressed to his head, "You *mother*fucker. You little mother*fucker*." Then he pushed his gun into his shoulder holster and pulled out the cuffs, yanked the kid's arms behind him, handcuffed him, and jerked him to his feet. The kid was a tall, handsome Latino, seventeen or eighteen years old, and he was staring down at the crack vials on the sidewalk as if they had betrayed him.

The cop was on a handheld radio now, and in no time uniformed cops were there too. One of them swept the drugs back into the dealer's paper bag, and then they were gone and it was over, the sidewalk filled with only stockbrokers now. On my walk back to the Upper East Side, all I could think about was how I seemed to be the only one who had stopped and watched that scene play out. Was it because I wasn't a New Yorker, and New Yorkers saw that kind of thing fairly often? Or did it have more to do with how many drug busts and guns to the head we all see on TV and in the movies hundreds and hundreds of times every year? But that had been no show, and it would've taken very little for that .38 to have gone off, its zipping bullet piercing the skull of a boy none of us would ever know or care much about.

———

ONE NIGHT AFTER ONE OF THESE LONG WALKS, JESSICA WORKING at the bookstore, I came back to our apartment, and it was dark and too quiet. I had just shut and locked the door behind me. There was only the dim light of the streetlamp coming through our barred window, and from the center of our shallow kitchenette there was the blinking red light of the answering machine. I pressed its button, and it was Jessica. "Honey, I tried to—" Something slapped the back of my head and I wheeled around and threw a punch at empty air. There was a soft frantic fluttering, and Jessica's voice in the dark was telling me about the bird in our apartment, how she tried to catch it but couldn't. My heart was thumping in my throat and fingertips as I fumbled for the light switch, and there it was, sitting on my desk under our loft, a brown bird. I did not know anything about birds, but it was bigger than a pigeon and it was brown, its wings folded until I took a step forward and it launched itself into the air, the flapping of its wings surprisingly loud. It grazed the top of my head, and I ducked and now it was skittering along the top of the wall at the corner of the ceiling, its tiny clawed feet tap-scraping the plaster, a few feathers floating down to our couch.

I unlocked the door and jerked it open, then I grabbed our broom and tried to lightly swat the bird toward the doorway, but it swooped behind me and crashed into the TV, dropping to the floor on its side before it righted itself, its small head pivoting on its neck. I ran into the bathroom for a towel to throw over it, but when I came back out the bird was perched on the railing of our loft. I lunged at it with the broom and it dipped right for my face and now I was scared. Later, I would think back to this moment, that that's when everything changed. When I began to fear this bird trapped in our apartment.

Now it was flying in tight circles above me. I put my back to the loft and raised the broom and tried to swat the bird once more toward the open door, but it plummeted and hurled itself along the top of the couch and into the crack of air between one of our bookcases and the wall. For a second, there was stillness and quiet, and I couldn't believe it had been able to squeeze into that narrow space. I thought it must have broken its neck. But then came the soft and muffled struggle of its wings. It was clear it couldn't open them, and their futile movement sounded to me like the strangled beats of a heart where there should not be one, and it was terrifying and I just wanted this bird gone, and that's when I remembered my rifle.

I dropped the broom, climbed the ladder to the loft, and grabbed my gun. The hallway outside our doorway was empty. I swung the door closed, lifted the rifle, flicked the safety off, then aimed at that muffled flutter of folded hollow bones against books and plaster and I squeezed the trigger, a loud crack in the air like news of some sudden but eternal admonishment. There was a slight ringing in my ears, the spent-shell scent of hot metal, and now all was truly still and truly quiet.

I lowered my rifle and set it down. I stepped over the towel on the floor and moved past the broom on the couch and put both hands on the top corner of my bookcase and dragged it away from the wall. There came the thump of the bird hitting the floor. I switched on my desk lamp and pulled the bookshelves farther back. On the floor the dead bird looked smaller than it had earlier. On the second highest shelf of my bookcase, bits of the bird's feathers were stuck to spots of bright blood on my hardcover Faulkner, Tolstoy, and Chekhov. Then something made me look at the wall facing the street. It was the severed cord of our clock radio, the bullet having passed through it into the Sheetrock and brick beyond. I thought how reckless I'd just been. I thought of how a .22 bullet left the barrel at 1,300 feet per second and how it could go over a mile before it stopped. And how did I know it couldn't have made it through Sheetrock and mortar between two bricks into the chest or head of a fellow human being just walking by? I was tempted to look out the window but did not.

I got down on my hands and knees, reached under my desk, and unplugged the live cord lying on the floorboards. In the kitchenette I grabbed a handful of paper towels and a plastic garbage bag, then I crawled behind the bookcase, laid the paper towels over the dead bird, wrapped my hand around it, and picked it up. The bird felt heavier than I would've thought, its small head and beak lolling back as I stuffed it quickly into the garbage bag. I backed out on my hands and knees, and then I was outside on the—thank God—vacant sidewalk pushing the wrapped bird deep into one of the trash barrels that would be emptied the following morning. I looked up and down 82nd Street. There may have been a few people coming and going, but nobody seemed to notice or care what I was doing, and I hurried inside, where I took more paper towels, wet them under the faucet, then squatted behind the bookcase and scrubbed the blood and feathers off my books. I wiped the floor, pushed the bookcase back to the wall, then stuffed those damp paper towels deep into the trash bucket under the sink.

On a shelf there I found a roll of electrical tape, and I took one of our sharpest knives and used it to slice and peel back the rubber coating on the alarm clock cords, twisting the wires back together, then wrapping the black tape tightly around the copper wires until they were completely covered once again. I crawled back under my desk and plugged in the cord. Then I picked up the towel off the floor, put away the broom, and carried my rifle back to its place on my side of the bed.

Jessica would not like what I'd done. I was considering maybe lying to her, telling her that the bird had left the way it clearly had to have come in, through one of those spaces between the black iron bars in front of our open window. And that is when, as I laid my rifle down, I remembered the padlock I'd put on those bars. That's when I remembered the small key on my desk that would've unlocked that padlock and allowed me to swing open those iron bars through the ivy, that would have allowed me to make a three-foot-wide-by-four-foot-tall opening to the outside air the bird surely would have sensed and flown away to.

I lay down on my mattress and stared at the ceiling two feet from my face. I thought about that a long time, that the mere presence of my loaded and illegal rifle had called me to it, had blinded me to a more creative and humane solving of my problem. I thought of nuclear weapons then, of how messy and difficult and compromising diplomacy was, of how much easier and cleaner it would be for a man or woman not so different from me to just push that damn button.

When Jessica climbed into bed hours later, she woke me and asked how I had freed the bird. I lay there, not sure whether a lie would come or the truth. Then she asked why the alarm clock was blinking and why it was hours behind, and I told her the whole story, and she spoke very little to me for days. The last thing she said to me before falling asleep, her back to me, was, "I can't believe you *killed* it."

A week later an Iranian friend of mine from college visited me. Over a pitcher of beer at a bar on Third Avenue I told him the story of my gun and the bird. My friend shook his head. He stroked his mustache and looked out the window at the taxicabs rushing by out on the street. He shook his head again. "My brother, in my country, if a bird flies into your home, it is an angel who has come to bless you." My friend looked back at me, his eyes dark with worry. "And you *killed* your angel."

III

On the afternoon my father nearly killed me, his oldest son, we were installing new trigger guards on his guns. It was a Sunday in late spring or early summer, the maples outside his window fully bloomed, their leaves greener than the lawn sloping down the hill. My father had transferred from his wheelchair to his bed, and he'd propped his surviving leg on a pillow, the stump of his amputated right leg wrapped with a bandanna to keep his folded sweatpants in place. On the bed beside him was his metal lockbox that held all eight of his handguns, and he and I were pulling them out one at a time and fitting each with a trigger guard. It was a two-part metal device that once attached to the trigger was locked so the trigger could not be pulled until the lock was taken off the gun, which would require a key. We were doing this because our lives and my father's house that very Sunday were filled with young children.

The summer of 1989, I married my wife Fontaine, and now, six years later, we already had two of what would become our three children: a three-year-old son and a newborn daughter. My father's third marriage was over, but it had given him two more daughters, the oldest thirteen and the youngest eight. As I stood at the foot of my father's bed fitting a trigger lock onto his 9-millimeter, I could hear their laughter behind the closed bedroom door and down the hallway. It sounded like they were playing with my son and taking turns holding our baby girl, and I was thinking once again how I still owned that .22 rifle and it was time to get rid of it.

Fontaine and I lived nine miles east in Newburyport, an old

shipping town at the mouth of the Merrimack River, and we were renting a narrow half-house with two bedrooms and one bathroom. It had an unheated attic I used for my writing room, and there was a closet where I kept my unloaded rifle zipped up in its case. But my son was growing so fast, and it was only a matter of passing days and nights before he'd find it, I was sure, and would take it out and play with it, maybe discovering its bullets and—no—kids and guns just did not mix. It was past time to sell it.

My father felt the same way. He had just written an essay called "Giving Up the Gun," and it was to be published the following winter. In it, my father writes about my sister being raped at knifepoint, though in the essay he simply describes her as "someone he loved." He goes on to write how he went to his local police chief "and told him I wanted a license, and that my father had taught me to shoot, and the Marine Corps had, and I would safely own a gun, and no woman would ever be raped if I was with her. I cursed and wept and he was sympathetic and said he would immediately start the background investigation by the state." My father was given a Massachusetts license to carry. "In the space on the card for occupation, a police officer had typed *Author*; in the space under *Reason for Issuing License*, he had typed *Protection*."

My father goes on to describe living the next thirteen years as an armed man. He writes how at first he only carried a gun when he was on a date with a woman in Boston, but then he begins to carry it elsewhere, then nearly everywhere, and the essay culminates in his pointing his loaded Derringer at a college kid who'd pulled a knife on a young black man and kept calling him "nigger."

This happened in Tuscaloosa, Alabama, in 1985. My father was less than a year from being run over, and he and his young family were there because he'd been invited to be writer-in-residence at the University of Alabama for the fall semester. In my father's essay, he writes of that night: "My hand aiming the gun was steady and I said loudly: 'Put away the knife.'

"He looked at me, recognized me, and said: 'Fuck you.'"

This became a standoff that ended only when the young man's friends talked him down, the cops on the way, but my father was shaken, for he'd come very close to killing someone, a drunk college kid at that.

Later that night he called me. Jessica and I had not yet moved to New York City, and we were house-sitting that fall for my father and his wife. It was a good way to save money, and I was working five shifts a week as a bartender at a roadhouse a mile away. Because my father lived out in the country, I didn't like leaving Jessica alone, so I'd given her my father's .38 snub-nose to keep close by until I got home each night. She had grown up in a military family and was comfortable around guns, and said little as I set it in the drawer of the bedside table under her reading lamp. When the phone rang it was after midnight, and while I don't remember my father's exact words, I do remember this: "I pulled my gun on a man tonight, son. I just needed to talk about it." His voice sounded high in his chest, as it did when he was passionate about something, like any story by Anton Chekhov, or when he was spent and beyond tired, all his reserves gone.

I asked him what happened, and he told me, and I think I told him he'd done the right thing, that that racist son of a bitch might have stabbed that young black man. I know I said something like that, but what I did not say was "Of course." I had not yet moved to New York and shot that bird in our apartment, but I had already begun to sense that guns, especially loaded ones, call us to use them. And more than once that fall, when I came back to my father's house at 2 a.m. after a night shift at the bar, I'd hope the sound of my key in the door lock would be a signal of safety to my sleeping girlfriend and that she would not be in the shadows in her nightgown aiming a loaded .38 at my chest.

On the bed now, installing those trigger locks, my father had moved on to his Argentinian single-shot rifle. Beneath the barrel was the tube that held dozens of rounds, and he had just pulled it out to make sure it was empty, and now he began to reach for the lock, the butt of the rifle's stock pressed against his upper leg, the barrel pointing at the ceiling. I had just finished with the 9-millimeter, and I was getting ready to lock the .32-20 revolver. It was a heavy gun, and I always liked its balanced weight in my hands. I grabbed a new lock, pulled it apart, and began to fit both pieces onto the trigger guard, and I recalled that fall when Jessica and I had lived in this house. She was gone somewhere, and I was sitting at my desk in the basement bedroom working on what would become my novella *The Cage Keeper*. In the climax of the story, one of the main characters is shot by a .32-20, and I wanted to try to capture the sounds of those shots, then I remembered that my father owned one in this very house, and I walked upstairs and into my father's empty bedroom, pulled his gun box out from under the bed. I found the .32-20, loaded the chamber, then I was outside under the sun, pointing the gun at the ground and pulling the trigger fast three times—*thack, thack, thack*. Those are the words that came. But as I turned to hurry back inside to my writing desk, I could see through the trees my father's neighbor and his wife and a few friends sitting on their rear deck, all their heads turned toward this young man who'd just shot live ammunition not thirty yards from where they sat. I had wanted to stop and explain myself, to perhaps utter some words of apology, but instead I rushed back inside the house, the word *thack* in my head.

A .22 being fired is no louder than a firecracker or a big man slapping his hands together at a microphone, and that was the sound that filled my father's bedroom as he pushed the trigger guard into place, the smell of cordite in the air. I looked down at him. He was as still as an image in a photograph, his eyes on the small hole in the ceiling three feet beyond my head. Then he looked at me, and I looked down at the barrel of his rifle. It was still pointed at an angle toward the ceiling, and I could see that I'd been standing directly in its path and if my father had lowered it only two or three inches, that small hole would have been in my forehead.

I have no memory of what words passed between us then. My father may have apologized or maybe I did for standing where I had been, but what comes more clearly is my father's deeply reddened face, the way he lowered the rifle and looked down at the locked and unlocked guns around him as if they were scorpions he had once considered pets.

I felt oddly calm, but my mouth was drier than it had ever been. I told my father I was going to get us some glasses of water, and I laid the locked 32.20 on the bed, then left my father's bedroom and moved quickly down the hallway, for all I wanted to do was to find, and to hold, my children.

IV

And now their maternal grandfather wanted to bring a loaded gun into our new house.

Ten years had come and gone. My father had died of a heart attack at age sixty-two, and my third published book had become a bestseller, and for the first time in my life I had money and was able to build our first home. Fontaine and I had three kids now, Austin, twelve, Ariadne, ten, and Elias, eight, and we were still renting that narrow half-house in Newburyport. It had one small bathroom, the floor beside the bath so rotted there was a hole where you could see exposed joists beneath it, the water from our showers dripping down the kitchen wall below, buckling the faded yellow wallpaper that had been there for decades. There were two other rooms downstairs, and because this was a half-house, there were only windows on one side, and so the rooms were always in shadow. On the worn floors were carpets that had been there since long before we moved in, and no matter how many times Fontaine vacuumed and washed them, they still held dust mites that nearly closed our oldest son's eyes and made him sneeze day and night. In the living room, a few of the windowpanes were cracked, and my elderly landlord promised to come replace them but never did, though he finally did do something about the exterior lead paint flaking off the clapboards outside because I threatened to call the state on him if he didn't.

One late afternoon, as I pulled into the driveway after one of my college adjunct teaching jobs down in Boston, a crew of three men were nailing vinyl siding onto our home. It was starkly white and smelled like plastic and it was like covering up a lie with yet another lie, but at least now our kids were safe from being poisoned in their own yard.

Still, this neglected, dark, and cluttered half-house we'd lived in for eleven years was as good as, if not better than, a lot of places I'd lived in growing up with my brother, two sisters, and single mother. At least its street and neighborhood were safe, nobody yelling at each other late into the night, nobody fighting or picking fights, no loud motorcycles or lowriders driving by fast at three in the morning, an empty bottle thrown out the window at whatever would smash it to bits.

But Fontaine was unhappy in that place, something I'm ashamed to write I did not see clearly until we'd moved to the house I hired my brother to design and that he and I and a rotating crew of friends and family built over three years. We worked six days a week, ten hours a day on this house, and when it was finally done, it was move-in day—not for us—we would move in two weeks later—but for my wife's mother and father.

Fontaine and I had never talked about it privately, but whenever we visited her aging Greek parents eighty miles south, after we'd eaten the Sunday dinner my mother-in-law Mary had cooked for us all, after she'd served us pie and ice cream or her home-made baklava, our kids would play in the small living room of my in-laws' apartment, and we four adults would linger at the table, sipping coffee and talking about whatever came up, family mostly, or our jobs—Fontaine as a dance instructor and the artistic director of her own modern dance company, me as an adjunct writing professor and self-employed carpenter—and nearly always I'd hear myself saying, "If we ever own a house, there'll be an apartment in it for you two."

I'm not sure why I kept saying this. Maybe just because I was so fond of them both, especially my mother-in-law. Mary was a petite, warm, and vivacious woman, a first-generation American who grew up in Boston, one of eight children her mother raised alone after her husband died in his forties. Mary had a thick Boston accent and treated everyone with respect, and when she smiled, which was frequently, her eyes became two upside-down crescent moons, and she looked at you as if you were the finest person she'd ever met. Maybe that's why I kept promising them an apartment near us. Or maybe it was the way Mary often spoke of how much she loved the coastal town where we lived, that she was sorry she and her husband, George, had ever left there years earlier. Or maybe it was the sad light in her eyes when we all hugged and kissed her goodbye, and she'd say, "I wish we all lived closer to each other."

My wife's father, George, had worked as a small businessman

in the Midwest and New England. His parents had emigrated from Greece, and he was born in Chicago in 1919, just two years after his sister. But their father died young, and my future father-in-law was just ten years old when one morning after a gunfight in the street outside their home—between Al Capone's men and another gang, my father-in-law always said—his newly widowed mother, dressed in black, walked out to the oak tree on their sidewalk, stuck her finger into each of the fresh bullet holes in the bark, then turned to her small children and said, "That's it, we're going back to Greece."

George lived there until he was old enough to be drafted into the Greek army. But in the 1930s, Hitler was on the rise, so George stowed away on an Italian cruise ship and made his way back to America, where he eventually met Mary, and they married just before the Japanese bombed Pearl Harbor. George enlisted and served in the army all through World War II. He was stationed stateside and one of his duties was to lay mines in Boston Harbor for German submarines. Between that war and the next, Mary and George had a son and a daughter, my future wife's older siblings, and George took their photographs with him to Korea, where he was a supply sergeant on the front at the 38th parallel. Decades later, he showed me black-and-white photographs of blown-up jeeps and overturned trucks and dead dogs on the frozen ground. He told me of a young Korean woman crying and pushing a baby at them as they marched by, a little girl wrapped in blankets.

It seemed that George was always showing me things. Sometimes on those Sundays after dinner, he and I would walk out to the parking lot for some air. My father-in-law was small-boned but had a deep, resonant voice and a midwestern accent he'd gotten from living in Chicago as a boy. He also wore thick glasses, and for his entire adult life, except for when he served in the army, he had worked for himself—co-owning a bar in Indiana, delivering pressed linens to restaurants in and around Boston, then later, running a fruit and vegetable stand north of the city. But he'd never made much money doing this, and in his presence, this affable man in his eighties who was my wife's father, he often appeared to me as a man who'd like just one more crack at it. Give him the chance, and this time, *this* time, he'd come out ahead.

We'd walk out to his old delivery van, and he'd reach inside and pull out a worn handball glove, smiling at me. "Yeah, I was in shape. I was in shape."

He'd show me other things, a framed newspaper story of his father, a successful entrepreneur in Chicago. The headline read DOLLAS LEASES FRIEDMAN BUILDING, and beside this hung a black-and-white photograph of a handsome young man in a coat and tie, his black hair combed back, staring into the camera as if he had little time for this, for he had an empire to build.

"My father was somebody. He was—" Sometimes George wouldn't finish what he had to say, but it was hard to miss the boy inside him comparing himself to the man in the photograph in that framed and aging newsprint.

One Sunday afternoon after dinner, he walked me out to the hallway of the apartment complex to his and Mary's extra closet. Winter coats and suit jackets hung in there, and beneath them were stacked taped cardboard boxes. But George was reaching up to the shelf above, then he was holding an old cigar box and pulling out a small semiautomatic handgun. Its short barrel was silver, and it had pearl handgrips, and the magazine that held the bullets was in that handle where it should not have been. "Is it loaded?"

"Sure, I always keep it loaded."

I could also see that the safety was off, but before I could say anything more, he smiled and closed the box and pushed it back onto the shelf. "I used to carry cash. That's why I bought it."

George locked the closet door, and we both walked back into his and Mary's apartment, my and Fontaine's three young kids looking up at us from the couch as we came through the door, their father and grandfather, their protectors.

That night, back home and lying in bed, I told Fontaine about her father showing me his loaded gun, and how I felt like a coward that I hadn't asked him to switch the safety on and to keep it unloaded. She said that when she was growing up he'd always had that gun, that one weekend afternoon when she was sixteen, she and her twin sister were sitting on the couch of their apartment watching TV, and their father walked into the living room carrying his pistol, saying something about it she couldn't quite hear. Then he walked past the TV, slid open the glass door to their small third-story balcony, and stepped outside. A second later came the shot, George backing into the room, his face drained of color. He said he thought it wasn't loaded, that he shot into the air, but he thought it wasn't loaded.

———

WHEN WE ASKED MY BROTHER JEB TO ALSO DESIGN AN APARTMENT for George and Mary, we told him that this would probably be their final home on this earth, and that we wanted it to be as nice as possible. ("Nice" was a word that Mary used a lot, and these days I found myself using it a lot too.) Their apartment would be on the first floor with no steps to climb anywhere, and they would have an open kitchen and dining room, two bedrooms, two full bathrooms, a large living room beneath ours, and six-foot windows to let in the light from their back screened porch. In the last weeks of construction, Fontaine helped me lay the floors and paint the walls, and I tiled the bathrooms with Greek and Italian tiles Mary and I picked out together. Now, after all this work and more, it was moving day, but all I kept thinking about was how I did not want my father-in-law's gun in our house.

I already knew how a gun's very presence drew you to it, and years earlier I'd read a statistic that if you own a handgun, then you are four hundred times more likely to get shot. There was also Fontaine's story about her father and his gun, and there was him showing it to me, fully loaded and with the safety off. I kept picturing him mishandling it and firing a round through his ceiling into where his grandkids lived. Or I pictured my kids finding it, and then I wouldn't allow myself to picture anything else. No, the spacious apartment on the first floor of our new home was George and Mary's, but I could not allow him to bring that loaded gun with him.

But how was I going to tell him? How was I going to do it with the proper blend of respect and steadfastness? How would I do it without humiliating or emasculating him? This old man aging in a culture that patronizes and warehouses and dismisses the elderly? What was I going to *say* to him, and how would I say it?

Move-in day was a cold Saturday in February, the sky clear and blue. For nearly the last two years, George and Mary had been living with their son and daughter-in-law just a few miles from where we were building our new home. My brother-in-law, Chris, seventeen years older than my wife, was a warm, caring, and deeply likable schoolteacher, and on that morning when I was dreading telling George what I had to tell him, Chris and I and his two grown sons began to load up the U-Haul I'd parked in their driveway. George helped, too. He was in his mid-eighties and walked with a limp, but throughout that morning he'd come out of the house in a cap and his winter coat and light gloves carrying a taped box, or a lamp, or a kitchen chair he held with both hands, his glasses slipping down his nose.

George and Mary did not own a lot, but I'd rented too small a truck so now we would have to do two loads back and forth. It was late morning, and I could feel the sweat cooling under my clothes. My nephews were already on their way to my house in the older one's pickup, and my father-in-law was about to get into his son's car when I called to him, "Hey, George. Want to ride with me?"

He looked over at me and pushed his glasses up his nose, then he smiled and nodded, and now he was buckled in beside me in the U-Haul, my heart beating in my fingertips as I followed my brother-in-law's car down the road. We passed clapboard houses, their small yards covered with an inch or two of snow. A plumber's van sat in one driveway, a covered motorcycle in another, and behind these houses was a stand of pines, their green limbs dusted white. Then we were crossing an old stone bridge, the brook below gurgling beneath ice, its banks lined with hardwoods whose bare branches caught the sun. George and I were making small talk of some kind, and I knew there were only a few more miles to go before I would turn down our long gravel driveway in the woods, and this could very well be my one chance with my father-in-law, so I turned to him and said, "George, I need to talk to you about something."

I'm not sure if these were my exact words, but George turned to me, his eyes large behind his thick glasses, then said in his low and resonant voice, "Yes?"

"I can't have a gun in my house."

At first he looked confused, as if he thought that I was thinking of buying a gun and then had changed my mind. Or was I talking about *his* gun? Yes, I was, wasn't I? I was talking about *his* gun. He parted his lips to speak, but I cut him off and began to talk too fast about too much all at once. I told him how I'd grown up with guns, that I shot my first one when I was only six years old. I reminded him that my father had been a Marine and had owned quite a few guns himself, that when I turned nineteen he'd bought me a rifle that I owned until Fontaine and I had our kids, then sold on the same day my father sold all of his handguns. And while I did not tell George the details, I remembered driving my father up to the Trading Post in Kittery, Maine, on a lovely fall afternoon. This wasn't long after the day we'd both put trigger guards on his guns and my father nearly shot me in the head. I remembered pushing my father in his wheelchair across the Trading Post parking lot, his lockbox of handguns across his lap, my .22 rifle and his Argentinian pump resting across the wheelchair handles behind his shoulders and head. I remembered how my father, cheerful and expansive, his thick beard neatly trimmed, wheeled up to the glass gun case, lifted his box of guns onto it, and said to the salesman in a heavy wool shirt, "I don't care what you give me for these, I just want enough to buy a new coat."

I was used to this kind of generosity-fueled financial reckless-ness from my dad, but I stepped up with the two rifles and said, "He's kidding. We'll take market value for everything."

I did not tell my father-in-law any of this, but as I steered down the road that was taking us closer to our new home, matted salt marshes stretching out to the west and the east, I missed my dead father deeply, and again, I could feel the attraction I still had for these well-made objects called guns, but more, there was the iron-fused belief that they were the worst our collective human ingenu-ity had ever invented, that they could only bring about blood and pain and loss.

I wanted to say more to my father-in-law. I wanted to tell him how I almost cut Jeb in two with a shotgun. I wanted to tell him how I'd risked prison to take my illegal rifle to New York City to pro-tect my girlfriend and perhaps any woman running from a madman with a knife. There was so much I wanted to tell George, but now he was staring at me like he was stunned that I was actually saying this to him, that I was giving him an order of some kind, that I didn't trust him.

"But I always keep it locked up."

I pictured the cigar box in which he kept his loaded semiautomatic, the closet he'd locked it in.

"But there aren't any locks on your new closets, George, and even if there were, it's still too dangerous."

"Well, I'll buy a gun box." George's tone of voice concerned me for he sounded anxious, as if I, his son-in-law, was backing him into an unfair corner.

"I'm sorry, George. This is going to be your and Mary's apartment, not ours, but I just can't have a loaded gun in the house. Not with young kids. I just can't."

"Well then I'll keep it unloaded."

"No, I'm sorry. I can't have it." Because I knew how easily unloaded guns could be loaded. My face heated. Chris's van was taking the turn onto our road, a narrow asphalt lane that curved through woods, the winter sun shining onto bare oaks and maples, a few lone pines among the thickets as if they'd been left behind to take some sort of stand.

"But." George's voice was higher now than I'd ever heard it, and he seemed to be sitting back against the seat as if he were being held there. "What if Mary and I want to fly to Florida to visit family? I'll *need* that gun."

"They wouldn't let you bring it on the plane anyway." I began to feel like a bully, as if I were boxing old, frail George, and he was too easy to hit, but I kept hitting him. I wanted this conversation to be over, and I was surprised by how much George wanted—no, *needed*—that gun. But why should I be? I had grown up knowing physical danger all too well, and once I'd changed my body from soft to hard, once I'd learned how to throw a punch that could knock a man down, I could forever feel that nascent punch in my right hand and hips and feet like a loaded pistol in my pocket.

"But you're well known now," my father-in-law said. "What if somebody tries to rob you?"

"Then we'll take him on with baseball bats, George. I'm sorry. I just can't have it."

I turned off the road onto our long gravel driveway and followed my brother-in-law's car. His sons were already unloading their pickup, and my elderly mother-in-law was holding the door for them and smiling widely in her wool winter coat. She had been waiting for this day for a long time, as had her husband, and I was putting a damper on it all.

We spent an hour or so carrying George and Mary's things into the various rooms where they belonged. Then we drank glasses of water Mary poured for us from a jug in her new refrigerator. On her kitchen table was a vase of roses my wife had gotten her. Tied to the back of one of the stools at the peninsula were red, white, and blue helium balloons floating above the heads of my nephews, one of whom was laughing loudly about something, Mary reaching up and pinching her grandson's cheek. The sun was shining through her tall front windows across her brand-new floor, and the air itself felt celebratory, but George, still in his coat and hat, sat quietly at the table, and he kept looking over at me from behind his thick glasses like he still couldn't believe I was doing this bad thing to him.

It was time to head back to my brother-in-law's for the second and last load. Chris asked his father whom he was riding with, but I answered before he could. "He can ride with me."

Then George and I were driving back down the driveway in the U-Haul, and I was about to tell him that I meant no disrespect, that if we didn't have kids, then maybe I wouldn't feel so strongly about this. But I knew that was a lie. I still didn't want a loaded gun in our home, especially in the hands of this old man who years ago accidentally shot it into the air over a town full of people. But as I made the turn onto asphalt, George said, "I'll keep it in pieces around the house." His voice sounded pleading now, its normally low resonance gone. I started to shake my head.

"Then I'll bury it in the yard."

"What if one of my kids finds it?"

"I'll bury it in pieces."

I accelerated down the road, then looked over at him. His wool hat was pulled low over his ears, and he was staring at me from behind his thick glasses, and I was beginning to feel like the thief of whatever power he had left.

"I'm sorry, George. But I'm not going to change my mind on this." Up ahead, the early afternoon sun lay across the railroad tracks, its steel rails glinting dully as I drove over them. I could feel George's eyes still on me. I glanced over at him, and he nodded once. It was as if I'd shown him something about me he should have seen earlier but had not, and now that he had, he didn't like it. He didn't like it one bit.

The rest of the drive was quiet, too quiet, and I wished the radio worked, but it did not. Finally we were driving up the steep paved driveway to my brother-in-law's house. My wife's father turned to me. "All right. It's your house. But can I at least keep it tonight?"

"Why?"

"You people haven't moved in yet. Please. Let me keep it tonight."

He was referring to him and Mary being in a big house in the woods alone. He was referring to wanting to keep them safe, but my mind went to a dark place, to old George just ending it all on his own terms in this brand-new apartment we'd built for him and his wife of over sixty years.

His eyes were big behind his glasses, and I could hardly bear how much power this man—born forty years before me—had just given me. "Sure, no problem."

I told him he could give it to me the next day, Super Bowl Sunday, when I would pick him up and drive him over to our rented half-house, where we would watch the game with my two young sons. I went on to tell him that I had a friend who had a license to carry and he could sell it for us, but George was already out of the truck and walking back to his grown son's house.

Over an hour went by, but there was no sign of George. Chris and my nephews and I had loaded the rest of George and Mary's possessions into the pickup and U-Haul, and as I finished wrapping a moving blanket around Mary's large living room mirror, I asked my brother-in-law where his father was. Chris just shrugged and said, "Resting, I guess."

Again, my mind went to a dark place, but this time I imagined old George coming out of Chris's house only to aim that loaded gun at the man who was taking it away from him, then squeezing his trigger until that man lay dead in the back of his rented U-Haul.

I was pulling the van's sliding door down into place when George walked across his son's concrete patio to where we were. His wool cap was pulled low over his ears, his glasses fogging up slightly, and with both hands he held that cigar box in front of him as if it carried the ashes of his ancestors.

————

ON THE DRIVE BACK, GEORGE KEPT HIS EYES ON THE ROAD, BOTH hands folded over the box on his lap. He was sitting straight in his seat, but he looked smaller somehow. The air between us was heavy and still. I was tempted to fill it with small talk, maybe about the football game the next day, but to do that would be like chatting mindlessly over an open casket at a wake, for that's what this ride felt like: my elderly father-in-law was in mourning; he was mourning the last bit of potency he had left.

The next day was cold, and I spent it inside playing with our kids, catching up on bills, cooking chili to eat with the game. Fontaine told me that her father and mother had both been in church that morning with her, and then she had gone over to their new home and helped her mother for a while, but all day long I kept hearing George's voice in my head, *Please. Let me keep it tonight. Please. Let me keep it tonight.* Now the sun was going down and it was time to go pick up George and collect his loaded gun.

On the short drive over there, I decided to keep it locked in my truck until the following day, when I'd drive it over to my friend who would sell it for us. I felt determined yet guilty, sure of what I was doing but also wishing somebody else were doing it. But who would that be? I was my children's father. It was my job to protect them. It was my job to keep them safe. And did it matter if someone got hurt in some way while doing this?

Then I was turning down the gravel driveway of the house I'd been building in the woods for three years, Mary and George's front porch light on, their brown Buick parked up against it like it was meant to be there. Beyond that rose the concrete retaining wall and hill covered with snow, the deep stand of pine and maple, the sky purple and red through the bare branches of the hardwoods. Standing in the lighted windows of their new kitchen was Mary, smiling and waving at me. And George was already stepping outside in his cap and coat, that cigar box under his arm as he pulled the front door closed and started to make his way over to my truck.

I turned it around, then got out and walked to the front of my hood and said, "Hey, George. Ready for the game?"

He didn't say anything, just kept walking toward me, his eyes on the uneven gravel and patches of ice under his feet. When he was close enough, he raised his head to me and held out the box. His glasses were fogged again, and I took the box with both hands. It felt lighter than I would've thought. "Thank you." I felt I should say more, but what?

George said, "The bullets are there."

Then he moved past me and climbed up into the passenger side of my pickup, slamming the door before I could even get close to my own.

———

MY FATHER-IN-LAW LIVED WITH US FOR NEARLY SIX YEARS, THEN died in his sleep at age ninety. And it was a good six years. Often, I'd come home at night, and our three kids would be down in their grandparents' apartment, eating cake and ice cream, playing games or watching TV with George and Mary. We all became closer in many ways, especially George and me. He began teaching me some Greek, and whenever I saw him I'd call him *sevestai petherai mou*, my respected father-in-law, and he would call me *gambros*, son-in-law, or *masterah*, master of all trades, because he'd see me running around doing all kinds of work on the house—finish carpentry, more tiling, painting. On Friday nights, I'd go down to their apartment after dinner, and George and Mary and I would scratch lottery tickets. We rarely won anything. More than once, George and I would sit at their kitchen table over cups of coffee and he'd show me those black-and-white photographs from Korea, his liver-spotted hands trembling slightly as he pointed out an image of his much younger self, a thirty-one-year-old supply sergeant in thick glasses smiling into the camera.

Mary lives alone now. She's ninety-six and does all her own cooking and cleaning. Every Monday she drives to the Greek church and helps serve lunch to people in need in some way. A few years ago she had a mild heart attack, so now twice a week she drives herself to the hospital rehab and works out for nearly an hour. She's made new friends there, men and women younger than she whose ailing hearts have forced them to look directly at their own mortality. On Friday nights, I still go down to Mary's place. She and I sit in her living room and play music from the forties and scratch tickets and talk about whatever comes up—our families, old friends, often people whose lives have been harder than others'. Sometimes she'll leave the TV on, and we'll turn our attention to the news and to the terrible things we see there.

School shootings. Mass shootings. There's the daily sense that things have gotten uglier, more dangerous, that the school bullies have broken into the principal's office and taken over.

Our three kids are grown now, and I can feel my own body slowly aging. There are the daily pains in my knees and back, the nightly trips to the bathroom, the fact that I need to wear glasses all the time now, and not just when I read. I still work out hard five days a week, as I have all my adult life, and I may be lying to myself, but I can still feel in my right hand and hips and feet that dormant right cross should I ever need to throw it. But at what? And whom? Some heavily armed man in a Kevlar vest bent on murder? Some tiki-torch-carrying white supremacist?

Since that year I first shot my father's .22 rifle at a pine tree in the New Hampshire woods, the same year that we lost Martin Luther King Jr. and Robert Kennedy, there have been more than 1,516,880 deaths by guns in our country. This is more than all the war deaths from all the wars we've ever fought: in Iraq and Afghanistan; in the Gulf War and Vietnam; in Korea and World War II and World War I; in the Civil War and the Mexican War and the Revolutionary War—combined. Each year, we lose roughly 33,000 people to guns, and two-thirds of these deaths are suicides.

A few months ago, I went to the funeral of a high school friend's younger brother. He was in his forties and had had a bad day at work, one of many, I'd heard. So he drove home and got his hand-gun, then went back to work, where—in front of his coworkers—he shot himself in the chest. In the coffin, his handsome face made up, his hair combed back, he looked like a man at the peak of his powers.

Yet part of me, inexplicably, still loves guns. Their reassuring weight in my hands, the gleam of their polished wood stocks, their straight barrels and lead bullets, the smell of gun oil, the pulse of the trigger, the crack and kick of the shot as it flies.

A few nights ago at two or three in the morning, I lay in bed in the dark beside my sleeping wife of nearly thirty years. I had gotten up for the bathroom, and now I couldn't sleep. I lay there and stared into the darkness. I listened to my wife's shallow breaths, then I heard a car coming slowly down our long gravel driveway, and I sat up and nearly reached for the baseball bat I've always kept beside my bed. I imagined a car full of young men, their eyes on this big modern house in the woods, and now my heart was an echo in my ears and I was just about to rise from my bed and reach for that bat when I heard the rolled newspaper hit Mary's front porch down below, the woman who delivered that paper turning her car around and driving away.

One day it may be just me and Fontaine out here in the woods. And maybe it'll be my time to be old and frail, and I'll want that loaded gun in my hands. I will. But I can't and I won't. I will not have it there calling to me the way guns do.

BENEATH

—⟪•⟫—

Early in her writing life, an old friend of mine bought herself an expensive and ornate hardwood desk. It had a green felt surface and smooth-sliding drawers for paper and pens and manuscripts, and she put this desk in a library of books, then bought a fine brass lamp and set it on this desk, and that is where she planted herself each morning and wrote.

This was more than thirty years ago. In those days, I could not afford a desk and lamp or a library to put them in; but even if I could, I believe I would have run from that. I preferred to travel lightly, to carry only pencils and a notebook and shadow my nascent fiction like a hunter or neurotic lover. If I were to set up shop like my friend, it would be a naked declaration that I was committing myself to writing, that I had even created a shrine to receive it, but that was where the trouble began: at a deep and not-so-deep level, I did not feel worthy of receiving it at all.

Who knows where this came from? My father of the same

name was a master short story writer, though when I wrote, I rarely thought about him or his work or any other writer, living or dead. I did not even feel their presence. What I was trying to feel, instead, was the presence of these half-born beings called characters.

This sense of unworthiness lasted years, and I suspect it had to do with the kind of New England working-class neighborhoods I was raised in, places where bright boys and girls hid their brightness so they would not be seen as "conceited" or "stuck-up." It was why I hated the word *author*, which sounded elitist to me. The better word for me was *writer*, because it seemed to more directly express the honest labor of writing itself.

———

MAYBE I BELIEVED MY FRIEND WITH THE FANCY DESK WAS TRYING to look like an author every time she sat at it. But I did not even want to be an author. I just loved writing words, the true words that became true sentences that then somehow seemed to both penetrate and then become these now-living spirits called characters. I would watch as they would start to say and do things, and their stories would begin to emerge like driftwood on a beach at low tide, and I would follow them with my pencil and paper, for what I loved more than anything was this following, this half-trance that seemed to come more frequently if I did not think too much about it or force it in any way.

So I traveled light. I wrote wherever there was a flat surface on which to rest my notebooks: For my first book, a collection of short stories, I wrote at a metal library carrel I stole from a local college's dumpster and hauled back to my apartment over a shoe store and barroom. The desk leaned to one side, and I shimmed that leg with a phone book and got to work. Another story I wrote at the cigarette-burned desk of a motel room I rented in Boulder, Colorado. Another, the first I'd ever written from the point of view of a woman, I wrote in a friend's apartment overlooking San Francisco Bay, but that apartment was small and held a family of five, so I'd sit on the floor of the guest bathroom and write with my notebook resting on the closed toilet seat. This felt to me like just the right place. Why? Because it was about as humble as you could get, and what I kept finding again and again, even now, all these years later, is that if the writing of fiction is anything, it is an act of humility, an act of surrendering yourself to something larger than you are.

Those rare days when I sense I might be writing well, there's a forward pull into an unfolding that feels inevitable, and it's as if I'm unearthing my story, not creating it. Over the years, as I've practiced daily this digging for what lies beneath, that tug of unworthiness has weakened, and it's been replaced by a dogged desire just to get to work, to find those essential details that pump blood into the veins of breathing, thinking, feeling people who begin to move through their very real stories.

For this I need quiet, no human voices, no music, which is why I wrote my third book in my parked car in a graveyard not far from my rented house. In the winter, I turned on the heat and wrote in the dim glow of the interior light. In the summer, I opened all the windows and sprayed myself with mosquito repellent. Those days I was working as a self-employed carpenter and as an adjunct writing teacher. My small used Toyota was littered with student manuscripts, power tools, and sawdust. Sitting behind the wheel of my parked car, I wrote in those same composition notebooks, and I sharpened my pencils with the U-knife from my leather carpentry belt.

After three years of this, I had filled twenty-two notebooks with a beginning, a middle, and an end. It took me a year to type these. My agent sent it to twenty-four publishers, and when the twenty-fourth published it, it sold so many copies I had enough money to build my family our first home. My brother designed it, and when he asked me where I wanted my writing office, that old sense of unworthiness and that desire to travel light welled up in me again, and I told him not to worry about it; I'd find someplace to write.

This turned out to be our future master bathroom. I wrote at an unvarnished plywood desk I put right over where the toilet would go. When I finally hired a tile man to come in, I found a space in my basement where I built a small, soundproof room with a port window I cover every morning with a blanket. The ceiling is low, and my unvarnished desk sits before a blank wall, and this is where I sit now. It's where I've written two more books, and it's where I'm deep at work on something new. I have planted myself in one place like my friend so long ago. And because I no longer travel light and track my stories like a trapper, I, too, have created a shrine to receive them.

Up against that blank wall is a corked bottle of water from the oracle's spring at Delphi a poet friend brought me from Greece. There's an open box of unsharpened Blackwing 602 pencils and a short length of alderwood one of my Louisiana cousins drilled two holes into as a pencil holder for me more than twenty years ago. There's a fragment of trilobites another friend gave me after I gave him a copy of Breece D'J Pancake's short story "Trilobites." It was one of the first stories I read as a young writer, and it pushed me to write about people and places I knew and cared about. There's a flat, heart-shaped stone from Moosehead Lake, Maine, that Fontaine, my wife of twenty-five years, painted blue and yellow, enclosing our initials in red. There are the two stones she gave me before we'd even married and had our three miraculous children. One of the stones is rose quartz and is supposed to resonate love, the other is aventurine, a deep green, and has something to do with creativity, I'm not sure what, though I keep these stones on my desk as if they're gifts left out for a stranger.

There are two magnifying glasses that once belonged to my father-in-law, and on the wall ten feet behind me hangs a bowie knife in its sheath that my older sister and I gave our late father on his sixty-first birthday. On the wall to my left are two shelves cluttered with manuscripts and contracts and travel schedules, the top one weighted with dozens of volumes of poetry. It's how I start each writing day, by reading a few poems, that distilled and essential verse of the finest writers among us; it pulls me down and in, and it makes me reach for headphones that hang on a hook in the wall to my right. They're the kind I used to wear when working with loud power tools, and they make my quiet writing cave grow even quieter. Next to that hangs an etching a friend did of a twelve-paned door in an old clapboard house. Sometimes I stare at it, my cave so silent I can hear the air go in and out of my lungs, the beat of my heart, all these talismans on my desk as still as if they're waiting for something. Then I open my composition notebook and reach for my pencil, push its point into the black Ranger sharpener screwed into the wall, and I crank until my pencil is sharp enough to puncture and to penetrate, to enter one true word at a time that dream world that lies beneath the surface of wherever we are, talismans or not.

HIGH LIFE

— ‹‹●›› —

t's the summer of 2001, and I'm trying to check into the Royalton on 44th Street, but my credit card has been declined. The receptionist is in a silk blouse, and she glances behind me at my road-tired, happily expectant family: at my wife and three young kids, at my mother and older sister, her toddler daughter in her arms.

"I'm sorry, sir. Is there another I might use?"

On her face is an expression I know well, for I grew up with it. It was on the faces of the mechanics who'd shake their heads at my young single mother when she asked if she could pay for a car repair in installments; it was on the faces of teenagers working the cash registers at grocery stores when, once again, the total would be too much, and I and my siblings would have to set aside the eggs and the peanut butter, the apples and the cans of soup, sometimes even the milk; it was on the faces of gas station attendants when my mother would scour through her purse and ask for "A dollar and thirty-seven cents worth of gas, please"; and it was on the faces of landlord after landlord as they stood in our doorways asking for the rent, which was late yet again.

Now, on this hot evening in the lobby of the Royalton, I ask my mother and my sister if they have a credit card for the deposit. They do not, but my mother, sixty-three years old and still working, her hair just beginning to gray, is smiling at me. She knows that this time will be different.

I say to the woman at the desk, "Will you take cash for a deposit?"

"Well, that would be a sizable amount, sir."

"How much?"

She looks at me as if I can't be serious. "Four thousand dollars."

I reach into my backpack, pull out a wad of cash, and begin laying down forty hundred-dollar bills. At first the woman acts as though I'm doing something obscene. But then she's all business. She sweeps the bills into an envelope, and now her expression is a different one altogether. It's one that I'm still not used to. It says, *Welcome. Please, won't you come in?*

Our rooms are suites, air-conditioned marvels with king-size beds and colorful pillows, with deep sofas and chairs, with paintings on the walls that look like real art, and with tubs that can easily hold all of our kids and at least one grown-up. But there isn't time for that. We need to get cleaned up, and then climb into the stretch limousine I've hired to take us to LaGuardia to pick up my blind aunt Jeannie. It's why we're here in the first place, to celebrate her seventieth birthday.

The plan came to me when I called Jeannie back in November. I was in northern Massachusetts, sitting in my brand-new pickup truck, and she was down in Kentucky, where she lived near her eldest son. She had reminisced about all the places she'd lived: Louisiana, Texas, Mexico, Oklahoma, Australia, even Brussels. Yet she had never been to New York City.

"Really? Not even the airport?"

"Maybe the airport, but that's it."

The truck I was sitting in still had that new-car smell, and I couldn't believe that I owned it. I had been writing daily for nearly twenty years, and now my third published book had become a major bestseller, and I—who at forty-one had never had more than three hundred dollars in the bank, whose mother once had to prepare for me and my siblings a dinner of saltine crackers spread with butter—heard myself telling my dear aunt Jeannie that I was going to fly her first class to Manhattan, to celebrate her birthday in style. I wasn't sure what "in style" meant, except that it should have something to do with the word *luxury*. When I typed that into my computer, I was led to the Royalton and then to the Plaza, where we'd be staying our second and third nights in the city.

Like nearly all my relatives, Jeannie was from Louisiana. In her late forties she became a widow, and in her fifties she lost her eyesight, but she was still active in her progressive church. She cooked her own meals and listened to biographies and the *New York Times*. To everyone she met, she was warm and friendly, her blindness somehow not robbing her of her gratitude to simply be alive, which is on full display as our family cruises away from the airport.

Sitting in low, plush seats, Herbie Hancock on the stereo, I pour my aunt a glass of her favorite bourbon and hand it to her with a kiss on her cheek. The sun is down, and as the silhouetted skyscrapers of Manhattan come into view, my oldest two kids take turns describing them to her. She's sitting next to my mom, both of them laughing and sipping, smiling in wonder.

Seeing them so close together brings back another image: my

aunt and her husband wedged on the only living room furniture my family owned, a yard-sale wicker settee, my mother sitting across from them in her own wicker chair. At the time, my aunt and uncle lived down in Texas, in a house filled with long, soft couches and leather recliners. Parked under their carport was my uncle's new sedan and my aunt's Opel GT. It was rare for them to visit us in our Massachusetts mill town, and in the days before their arrival, my mother bought a pot roast she could not afford, along with a bottle of Johnnie Walker Red Label. Now the roast was cooking, its holiday scent filling the house, and my engineer uncle sat in his blazer on that squeaking settee, sipping his Scotch from a jelly glass.

Somehow the subject of money came up. After my parents' divorce, my mother took any job she could find: a waitress, a nurse's aide. Since earning her degree, her work had been helping poor families—first as a director of Head Start, and now as a lead-paint inspector for the Commonwealth of Massachusetts, often taking slumlords to court. She said with some pride that she was making twelve thousand dollars a year, the most she'd ever earned.

"Twelve thousand dollars?" my uncle said. "With four kids? Nobody can live on twelve thousand dollars. Hell, I make sixty and that ain't enough."

Sixty? Sixty *thousand* dollars?

I lean toward the limo's glass divider and ask the driver to take the long way to Midtown. My aunt can still see what's in the periphery of her vision, and I want her to take in the lighted buildings as we head down FDR Drive, the East River glistening to our left. Sinatra's singing now, and while I'm talking and laughing, topping off my aunt's drink, she says something like, "Well, this is already the best summer vacation I've ever had."

And we haven't even got to our hotel yet, or the restaurant we'll be going to later. In my research, I discovered something called

Michelin-starred restaurants, places so fine and rare there were no prices on the menus. That night, and the next two, we'd be going to three of them. But the phrase *summer vacation* is in me like a rusty hook.

Growing up, summer vacation simply meant no school. As I got older, I would meet people who'd gone to camps, whose families could fly to Disney World or Europe, who rented cottages on the ocean. But all I and my siblings did was roam the back streets of our town, trying to avoid trouble or go looking for it. Once, my mother bought a few fishing poles and a small tent on layaway. She packed a cooler with sandwiches and Cokes, and the five of us spent three days in a campground close to the highway. The brook near us was shallow, lined with car tires and empty beer cans. Just a few yards behind us was a family's camper, and I remember the wife yelling at her husband a lot, and their TV blaring as we tried to sleep on the roots of a big pine tree. We caught no fish, but we cooked hot dogs over a little fire. We drank too many Cokes.

Now, in Times Square, the tinted windows of our limo come alive with bright neon, and the kids let out such happy sounds that I lean over and kiss them. We eat dinner under a high ceiling of hanging Italian linens, the waiters in tuxedos. When the bill comes, the total is more than I used to make in a month, but I pull out my cash and tip 40 percent. On the way out, I give the busboy a hundred.

At the Royalton, I hand my mother and aunt four hundred dollars each, for pocket money. My aunt kisses and thanks me, then folds the bills and pushes them down her bra. She will eventually lose the cash, and I will hand her four more hundred-dollar bills. "Good Lord, Andre," she'll say. "I'm going to leave this trip with more money than I brought with me."

The next day is cloudless and humid, and we take one of those open-topped-bus tours so that Jeannie can hear and smell and feel the city. The bus drops us off in Chinatown. The day has become hotter, and we walk through narrow streets that smell of rotted produce and pigeon shit. We find a restaurant that is also hot, with a stand-up fan blowing warm air. We eat quickly, and there comes the deflating feeling that for the past twenty-four hours I've been the master of a grand circus, but now half the tent is collapsing and some of the lions are getting out. I wave a fly from my face and pay the bill.

We walk down the shadeless sidewalks of Canal Street, heading for Little Italy. Taxis and trucks drive by. We pass a bald man in a visor hawking dozens of sunglasses. Beside him, on the concrete, is a thin woman with dreadlocks, a sheet in front of her covered with old paperbacks and a box of candlesticks. I want to make a contribution, but my wife and kids are walking ahead, and the sun is on us too directly. I'm sweating, and I see that my mother and aunt are sweating, too. My niece has begun to cry, and my sister picks her up and says to me, "Maybe we can cool off somewhere?"

It's what we used to do if our mother had one of her Head Start vans for a summer weekend. She'd take us on what she called a Mystery Ride, which was really just a chance to put on the van's AC, if it was working, and get out of our neighborhood of peeling clapboards and cracked windows. Sometimes she'd drive us to back roads lined with deep woods, or north up the coast, the ocean smelling like some bright, expansive future.

But one July night, all five of us in the van, the engine took a long time to start, and when it did my mother couldn't go faster than ten miles an hour. Finally, she had to leave it in the street, and we climbed out and trudged back to our hot, airless house.

That feeling, of a magic promise shattered, is coming back to me now. But near the corner of Mulberry Street we find an air-conditioned restaurant, its interior dark walnut, and suddenly I sense it again, all that money in my account. While the ladies order iced teas and the kids get root beer floats, I step outside and call the Plaza. I hear myself telling the concierge that we have three suites reserved for the next two nights, and is there any way they can send a car to the corner of Mulberry and Canal?

The concierge does not check the useless credit card I used to hold the suites. He says, "Yes, sir. I'll send a car right away."

The car is another stretch limousine, and it pulls up before the kids have even finished their floats. The driver is a handsome young man, and as he holds the door open, bowing slightly, I push two hundreds into his hand.

A piano concerto is playing inside, and there are strips of purple light in the padded ceiling. The bar's stocked with ice and glasses and bottles of water. I pour some for my aunt and my mother, and they smile at me with such pride that I have to look away.

My wife, Fontaine, leans close and says, "Honey, can we afford all this?"

"Of course. It's crazy, but yes, we can."

In her voice, though, I hear a note of warning. She grew up in a family with little money herself, and maybe she sees what I do not yet see, that all this abundance has made me a little insane. In the past few months, I've given a lot of money to a lot of people. When I discovered that my best friend's mother-in-law had never been to a Red Sox game at Fenway, I bought her and a dozen of her loved ones tickets, and then we took a limo into Boston, where I gave everyone two hundred dollars each for beer and hot dogs. When another friend needed a loan, I gave him the money as a gift.

But for some time now, I've felt deeply disoriented, as though I'm walking on a ship rocked by high seas. Many times a day I've had to sit down, close my eyes, and take deep breaths. I reach for a fork and my fingers drop it. I don't sleep much. Before all of this,

anxiety was Fontaine's problem. To support my writing and her
work as a modern dancer, we cobbled together a string of temporary jobs. I worked as a carpenter and an adjunct professor of writing; she taught dance classes and learned to upholster furniture. But
we often came up short, and late at night she'd find herself unable
to sleep, thinking about how we owed the electric company $34.75
by Friday. She'd say this to me in a small voice in the dark, and I'd
tell her not to worry: I had just got a new deck-building job, and,
yes, we'd be late, but not by much. It felt like we were speaking the
language of scarcity, the only language we had ever known.

For ten years, we have been renting a dark, narrow half-house
with lead paint peeling off the clapboards, the landlord refusing
to address it. There's one bathroom, and its pipes leak down into
the kitchen, the wallpaper behind the stove bubbled and streaked.
When my book took off, Fontaine quickly found us two acres of
land. For me, the money meant time to write; I never imagined it
would change how we actually lived. This was how I'd grown up.
But we made a down payment, borrowed the rest, then hired my
brother Jeb to design a house for us to build.

Now a different kind of anxiety was keeping me awake. I had
never known this kind of wealth, and who *was* I if I lived like this?

Our suites at the Plaza make our rooms at the Royalton seem
cramped. There are high, vaulted ceilings and carved antique
furniture. The living rooms are palatial, and the bathrooms are
filled with polished gold accents and softer, thicker towels than I
knew existed.

The receptionist needs even more of a deposit than the Royalton did, so after handing him my four thousand, still in its envelope,
I call my bank and tell the woman who answers that I'm treating
my aunt to a few days in New York City. Could I get my hands on
another ten thousand dollars?

She checks my balance and tells me that she's happy to take the cap off my daily withdrawal limit.

"So then I can just use my debit card?" I ask.

"With that balance of yours, you should be more than all set, sir."

Any door I want to open, opening. But what good is an open door? Growing up, I was often bullied, so I began to will myself from being passive to active, soft to hard. Yet none of that knowledge, none of that hard-earned change, would have come without resistance. These welcoming smiles, these soft comforts, feel like the beginning of atrophy, of danger.

The rest of our trip is a blur of excess. Checking into the Plaza, we had seen the horse carriages across the street, the drivers in top hats. So we take a ride through Central Park, my smiling aunt closing her eyes to the clomping of hooves, the thwack of tennis balls. There's a limo ride to the Museum of Natural History, our kids marveling at the *T. rex* skeleton. There's dinner at another Michelin restaurant, the musician Meat Loaf sitting right beside us. (After striking up a conversation with my aunt, who keeps calling him Mr. Meatball, he sends our table a bottle of Cristal.) There's a ride to FAO Schwarz, though Fontaine and I don't even consider buying any of the expensive toys.

The truth is, I'm beginning to regret exposing our kids to a way of life that I do not even remotely respect. On our last morning at the Plaza, we eat at the brunch buffet. Set among tall potted palms and gold-leafed columns are four tiers of linen-draped tables, with silver platters of eggs and sausages, prime rib and cured salmon, baked scones and tarts. A mountain of fruit sits in a bowl larger than the font in which my children were baptized. Having worked in restaurants, I know that whatever is left of this will be thrown out. For three days, I have tasted luxury, and I've had enough.

At the airport, we all hug and kiss Aunt Jeannie. I make sure she has a helper to get her to her first-class flight back to Kentucky. Then we catch the Amtrak home, my three kids falling asleep almost immediately, my sister and her daughter, too.

Beside me, Fontaine's reading a book, and across the aisle my mother sits at a table with her cup of coffee. She smiles brightly at me, and I smile back. I'm calculating that in three days I have spent what I once made in an entire year. Is that possible?

In one way, I feel fine about this. I was able to give my aunt a weekend she'll never forget. Throughout my childhood, there was the jagged feeling that I was waiting for something, or someone, to come take care of us. I had no idea that it would be me.

The boy in me can only feel dumbstruck at this, but the man is thinking of how hard I would have to work for all the money I just spent. How it would be months of getting up before dawn, of ten-hour days under a hot sun, taking Sawzalls to half-rotted clapboards, swinging sledgehammers into hundred-year-old studs, prying out windows and horsehair plaster along walls. There were the newspapers used as insulation, stuffed with ancient straw and mouse shit, making my brother and me cough. There was getting down on our knees on protruding nail heads. There was covering a roof with asphalt shingles, humping each heavy bundle up a ladder over one shoulder, our thighs burning, the air squeezed out of our lungs. There was taping and mudding and sanding. There was laying tiles on wet mortar we'd mixed from eighty-pound bags. There was hanging new cabinet boxes in the kitchen, and there was standing at the new island and discussing final paint colors with the owner. Man or woman, they tended to carry the no-nonsense air of one accustomed to big projects, and no matter how skilled I or my brother might be, no matter how much we might know about our work, these owners always talked to us in the same way: as though we were less than they were, and always would be, because we worked with our hands.

A week of that work might pay five or six hundred dollars before taxes. This weekend I tipped that amount a few times over, which felt partly like solidarity. All those hundreds went to waiters and busboys, drivers and porters, people who would always be seen as *less than*. Sitting on the train, I can still feel in my body the toll of such work. The wealth created by my novel, meanwhile, just doesn't feel real. I spent four years on the book, writing it longhand in my parked car, my agent sending it to nearly two dozen publishers over two years. During that time, I built things and taught classes. I started a new piece of writing, and began to expect that the novel would never be sold. So when that door did swing open, when I and my family were pulled into a land where no one spoke my mother tongue, why *wouldn't* I try to go back to where I used to be?

Still, Fontaine wants a home in which to raise our three children, a home that belongs to *us*. In the soft rocking of the train, I sense that my wife is learning to speak a new language, and that it's time for me to learn it, too. I tell myself that, when I get back, I will stop spending all this money. I'll acquire the permits we need to build the house. Yes, it will be the first house any of us have owned, but it *will* happen, though not for many months, months when I and my brother will haul lumber to be measured and cut, where we'll load our nail guns and strap on our tool belts. And something strange will happen to me. With each wall my brother and I raise, with each nail I drive, I'll begin to feel grounded again. I'll feel the presence of the boy inside me who wants a home.

My mother's smiling at me again, and I smile back.

Sometimes a car will roll slowly down our driveway, and for a dizzying heartbeat I'm convinced it's the landlord coming for the rent we don't have. But other moments feel like luxury, filling me with a calming gratitude. When I want to visit my mother, I just walk down the stairs to her apartment stuffed with her plants and her books, her photos of us when we were young and often so unhappy. Before sitting on her sofa, a real one, I pour her a bourbon, and I pour myself one, too, and my mother and I sit and catch up on the labors of our respective days, on my brother and sisters, on my kids and her grandchildren, on all these people we love, high times or not, a smile on her lovely, aging face.

RISK

— ‹‹•›› —

Horror walked into the offices of *Charlie Hebdo*, then a café in Copenhagen, then the Bardo Museum and a resort beach in Tunisia. There came the Russian airline flight over Egypt, then the madness of a Parisian night, and in just a few months, as quickly as the young and lost can pledge allegiance to a new state, over five hundred men, women, and children were gone, and my wife of many years, a performer and the owner of a dance studio, tells me she is taking twenty-one teenage girls to Barcelona to dance. Do I want to chaperone?

I asked her if she really needed to take them to Europe. She said yes, we can't let them stop us.

I told her I would go.

In the months leading up to our trip, there came the suicide attacks at the Brussels airport, then the carnage in Istanbul. In July, one week before we were to fly to Europe, a young man in Nice used a speeding truck to kill eighty-four more human beings, and yet we were going. And yet we went.

As I boarded the plane with our lovely, passport-clutching young dancers, I felt I was an accomplice to exposing them to something terrible. In Zurich, then Barcelona, I kept scanning terminals and open squares and hotel lobbies for any man or woman with death in their eyes. But what would I *do* anyway? Hurl myself at them and shout at our young dancers to run?

But they did not run, they danced. Under the sun, in front of hundreds of happily attentive people.

Then it was over, and we were back at the airport in Zurich. We had a long layover, and we were in a quiet and empty part of the terminal, our twenty-one dancers sprawled in small groups. But a few of them kept looking over at the wide expanse of floor, its surface hard and shining, and one of them said, "You guys, let's do our *show*." My wife stood and opened her laptop and began to play the music these kids knew so well. It was hard for the rest of us to hear, but it didn't matter. Our young women were dancing at the airport, their long hair flying, their shoulders and arms whipping out from their torsos, and now weary-looking passengers were leaving a plane, many of them middle-aged men and women from all over the world, and their faces began to soften with smiles, with looks of wonder and gratitude as they walked right into it all, this explosion of resolve, and hope, and joy.

A LETTER TO MY
TWO SONS ON LOVE

—◄•►—

My Beautiful Sons,

You're young men now, twenty-eight and twenty-three, and you're both more perceptive than I ever was, especially when I was your age and older, when I was full of rage. So, because you are—both of you—smarter and more whole than I was at your age, you probably won't be surprised to hear that the notion of truly loving someone, and being loved back, terrified me.

The first time I ever went to a therapist I was twenty-four or twenty-five. This was in my hometown, her office not far from the Y where I lifted weights and hit the heavy bag and kept myself ready for the next fight. A block or two south was the convenience store with cracked front windows and mostly empty shelves that everybody, even the cops, knew was a front for bookies and drug dealers. Across from it was a Laundromat where young mothers washed the clothes of the kids they let run wild through the streets, and to the north was the park where the drunks slept on the ground in the summer on a hill overlooking the Merrimack River.

The lady who became my therapist for the next few weeks seemed old to me then, though she was only in her early sixties. She had a lined face and wore cardigan sweaters and skirts and nylons. Her eyes were gray but warm. She asked me why I'd come to her, and I wasn't sure. It wasn't because I couldn't stop looking for victimizers to victimize, and once almost beat one to death and nearly got beaten to death myself. It wasn't because I saw the world as a dark place, or that I expected disaster at every turn. It was because more than one girlfriend had said to me, in various ways, "You don't let me love you."

It was true. I would much rather do the loving, the rescuing, the tending-to than have it done to me. But as I explained to that smart, kind woman in her small office so many years ago, I knew that if I surrendered to love that I would die. And then this image came to me: a clear glass of warm water and a dissolvable tablet. The water represented the sort of love required of me, the kind where you open your heart fully to the other. The tablet was me. This young man who still remembered as a boy his mother crying herself to sleep in the weeks after his father drove away, this young man who couldn't get all the fighting out of his head, his mother and father throwing things at each other, swearing, screaming, slamming doors. This young man who watched his still-beautiful young mother date man after man after man and asked very few of them to stick around. This young man who, like his brother and sisters, felt tossed out on his own.

We human beings are all a multitudinous mystery, so I reject the notion that it was my childhood alone that formed me into a hard tablet who wanted no part of a glass of warm water, who would rather love than be loved, who would rather hug a woman with one arm because he had to keep the other free to ward off the danger that was surely coming.

I don't remember what my therapist said to me about this image, but as it hung in the air between us, I knew I did not like what it revealed about me, that I did not trust the good things in this life, that I would rather not love, as the wise saying goes, than lose and hurt again.

Then I met your future mother.

When I first saw her, she was doing that thing that made her *her*: she was dancing onstage, and I was in the audience and I could not take my eyes off her. I was drawn not so much to her physical beauty as to the power she exuded as she moved. As if she needed no one. Like the world was hard, yes, but *dance*.

Then, months later, meeting her for the first time, I found myself sitting next to her in the backseat of my friend's car on a four-hour drive south to New York City. I was heading there to do a reading with your grandfather. She was heading there to visit a friend and to dance. I hadn't slept much the night before, and she was getting over the flu, and so we both laid our heads on the seats and talked quietly to one another. And the thing is, as I looked into her brown eyes, as I listened to her talk of wanting only to dance and to draw, I *recognized* her. From long, long ago. From before I was born.

On our first date together, a lunch where I was so nervous I ate only salad, I had to keep looking away from her face because tumbling down through my head was this sentence: *God, that's my wife.*

I'd never wanted a wife. I never wanted marriage, and I sure as hell wasn't looking for one. But when I was in the presence of this strong, creative, and beautiful young woman, it was like hearing once again the strains of an ancient music, and I knew I was supposed to move to it, to join myself to it, whether I wanted to or not.

I could have proposed to her that very day, but my fears began to stalk me like a gang of young men years earlier who'd cruised the streets looking for me for weeks. Then a cold February night, ten months after we'd met, I finally got down on one knee and asked her to marry me. She punched me in the shoulder and said, "What took you so long?"

That night was thirty-one joyous years ago. All the way to our June wedding, I vacillated between hope and black terror. What good could ever come from marriage? What could ever come from love but pain and loss and an acute loneliness? But whenever I was with your future mother, the parts of me I was ashamed of— my lack of faith, my short fuse for bad behavior of any kind—felt smaller around her. And the parts of me that I was not ashamed of—my desire to create art, my tendency to feel compassion for others—felt larger. By opening myself to her love of me, I was opening myself to also loving the boy whom I had stopped loving to protect myself from it all.

Then I was stepping into that terror the same way I learned to square off with a man who had every intention of doing me harm; on a hot, cloudless day in early summer, your mother and I vowed to love one another in her Greek Orthodox church in front of two hundred and fifty people who loved us, including my mother and father, who had gone on to love other people a few times over yet still loved one another, hugging and kissing and teasing each other whenever they could. And, my sons, it is my love for this one woman all these years that has carried me into some eternal village of spirits, where I have not died but lived far more fully and acutely than I would have otherwise, and it never would have happened if I had not surrendered to the deep and terrifying and exalting mystery of love.

VIGILANCE AND SURRENDER

— ◂◦▸ —

t is a sort of elation, a razored clarity, and it magnifies every car on the road so that I see the minute scratches on their hoods, the caked mud in their wheel wells; it makes every masked woman or man in the grocery store nearly four-dimensional, the hairs of their ears visible though I might be six feet away or more; it makes each traffic light hanging over the street as close as if I am holding it in both hands, flakes of rust on either side of it, the glass lenses pointed at my vigilant self, who has always known the world would face a calamity like this, who has been waiting for it really. For since I was very young, I have been expecting disaster everywhere and at all times.

I'm driving south on 495, the April sun high overhead. My mask hangs loosely under my chin. It is a much-needed N95 mask that I pulled from the pocket of my leather carpenter's belt in the basement. I bought this mask months ago to protect my lungs from sawdust when I was building my family a dining room table. It can seat as many as twenty-four people, and it sits in our house in the woods forty miles north of Boston, a house I was so very lucky to have built with my own hands with my only brother fifteen years ago. He designed it, and then he and I and a small crew spent nearly three years making those drawings real. After cutting down trees and blasting into a hill of rock, we built the first floor for my wife Fontaine's aging parents, and then the three floors above were to hold us and our three children, who were twelve, ten, and eight.

When we were finally able to move into our new homemade house on a cold sunny March afternoon, I was forty-five years old and had never lived anywhere without a landlord. Late one of those first nights, lying in bed next to Fontaine, who was asleep, I counted the rented houses and apartments I'd grown up in and lived in as a young man. The number was twenty-five.

There are very few cars on this highway, though it is late afternoon on a weekday, the usual time for commuters to head home. At the Byfield exit, I take the ramp, pull over, and call my brother-in-law on my flip phone. He is a retired schoolteacher in his early seventies, one of the kindest men I know, and I'm calling him to tell him that I'm five minutes away, that I was able to buy all the groceries on his list except for the antiseptic hand wipes, which are gone, as is all the toilet paper on the store's shelves, and the flour and the pasta and the bottled water. I am shopping for my brother-in-law because he and his wife, also in her seventies, have the virus.

They believe that she probably contracted it where she works as a nurse in a home for the elderly. Her symptoms came before his did. She lost her senses of smell and taste, and then she started throwing up and couldn't stop and my brother-in-law drove her to the hospital, where they put her on an IV before sending her home. When her test came back positive, the town's Board of Health called and told them that they were to stay in their house for weeks.

The first few years of living in our lovely home with all of its windows and natural light, its wide-open downstairs where we hosted parties for friends and family all year long, inviting my in-laws up to join us, in this structure of wood and glass where our kids felt safe and loved, I'd lie in bed late at night unable to sleep, waiting for any rolling crunch of tires out in our gravel drive-way to be a carload of men come to beat me to death. Beside my bed leaned a baseball bat I was prepared to use, but most nights, instead of expecting the kind of street trouble I'd known as a kid, I feared it was the landlord coming for the rent I did not have. I'd have to tell myself that I owned this house, no one else, except for the bank from which I'd had to borrow. Then I worried about the bank coming to take everything, even though I paid my bills, even though I wrote and published books that sold well, even though I was a university professor, even though my wife now owned a dance studio downtown.

Such abundance, and I was used to none of it. I had grown up the son of a single mother in poverty in half-dead mill towns where I had had a violent youth, so that things going consistently well for me has been like living in a foreign country, one where I'm still try-ing to learn the language.

My brother-in-law thanks me and tells me he'll leave the garage door open. He asks if I'm sure I don't need any help with the gro-ceries. I tell him no, that I want to be a mile down the road before he even steps into that garage. We both laugh and then he starts to cough, and I hang up.

Until the wild success of my third book, I'd never had more than three hundred dollars in the bank, and then I had so much more than that, I could not get rid of it fast enough. I treated friends and family to trips and ball games and boat rides. I bought my mother—a woman who never owned anything but used cars with well over 150,000 miles on them—a brand-new pickup truck. I'd lend friends thousands of dollars with them barely even asking for it. And as I was doing all this, I seemed to be operating under a dual awareness of myself: half of me took joy in the good times I was finally able to spark and spread around, but the other half could see that I would not feel like myself again until I was broke. Those days, I often felt like I was walking on a boat drifting through high seas.

When I pull into my brother-in-law's driveway, the late afternoon sun is shining on his new toolshed, on his well-tended lawn and flower garden, on the clapboards of this new home he and his wife built for their retirement. I turn my truck around so that it's pointing back to the road, then I pull on my mask and a fresh pair of latex gloves, leave my engine running, and in two trips carry a dozen bags of groceries into my brother-in-law's garage. As I climb back behind the wheel, he comes out on the front porch in his mask and thanks me, waving as I drive away.

The backseat of my truck is now empty of my brother-in-law's groceries, but in the front are the ones for my mother and my mother-in-law, who is nearly ninety-nine. We are particularly worried about her catching this thing, this widow of nearly eleven years who still does all her own cleaning and cooking, who drives her sporty leased Toyota to the gym twice a week, who goes to church on Sundays and on Friday mornings helps my wife at the dance studio, where she enters into the ledger all the people who have shown up for Zumba. We have been living quite happily together for fifteen years, and she's become one of my best friends.

When I show up at her door with her groceries, wearing my mask and a new pair of gloves, she greets me from only two or three feet away, and I have to tell her to go to the other side of the room. "Oh," she says, "I keep forgetting." She asks for my receipt and insists on paying me back in cash for her groceries before I even finish unpacking them. As I do, I know that she does not forget about the virus because daily she is moved to tears by all the dying she sees on the news. "Why?" she'll ask me. "Why has this *happened*?"

I ask her to leave the money on her kitchen table, then please step into the hallway before I retrieve it. She thanks me in Greek, and says, "*S'agapo*," I love you, and I say it back.

Then I'm in my truck again, driving along the Merrimack River, the late day sun glinting off its swirling surface. I pass a house with signs on the lawn thanking our doctors and nurses and essential workers, and I think how my younger brother suffers from diabetes and three kinds of cancer, how he's been told by his doctor that he has the immune system of an AIDS patient. At my brother's apartment, I leave my truck engine running, pull on new gloves and my mask over my face, then leave his groceries on his porch. As I put my truck in gear, his eighteen-year-daughter Nina comes outside and blows me a kiss before gathering up the bags and disappearing inside.

If I had not been a father and a husband, I believe I would have blown all that money twenty years ago. But Fontaine made it clear that it was time we had a home of our own, something other than the dark, cramped half-house we'd been renting for the past eleven years, our three young children sharing the same room. It took a while for me to imagine something different, to imagine that we might actually build something, that we might have a home of our own.

My next stop is my mother's place just a mile or so down the road from my brother's. She is eighty-one and last year had triple bypass surgery, though she still works part-time as an addictions counselor. She lives alone on the first floor of a house she owns, and when I pull up to my mother's I see that her car is in the driveway.

I'm relieved because I fear she leaves the house more frequently than she should.

I park on a side street, pull on my mask and a fresh pair of gloves, and call her on the phone so that she'll bring out to the porch her bags of trash and recycling. She does this, then waits inside until I've carried them out to the barrels in the driveway before setting down onto her narrow porch her bags of groceries. I wait on the sidewalk for her to come back outside, and we chat briefly from twenty feet away. My lovely mother's hair is white, and it pains me that I cannot hug this woman who raised me and my three siblings largely alone in one rented house or apartment after another, this woman whom we all worry about more than we ever have before. She thanks me, then says, "You're the family Sherpa."

And as I wave at my mother and drive away, I picture these Himalayan men, paid to haul climbers' food and supplies up steep mountains. It is an image that seems to ripple through me, for throughout this strange, hard time I've been thinking a lot about the words *love* and *family* and *friends* and *community*, and I think about our three children, who not so long ago were moving with us into our new homemade house in the woods, and now they are twenty-seven, twenty-four, and twenty-three, all three living full lives elsewhere, though the oldest two have come home for a while, and they do not like me being the one to shop for others. They tell me that I'm old and that I could die, and I see the same fear in their faces that I've held for so long in the depths of my own heart. But how can I tell them that I feel most at home when things are perilous, that all that is wonderful in this world is frighteningly temporary, and so when abundance of any kind comes, we must celebrate it, for what has saved me is my love for them and for their mother, for my larger family and many friends, and I want to hug my children and tell them that it's okay, but we cannot hug, can we?

And so we have to show our love in other ways. We have to climb the mountains rising up before us, food strapped to our backs, our faces covered with masks, as we say, "Stay safe. Stay healthy." Don't leave. Ever.

MARY

— ⋅‹‹•››⋅ —

One night not long after dinner, my mother-in-law's voice came over the intercom, and she sounded weak. "Can you guys come down? I fell. Twice."

My wife and I and our son Austin pulled on our masks and hurried down to Mary's apartment, where we found her slumped in her kitchen chair in her robe, her head resting on her arms. Her face was pale and in a slightly wavering voice she told us how she fell off her step stool trying to pull her window shade down, that she hit her dining room table and then the floor only to get back up and climb that stool and fall the same way again.

While my son and I helped Mary to the living room, Fontaine told her mother in a warmly teasing voice that she should have called us to help with the shade, though we all knew that Mary, even at ninety-eight, preferred to do things on her own. Then Mary said: "But you people don't come down here anymore."

She was right. We were two months into the pandemic, and

except for when I brought her her groceries while wearing a mask and sanitized gloves, we rarely went down there at all.

But it wasn't always this way.

In her first years living with us, I'd start my day by standing on the exterior steps leading to my front door and wait for Mary to come to her kitchen window. She lived on the first floor of our house, my wife and I and our three kids living in the floors above, and after I'd driven them to school, after I'd parked my truck in the gravel driveway of our home in the woods, I'd pause on those steps.

Mary would usually see or hear me pull in, but if she was finishing washing her breakfast dishes at the sink, then I would wait for her. Even if it was raining or snowing. Even if I needed to get inside and get to work. Because when Mary appeared at that window, it was like starting my day with some sort of blessing.

She was a small woman, her lovely face suffused with warmth, this life-loving, first-generation Greek American from Boston who had not only given me my wife but had also become one of my dearest friends on this earth. She'd wave and blow me a kiss, and I'd do the same. If I were wearing a hat, I'd take it off and give her a deep bow, which always made her laugh.

———

AT THE BANK WHERE SHE'D WORKED PART-TIME AS A TELLER UNTIL she was eighty years old, they called her Sunshine Mary. She appreciated this nickname but seemed genuinely confused about why she'd been given it. For those of us who knew her, however, there was no confusion. Because no matter whom Mary was talking to, whether it was a wealthy customer or someone just getting by, whether it was the bank president or the young janitor emptying the trash can near Mary's window, she turned that radiant smile on everyone, and the thing is, she *meant* that smile.

In the fifteen years she lived with us, she would say to me many times, in that strong Boston accent she'd had since the 1920s, "Oh Andre, I don't think it costs anyone to be nice. I take people as they are."

————

WHEN MY WIFE FONTAINE AND I DECIDED TO BUILD AN IN-LAW apartment into our home for her aging parents, I did not foresee how much daily joy they would bring to our lives, especially Mary. She was eighty-four years old when she and her husband George moved downstairs, but you would never know it. She did her own grocery shopping and cooking and cleaning. On Monday mornings she volunteered at the soup kitchen at her church, feeding men and women who quickly grew to love Mary as much as her bank customers had. On Monday nights she went to choir practice, for she'd been singing in her church choir since she was a teenager, and on Wednesdays she volunteered at a domestic violence prevention agency where she answered the telephone and stuffed envelopes and shredded documents and always walked in there with that smile and often her homemade baklava. On Fridays she'd drive to my wife's dance studio and sign in the ladies who took Zumba class, many of whom said they came to class mainly to see Mary.

Every holiday, Sunday dinner, or house party—of which my wife and I hosted many—Mary would walk up the interior stairs from her apartment, knock once on the glass-paneled door, then enter with that smile. She'd be in a perfect outfit for whatever occasion it was, mainly dresses and blouses and sweaters of all colors, her jewelry matching, her hair just right, and even if our kids didn't see her right away, they seemed to sense that their grandmother was in the house and they'd all go to her, hugging and kissing her and saying, "Hi, Yia Yia!"

For the dinners Mary would help Fontaine set the table, and she'd help me with appetizers or anything else that needed doing. My wife's a modern dancer and so many of those house parties were cast parties after performances, and while Fontaine would be finishing up at the theater, Mary and I would get the house ready, both of us in aprons, jazz playing, the tinkling of ice and glasses as I set up the bar, Mary cutting up carrots and celery and blocks of cheddar, and all the while she and I would talk about whatever came up—how I bought too many meatballs again, though she'd point this out with that smile. We'd talk about how wonderful Fontaine's show was, and Mary would say how she loved to brag about her "multitalented daughter." We'd talk about anyone in our families who might be suffering in some way, a subject that always made Mary reflective and momentarily quiet, for above all else she hated to see or hear of the suffering of her fellow human beings.

When her husband George had a hip replacement, it was Mary who tended the wound, and it was Mary who got him out of the rehab facility she was convinced was killing him. Then, after five years of living with us and after nearly sixty-eight years of marriage, Mary's husband George died in his sleep at age ninety, and now for the first time in her life she lived alone.

Fontaine and our kids would go down to her apartment and visit her, usually after dinner when Mary was watching her game shows. Grieving or not, she'd turn that lovely smile on them and talk over whatever show she was watching, her favorite being *Jeopardy!* If I wasn't out of town or busy with schoolwork, I would go down there, too, though every Friday night I'd visit her without fail and the two of us would scratch lottery tickets, winning very little over the years, but not losing much either. Mary would turn the TV to one of the music channels, one that played Big Band music from the forties, and she and I would finish our gambling and sit back and talk about our week, about my three kids and her four grown kids, about her grandchildren and great-grandchildren. About her late husband George.

———

WHEN THE PANDEMIC CAME WE'D KEEP THE NEWS ON MUTE, AND as the numbers of the infected grew, as the numbers of the dead grew, Mary would often be close to tears. "Oh, those poor people, Andre. Their poor *families*."

She was now ninety-eight years old, but she still cooked her own meals and cleaned her apartment and did her laundry. She still drove herself to buy her groceries, though in the last few years she'd been asking the teenage baggers to put less in each bag so that she could carry them, a request I'm sure she made with that smile.

I don't remember the moment we asked Mary to stop going to public places like grocery stores, but I do remember her quiet resignation about it. "But Andre, I worry about you doing the shopping. Are you *careful*?"

I *was* careful, though Mary was not. When I walked into her kitchen carrying her grocery bags, my mask on, gloves on my hands, Mary would walk right up to me to take a bag and I'd have to tell her to please stay back.

"But I need to pay you. Do you have the receipt?"

I'd thank her and ask her to stand in the hallway while I put the receipt on her table where she could leave the money, which I then told her I'd come get after she left the room. She did all this, though she seemed to think I was being too cautious, or maybe it wasn't that. Maybe it was something else. Many times over the years she'd say to me, "Oh Andre, I've lived my life. I worry about you people."

We were in full lockdown now: all of our town's restaurants were shuttered; Fontaine's dance studio was closed; and I was now teaching all my university classes online. As the numbers of the sick and dying kept rising and rising from coast to coast, we stopped going down to Mary's apartment altogether. One Friday night in early spring when we would normally be downstairs together, sitting under the lamplight scratching our tickets and talking and laughing, I called down on the intercom and said I didn't think we should do that for a while.

"You think so?"

"Yes."

"But why?"

"We don't want you to get sick, Mary. We love you."

"I love you too." Though she sounded far away when she said it.

Summer came, and we could visit with Mary on her front porch, though we would sit many feet apart and not linger for too long, and except for when I delivered her groceries we hardly went inside her home at all. Now tens of thousands of people had died, and Mary, who no longer volunteered at her church's soup kitchen because it was closed, who no longer sang in the choir either, who now had no office to go to or the dance studio, who couldn't even get out of the house to shop and run errands, she became quiet and withdrawn.

I'd stand at that kitchen window and talk to her through the glass, but even though she still gave me that smile, it seemed to rise up from a well of sadness.

Late at night, Fontaine and I would talk about how important it was to keep Mary from getting the virus, yes, but wasn't it also important to keep her from dying of *loneliness*? Because that's what seemed to be happening right there in our house.

———

THE MORNING AFTER SHE FELL TRYING TO LOWER THAT SHADE, her doctor paid her a visit at her living room window, and later that day one of our nieces, a newly licensed physical therapist, examined her too. It was clear that Mary had fractured her ankle and now she could no longer do her own cooking or cleaning or laundry, and so instead of staying upstairs and away from Mary, for weeks we took turns going down there at least four times a day: at seven in the morning to help her roll her walker to the kitchen for breakfast, then back to her living room and her husband's old recliner, where Mary would elevate her ankles and we'd ice and wrap her foot; at lunch and then dinner; and then later, one of us would help her to bed, and all the while we'd be masked but talking to her and listening to her, and despite her pain and discomfort, despite her constant apologies to us for needing help, apologies we would always tell her were not necessary because we *enjoyed* helping her, Mary's life-loving smile returned, as did her warm presence. In this time of such fear and isolation, of such hardship and daily loss, Mary falling off that stool seemed like the best thing that could have happened to her.

———

IN JUNE, MARY NO LONGER NEEDED HER WALKER OR EVEN A CANE and she turned ninety-nine years old. Fontaine invited friends and family to drive up to our house to celebrate Mary from their cars, and I rented a tent for shade and set out chairs under it for close family. Mary wore a gold crown and had big helium balloons tied to the arms of her chair, and even though she wasn't a drinker, I mixed her a piña colada with fresh pineapple while Austin played Frank Sinatra, Tony Bennett, and Big Band music on the sound system.

Over the course of that afternoon, the sun high over us all, thirty-five carloads of friends and family drove down our long driveway, then into the yard in a wide arc that brought them within feet of Mary, their horns honking, many of the cars decorated with glitter and balloons and handheld signs wishing her a happy ninety-ninth birthday as they shouted out their open windows, *We love you, Mary!*

And Mary's legendary smile had never been brighter. She kept dabbing at her eyes and saying, "I can't believe it. All these *people*. I just can't believe it."

The next morning, I called down to Mary's apartment, which was filled with bouquets and floating balloons and over fifty birthday cards. I asked her how she was feeling.

"Oh Andre, last night I cried myself to sleep."

"Why, Mary?"

"I just feel so *happy*."

———

TWELVE DAYS AFTER THAT PARTY, I WOKE WITH A BAD FEELING I couldn't shake. Instead of going straight to my writing room, I carried my coffee out to my porch, something I rarely did, and looked down at Mary's kitchen window. Every morning she would pull that window's shade up at just before seven, but now, close to nine, it was still covering the glass, and now I was running down the back stairs to her apartment, jerking my mask on as I hurried down the hall to her bedroom. All her shades were drawn there too and she was still under her covers from the night before. I called her name, but she could not answer.

We would lose her a few days later, though it was not the virus that took her; it was just her body giving out after nearly a century of life, a rich, people-loving life. And if Mary has taught me anything over the years, especially after watching her endure what we've all been enduring, this lovely woman born just three years after the Spanish flu, she has taught me this: We need one another. We need to spend time in each other's company. And we need to treat each other with respect and with kindness. After over a year of so much loss, we're beginning to sense a break in the trees of this dark forest we've been wandering through, our faces covered, our bodies far from the touch of another. And so once it's truly safe, let's take off those masks and turn to one another, and let's smile. And let us, like Mary, *mean* that smile.

GHOST DOGS

— ‹‹•›› —

Our dog seems to know that he's nearing the end. In the mornings or at night and often in the afternoons, he does something he rarely did much of before: he takes on the stairs and hobbles his way up them and scratches at our closed bedroom door. My wife Fontaine will let him in, and he'll follow her for a few steps, then sit on the rug. He'll look up at her or at me. Then he'll look off at nothing. And then he'll lie down. More than anything, he seems to want company.

He whines a lot, mostly at the front door to go outside, but then he'll barely leave the porch, barking into the night, and within a few minutes he'll be scratching at the door to come back inside. He often seems confused and forgets when he's eaten, even when he's just eaten. His hearing is going. His eyesight too. He is a small dog, a rat terrier mix, and he has a small face, as do I. My wife and grown kids say we look just like one another, especially now that I have a gray and white winter beard and Rico has a white snout.

Sometimes when he follows me down the stairs, we both take our time favoring our aching knees. He'll be gone one day. Maybe soon. But the thing is, I've never allowed myself to fully love this dog. I wish I could. Why can't I?

———

I WAS FIVE, MAYBE SIX YEARS OLD, AND WE LIVED IN A RENTED farmhouse out in the cornfields of Iowa. Though I did not know this at the time, my father had just left the Marine Corps to attend the Iowa Writers' Workshop. His rank had been captain, and some of my earliest memories are of living on Marine bases: My father's dress blues. His clean-shaven face and head. His bone-handled sword in its silver sheath. The cotton in his ears when he left for the rifle range. And my lovely mother, twenty-five at the time, crying in the doorway, holding my baby sister while on the floor my older sister and I were building a cabin out of Lincoln Logs, and my mother kept wiping at her eyes and saying, "They shot him. Oh God, they *shot* him."

I thought it was my father she was talking about, the man who shot guns every day, but it was the president, whoever that was.

Our first dog was big, and my father named him Gunny, short for gunnery sergeant. Looking through the torn curtains of the years, I see a German shepherd, though he could have been some kind of mix. What I remember clearly are his testicles and his tail, how both were always swinging, that dog in constant, loud motion. An overexcited bundle of muscle and fur and the daily joy of being alive. And I remember my father yelling at this dog. Trying to discipline it. To curb it. To calm it the fuck down.

One morning I was standing with my mother on the linoleum floor in the kitchen of our rented farmhouse. Out the windows on one side were the endless cornfields, though it was winter and there were only flattened brown stalks lying across frozen furrows. Out the other window were the pigpen and the pigs, who terrified me because one of them had bitten our landlord on the knee. He showed us his scar once, pulled his pant leg up to his shiny pink kneecap, a half-moon of stitching across it that looked to me like a baby's head.

My mother's voice was beseeching, and then my father was standing there in the kitchen with us, his face reddened the way it got whenever he yelled, and he was yelling now, calling our dog words I did not yet know. My father's mustache was thick and dark and he wore a coat and at his side was Gunny. A rope was tied around the dog's neck, and his expression is one I've never forgotten because he looked both scared and on confused alert, as if he was about to be called to do something only he could do.

My mother's voice was in the air, but I recall no actual words, just sounds of pleading. Then my father and Gunny were outside, heading for the cornfields, Gunny's tail wagging. My head felt hot and my eyes ached and there was one shot and then another and we never saw Gunny again.

———

I KNOW HOW MUCH PEOPLE LOVE DOGS, AND I KNOW MOST WHO hear this story will hate my father, a man who went on to be loving and generous and kind in many ways to many people in the decades that would follow. So I've kept it to myself until now. But it seems I may have also kept it *from* myself, buried it in some dark ditch of my psyche where other difficult things are buried.

When I was seven or eight, we lived in a house that had a pool and pastures and a herd of sheep and three dogs the landlords left with us for a year while they were away. Two of the dogs were dark brown German shepherds, the third sleek and black. Their names were Duke, Duchess, and Robin, and they would follow my brother and me out to the woods where we played, often sprinting with us across the fields. They would lie with us on the floor of our living room when we watched *Batman* or *The Green Hornet*. They would bark at the wind and rain pelting the windows. They felt like family to me, so why were we one day driving away from them and that old house and pastures, our dogs' faces in the windows watching us go?

The next year we got a golden retriever our parents named Steagle. He was big and gentle, his fur long and, yes, golden. This was the late 1960s. We lived in a rented cabin in the woods of southern New Hampshire, where we had a wide deck in the shade of pine trees that sloped down to a lake. In the summer we swam in the lake, and in the winter we slid around on its snow-crusted ice. Through the woods on the other side of the house was a slow-moving river, its banks soft with marshy reeds. There were many moments of joy in this place: building lean-tos and teepees with my brother deep in the woods; fishing from our dock with poles made from tree limbs; running with Steagle through the pines or rolling with him on the rug of our small living room. This was also the room where the Vietnam War was on TV every night. Where dead boys got zipped into body bags under whirring helicopter blades. Where men named King and Kennedy were shot in the head. Where there were riots in faraway streets. It was the room where my young mother and father argued louder nearly every night till one day our father drove away. And it was the room where my mother told me that a good friend of theirs, a poet who taught with my father at a college in Massachusetts, got something called cancer.

His kids—two girls and a boy—were our friends, and I knew from the boy that in the last months of his father's life he had a hole in his side where his shit would flow into a plastic bag taped to his ribs. And somewhere in all of this Steagle got sick and had to have an operation my parents could not afford, but they went through with it anyway, and the doctor had left an open hole in Steagle's throat that was supposed to heal on its own.

Steagle did not seem to know it was there, but I could not look at that dark hole in my dog's throat, for it was somehow also the hole in my friend's father's side. It was all the dead boys on TV. It was the darkness where my mother lay crying alone in her bedroom every night. And it was my father's absence from our small cabin in the woods.

I have written a memoir that covers some of these years, but I don't think I ever mentioned Steagle in it. And soon he was gone, too. He went outside and he never came back. And maybe it was then that I began to close my heart to these animals who had started to become frightening to me. No, not them, but my love for them.

———

A FEW YEARS LATER MY MOTHER AND SISTERS AND BROTHER AND I were living in another rented house in a half-dead mill town on the Merrimack River. My mother was working down in Boston for the Commonwealth of Massachusetts, forcing slumlords to rid their apartments of lead paint, and every night she'd come home tired but with the flush of one who knew that what she did all day had some kind of value. Our dogs then were two sisters we'd named Sonny and Cher, part collie, part German shepherd.

This was the winter before the Watergate hearings, and I was thirteen. Our mother could not afford to spay our dogs, so when they went into heat, our strip of yard became crowded with sniffing, whining, barking males. And then Sonny and Cher were both pregnant, and soon enough, they each had nine puppies: eighteen big-headed, tiny-eyed creatures I could not help but love instantly.

In the corner of the living room we set up nests of blankets where both mothers lay on their sides, nursing all those puppies and resting when they could. But one afternoon, not long after the puppies came, the snow slushy in our front yard, the sky gray, we let Sonny and Cher out to pee and they never came back. Neither one of them. Ever.

My brother and sisters and I must have looked for them. We must have walked up and down the streets calling their names, but I don't remember doing so. What I remember is my burning belief that somebody had taken them, because how could these two mothers just leave their babies like that? All eighteen of them, their tiny eyes nearly sightless as they whimpered and whined and crawled over one another, searching for the big, warm bodies that were gone.

What happened next I shoveled into that dark ditch of my psyche, and then I covered it with heavy stones, and it wasn't until more than twelve years had passed that I uncovered what I'd made myself forget I'd put there.

I was in my mid-twenties and living in a tiny apartment on the Upper East Side of Manhattan with my girlfriend, who happened to have grown up rich. She was athletic and lovely and smart and kind, and she had a $2 million trust fund in her name—something I could not stop holding against her. That, and her money-blinded vision of the world formed from private schools and ski slopes and sailboats and brand-new cars. I tried not to do this, but I did. Once, we visited one of her parents' five homes, where there was an aunt who held a furry white dog in her lap all day, even through dinner, and afterward, when my girlfriend and I were alone, I called that dog a name I do not recall, only that I said it with venom because I hated how much that little dog was being treated like a human being. I hated how my girlfriend's aunt cooed over it and stroked it. I hated how much this woman *loved* her dog.

We were back at our place, both drunk, and my girlfriend was screaming at me, "How can you hate a *dog*? She's just a sweet little *dog*!"

"Because—" I seemed to need more air than was in the room, and what came out of me next was as much a surprise to me as if I were turning the page of a novel I had never read. I was pulling stones off that ditch and showing my girlfriend what I had no memory whatsoever of ever putting there.

Hours after Sonny and Cher disappeared, the puppies' whimpering a constant and cruel symphony, my mother called a veterinarian, and then she drove to his office and came home with puppy formula and two plastic baby bottles with rubber nipples. She did not mention how much any of this cost, but I knew it was more than she could afford. She was forever having to decide whether the rent or the heating bill would be paid; if we would pay for our electricity or go to the grocery store; if she should put gas in her car or put a few dollars down on layaway for one of us to get a new pair of shoes. This bag of what we needed from the doctor's office looked expensive to me, but she said nothing about money; she just got to work pouring formula into the bottles and heating them in a pot of water on the stove. She showed me how to squirt some on my wrist, told me it should feel warm, not hot. And then I and one of my sisters sat cross-legged on the floor to feed these hungry, motherless puppies one at a time, the others clamoring blindly over our ankles and knees.

I was a small boy with small hands, but I could hold an entire puppy on its back in my palm, its legs curled close to its belly, its eyes closed as it sucked and sucked on that rubber nipple. If I had ever felt happier or more relieved in my life, I don't know when. As soon as one puppy had its fill, we'd grab another, until finally the whimpering stopped and all eighteen puppies slept in a heap in the blankets curled around and on top of one another.

That first night, our missing dogs' offspring safe and warm and asleep, I slept well too and woke with only the desire to rush downstairs to feed them again.

But something was wrong.

When I got downstairs, all eighteen puppies were whimpering, only louder now, and my mother was on the phone in her work clothes, a concerned look on her face, a smoking Pall Mall between her fingers. She was talking to that same animal doctor, and it was the first time I'd heard the word *distended*, which I took to mean swollen, bloated, because that's what those puppies were. I got down on the floor with them, and their whimpering was more strained, and when I picked one of them up, a moan seeped from its minuscule throat, its belly a tight drum.

Then my mother was off the phone. She stood there staring down at me and all those suffering puppies. Her expression was one I knew: it was the one she'd worn just before telling us that she and our father were "separating"; the expression she'd worn when she told us of my friend's father having cancer.

"They're too young for that formula, honey. They can't digest it."

"So what do we *do*?" There was a stark stillness in the air, a horrible flattening of what I saw and heard and felt. My brother and two sisters must have been in the room, but in my memory I see only my mother and all of those puppies.

"There's nothing we can do."

Maybe it was my mother's idea to rub their bellies to try to get them to poop. I don't know, but I do know that she had to go to work and that my siblings and I did not go to school. For hours we tried holding each puppy and rubbing their bellies, but the only thing that came from them was a kind of keening, their tiny eyes squeezed shut, their paws curled inward.

The first ones died within days. If we buried them, I have no memory of it. What I do remember is staying home from school for more than a week and trying to save every last one of those puppies.

After three or four of them died so terribly slowly and in such obvious pain, I found the veterinarian's phone number and called his office, and maybe because I was crying, his receptionist put me through. The doctor's voice was low and kind. He told me that there was probably nothing to be done, but I could try taking a bobby pin or something very small and put Vaseline on it and insert just a bit of it into the puppies' rectums to try to "loosen things up."

Nearly fifty years later I can still feel the warmth and slight weight of each puppy in my palm. I can still feel my fingers tremble as I push the tip of my mother's bobby pin into the open jar of Vaseline and then just a bit into the puppy's rectum, its curl of a tail quivering, its cry a blade slicing through the air.

But even though we were feeding them nothing, their bellies just got larger and harder, and if they opened their eyes, there was a look of desperate bewilderment, then more keening, and then, one at a time, so slowly, silence and stillness.

I stopped eating. I slept hardly at all. I would lie on those blankets with the ones who were still with us and they would squirm their way close to my chest and stomach, nudging their noses in search of a relief and comfort I could not deliver.

When the last one died, there was sudden quiet. That's what lingers: how horrifically quiet our house became.

What we did with all those small, still bodies, I cannot and will not summon. I do remember finally going back to school and feeling like a boy who had been very sick for a long time, a boy who would be forever weakened by it.

————

AFTER THIS, MORE DOGS CAME INTO OUR LIVES, AND I'M SURE that part of me must have taken some joy in them, but I remember seeing their presence in our succession of rented houses only as some kind of danger. Like poison under a kitchen sink. Like a can of gasoline near a campfire.

I have written about this time period in *Townie*, but when my daily writing brought me back to those years, I rarely even saw the dogs. Because during those years in the hard neighborhoods of that mill town, more than anything I wanted to become the kind of man who could protect my mother and my sisters and brother from street cruelty and violence.

The three dogs we owned then—Dirt, Dodo, and Oblio— clearly needed caring-for too, but I was done with that. I would save my love for people only. I would no longer waste it on dogs.

And then, on a warm spring afternoon when I was nineteen, backing too fast out of our driveway in my mother's ancient Toyota, I ran over Dodo.

Dodo was the oldest dog I'd ever known. A few years earlier, he'd been given to us by friends of my mother's from California who had already owned him for seven years, and he'd been given to them by friends of theirs who had also owned him for seven years, most of which they'd spent sailing around the world after finding Dodo in an alleyway in Singapore. He was a strange-looking dog. He had short legs and long ears and white fur with dark and light brown spots. He had sad, almost black eyes, and because he was very old, even when we first got him, he spent most of his time sleeping.

Despite having closed an iron door inside me to dogs, I couldn't help but kind of like Dodo. He needed little attention or care and seemed content simply to be a passive witness to whatever went on around him. He was like an old man, and maybe because I hadn't grown up around my grandfathers or uncles—all of whom had lived and died down in the Deep South, where my parents were from—Dodo's doddering presence seemed to partially fill a hole I had not known was there.

The day I ran him over must have been on a weekend, because my mother's car was available. Maybe I needed to drive across the river to the campus where I took classes, or maybe I was rushing off to visit my girlfriend, who lived in that part of town. All I know is that I was in a hurry as I backed up over a bump so large that I lost my grip on the wheel, and I stomped on the brake and shifted into neutral and jumped out of the car to see Dodo squirm from between the tires into the sunlight.

He looked vaguely confused, and all I wanted to do was apologize to him over and over. He turned and made his way haltingly up the steps, and I rushed to let him in, then knelt to feel his ribs and neck and legs. But all I felt were the tumors we already knew he had, and those tumors, not my having run him over, were why I had to drive him to the vet's office a week later to end what the doctor there had called his "suffering."

My younger sister, Nicole, loved our dogs more than any of us. It was she who fed them the most and who let them out to pee or walked them, even in the snow or rain. Maybe to spare her, or maybe because I had run him over, I was the one who volunteered to take our old dog on his last ride.

My girlfriend was with me. She was Iranian, and it was rare, given her Muslim culture, for her parents to allow her to be alone with me at all. But she was that day, and I could not enjoy being alone with her. In the backseat of my mother's car lay Dodo. When

I'd called to him to come for a ride, he'd perked up and climbed in so easily I immediately began to doubt we were doing the right thing. But we knew he had advanced cancer, and just because he did not cry out or whine did not mean that he wasn't in pain. I told myself this, even though I wanted to turn around and take him back home.

At the vet's office my girlfriend sat in a hard plastic chair in the waiting area while I carried Dodo into an examination room with medicine cabinets above a sink, gleaming floors, and a steel table on which I set Dodo, his eyes on me as if waiting for an explanation. But it was the doctor dressed in white who did the explaining, addressing me in that same low, kind voice used by the veterinarian from that other time, all while he pushed a needle into a small vial and instructed me to comfort Dodo, who had begun to breathe hard, his dark eyes on the wall and then up at me. It was clear that some ancient part of him knew what was coming, and I could hardly bear it. My body was trembling from my feet to my hands, and then the doctor pushed the needle into Dodo's right front leg, and Dodo was looking up into my eyes and then at nothing, his head dropping and the room going quiet.

On the drive home I tried to be stoic. I wanted my girlfriend to see only a strong man when she looked at me, a fighter, a protector, but it was like trying not to breathe, and then I was crying so hard I couldn't stop, and I almost had to pull over.

I kept seeing Dodo's terrified face, his hyperventilating chest, and then his head dropping to his paws. And when he'd looked into my eyes, it was with the trust that I, his owner, knew what I was doing, that I must be caring for him somehow. But look at what I'd done with that trust—look at what I'd *done*. My crying got so bad my girlfriend reached over and squeezed my arm, but I felt miles away from her then, because my tears seemed to come from far deeper than that afternoon; they seemed to go back years and years, and they were slowly opening that iron door on my love for dogs one last time before I closed and locked it for good, the combination lock spinning and spinning until it came to a stop.

Dogs became invisible to me. I knew they were in the world and often in the houses and yards of friends, but I did not see them or acknowledge them in any way, even when one was nudging my leg or sniffing my hands or barking at me. They held no more interest for me than a telephone pole. Dogs served some function, I knew, but not for me.

———

TWENTY YEARS LATER AND I WAS A HUSBAND AND A FATHER. OUR kids—Austin, Ariadne, and Elias—were fourteen, twelve, and ten at the time. Happy kids. Well-loved kids. It was Christmas, and Fontaine wanted them to have a dog.

I resisted at first, but I soon relented. Maybe from behind that iron door came the muffled echoes of Duke and Duchess and Robin barking at the rain, their warm bodies beside ours in the living room. Maybe behind that locked iron door Steagle was running beside me through the pine trees. Maybe I was there, walking Sonny and Cher, something I used to look forward to and did often.

"Okay," I said. "All right."

Because we wanted a rescue dog, the process would take more time than we had before Christmas, so we bought a stuffed dog and wrapped it, and when our kids opened it, we told them that this fake animal represented the real live dog that was coming. There was so much surprised joy in their faces that my eyes filled, but something I couldn't name began to move coldly through my arms and legs, and I stood and hurried past my kids and the Christmas tree to start breakfast.

We seemed to forget about getting a dog after that—or, at least,

I did. That stuffed dog and my children's joyfully expectant faces on Christmas morning faded like some dream that had left me feeling unsteady the next morning, somehow tilted sideways as if about to flip over into a ditch. A year and a half came and went, and during that time Fontaine bought the dance studio where she'd been teaching for nearly thirty years. When she wasn't creating her own pieces with her modern dance company, she was busy running the studio. Our kids' days and nights were filled with school and sports and friends and homework, and I had my full-time writing and teaching and public speaking duties, as well as a new book coming out.

Then, on a hot June afternoon, I came home from a book tour, and Fontaine picked me up at the airport. We hugged and kissed, and as she was accelerating into traffic, she glanced over at me in the passenger seat. "Um, there's something I have to tell you."

"Yeah?"

She smiled over at me, her dark eyes lit with mischief. "We got a dog."

"What?"

And she told me how she and Ariadne had driven to Maine to pick up a rescue dog they'd found while I was away. At first I felt a cool disappointment, then fear, and then a sort of mind-clearing surrender: we had promised them a dog, after all. I guess we now had a dog. Named Rico.

What followed I do not want to write about. I do not want to write it because I do not like how it makes me look, not just to the reader, but to my younger self, the boy who used to love dogs. I yelled at Rico so many times over the years that I'm convinced my kids saw a dark side of me they never would have seen otherwise. I resent Rico for this, and I want to apologize to him for this resentment. And I want to apologize to him for far more than that.

When our youngest son, Elias, was fourteen or fifteen, he said to me one day, "But Dad, look at Rico. Can't you see how *cute* he is?"

"Yes, I can," I told him, because I could. In that moment, Rico, with his small face and brown eyes, his lithe and perfectly proportioned body, was sitting on the living room rug, his front paws crossed, looking up at us with a kind of sensitive attention, a warm and alert presence that others would find adorable. But I went on to explain to my child that, though I knew Rico was cute, I felt nothing when I saw him. "I'm dead inside."

My son shook his head at this and went on with his day, but I was haunted by that exchange, because it was clear that he—and his older sister and brother—needed me to love this dog they loved so much.

I wasn't being fully honest either. When I was in the same room with Rico, I often did feel something: I felt annoyed. Except for a few times when he shit on the floor or chewed the legs of furniture and I yelled at him and held his nose to what he'd done, he was a well-behaved dog who seemed to need my family as much as they seemed to need him. All five of us would watch movies together, snuggled on the sectional couch of our TV room, and Rico would snuggle right in there with us, often moving from lap to lap, even to mine. When I'd pet him, he'd bring his nose close to my face and sniff this man he seemed to want to please the most, this man he seemed to fear, too.

I hated that more than anything: that this dog made me feel like a bully, the kind of man I'd always hated. As I stroked his short fur and muscled back, I tried to send him messages of love and acceptance, but I felt like a liar, like one half of a couple whose love had died long ago. My wife and children glanced over at us and smiled, the hope in their faces cutting me in two.

Maybe because my affectionate pats felt so forced, Rico stopped jumping into my lap, and I stopped calling for him to do so. As one season faded into another, he and I fell into a sort of daily routine that made me feel the way a racist must feel living beside people of color. *You stay away from me, and I'll stay away from you.* I mean this metaphor, for I do believe that my stance against dogs is a hateful one, a hatred born of fear.

And then one warm summer afternoon—and as I write this my face heats with shame, though even now I believe I was just trying to stop Rico from what he was about to do, not hurt him—I kicked our dog.

It was near sundown, and Fontaine and our three children and I were walking up the main street of our small town at the mouth of the Merrimack River. It's a narrow street of clothing boutiques and fine restaurants, of pubs and a bookstore and a movie house that shows international and independent films. We could smell the ocean just two miles east, and the geranium hanging from the lamp-posts, and Fontaine or one of our kids had Rico on a leash and he was pulling ahead, sniffing, sniffing, sniffing.

The sidewalks were crowded with men and women and kids enjoying this early summer evening, as we were, though I remember being tired and wanting to get home. Then Rico spotted a man ahead of us who held in his hand a bag of leftovers from a restaurant or snacks of some kind, I don't remember. I only recall Rico running ahead toward whatever was in that bag. I yelled, "Rico! No!" and then my foot swung into his small, bony rump, and Rico was yelping, and my wife was yelling my name, and the kids were yelling too, all of them looking back at me as if they had never known me and never would.

My remorse was instant, and it was worsened by the man's smiling at us with startled embarrassment for me. It was clear that

my vision of Rico trying to take something that was not being offered to him was wrong. It seemed that the man had *wanted* to share with Rico what was in that bag.

The ride home was filled with my wife and kids' justifiable anger. I had somehow become the man pulling his young dog out to the frozen cornfields, a pistol in my pocket.

Why had I gotten so angry at Rico anyway? Because the hunger and the need of dogs turns me away so fiercely: *Please don't ask me for anything*, I want to tell our dog. *Please don't need*.

That night or sometime the next day, when no one was around but me and Rico, I squatted and petted his head. He let me do this, which hurt almost as much as my remorse, and I told him that I was sorry, that I would never do that again, which in the many years since, I have not. And then I said, "It's not your fault you're a dog, Rico. It's not your fault."

Still, when I am gone from home for weeks and miss my family so much that my bones ache, I never, not even once, think of him. But why is it then, when I'm the one feeding him, that I can't bear to give him only a cup of dry dog food? Why do I chop up leftover steak or salmon or grilled chicken for him? And if we have none of those things, why do I find some cheddar cheese or expensive Gouda and give him that?

———

IT'S THE WINTER OF THE PANDEMIC, AND NOW THERE ARE TWO dogs in our house. Our daughter Ariadne, just twelve when she and her mother drove deep into Maine to get Rico, is now twenty-five years old and a doctoral student in philosophy in upstate New York. For the past eight weeks she has been home with us, and this second dog, a rescue from Texas, is hers.

Romy is an eight-pound Chihuahua with the tiny face of a newborn deer. Her ears stick up in soft points as she stands on her hind legs and straightens her back and stares at me with curiosity. She plays with chewy toys that squeak, and she runs around the house and onto and off our furniture so fast it is hard to follow with my eyes. When she's not doing this, she's usually curled up in my daughter's lap. Sometimes Romy will hear something the rest of us—including old Rico—do not, and she'll lift her small head and bark louder than a dog that size should be able to. My daughter adores this dog, and in those weeks when Ariadne's boyfriend is not with her in New York, I know Romy is keeping her from loneliness.

I cannot look at that little dog without smiling. One night, while I was watching the news, she stepped onto my thighs, her body so light it felt like some trick of the mind. She glanced up at my face, then curled up in my lap, her narrow back to me, her body warming my skin, and it was as if she was scratching on that locked iron door inside me, scratching to get in, though maybe Rico had already begun to unlock it.

———

IT WAS A LATE FALL AFTERNOON, AND ONE OF US LET RICO OUT TO pee, and he didn't return. Usually he'd roam our yard and woods for a few minutes, relieve himself, kick with his hind legs at what he'd done, then come back inside. But on this day it had been over an hour, then longer, and still he was gone. Fontaine and I called to him from the porch, but there was just our yard and gravel driveway and the empty road where the few cars that passed always seem to go too fast, and whatever I was doing that day I could no longer do.

I kept walking onto the porch and calling our dog. I hurried across the grass and dead leaves and peered into the woods and called his name, but there was only quiet and an unrelenting stillness and then a cold fear slithering through me, and I was no longer a man but a boy.

I climbed into my truck and started it, lowering all my windows so he could hear me as I called his name. I drove the back roads for close to an hour. Clapboard houses were set back in the trees, and I kept calling toward them, hoping my dog had found a friend, "Rico! Come here, boy! *Rico.*" Along both sides of the asphalt were ditches, their muddy sides the color of Rico's fur, and I couldn't look into them. I wouldn't look into them.

And then the sun was down, and I had to put on my headlights as I drove home. The gravel driveway was empty, as was the leaf-strewn yard, but there, sitting on the top step of the porch, was Rico, and as I got closer his tail began to wag, and he stood, his head up, waiting for me.

PAPPY

— ‹‹•›› —

I t was a winter afternoon in Louisiana when my grandfather told me that he may have killed two men. I was in my early twenties and Pappy was fifty years older than that and we were sitting in his pickup truck amongst the pine trees. Because his eyesight was going, I sat behind the wheel, my grandfather hunched on the passenger side. There was a month of white whiskers across his face and throat, and between us on the bench seat were copper pipe fittings and an empty tin of Skoal chewing tobacco, and even though it was cold outside, the oak cistern up against the cabin filled with thick ice, Pappy kept his window down so that he could spit out onto the gravel road.

Ahead of us the late sun shone down through the jack pines that sloped to a gulley of thickets and fallen hardwoods, and beyond these was a rise of more trees, ten acres of them. The summer before, I and my older cousins, Micky and Eddie Owens, the sons of my mother's sister Jeannie, cleared half an acre of Pappy's land in one day.

Eddie's friend Deke, a crop duster pilot, was there too, and it was so hot and humid it was like breathing steam, and we'd taken our chain saws to over two dozen trees, most of them oak and hickory, so there was no shade and that midday Louisiana sun was pressing its searing irons into us, but we didn't care. All four of us had our shirts off and we were slick with sweat and working in a kind of frenzy, Micky and Eddie shearing limbs off the felled tree trunks, their roaring, smoking chain saws spraying wood chips and oil as they then cut those trunks into three-foot logs that Deke and I would squat and grasp and heave onto our shoulders, half running with them, their bark digging into our bare shoulders and necks, before hurling them into the bed of Pappy's pickup. We'd do this again and again till Pappy's truck bed was low to the ground, and Deke and I would drive it fast back to my grandparents' camp, where we'd toss one log after another onto the pile between the carport and workshop, a tin-sided, corrugated-roofed building Pappy built with his own hands.

What was clear to me and probably to my two older cousins, is that we grandsons of Elmer Lamar Lowe were working in a joyous, suffering frenzy not for us but for *him*, a man who spoke little and who valued one thing in a man and one thing only: Can he *work*?

It was all he'd been doing since he was a boy, one who never went further than the third grade, a boy who at sixteen was a foreman for grown men laying train tracks under the punitive sun, a man who during the Great Depression was making an unheard-of sixty-five dollars a day, suicide pay for setting bridge piers in a diving bell suit in the muddy depths of the Mississippi. Many men drowned doing this, but our grandfather went on to become a pipe fitter who helped to build power plants throughout the South and

Mexico. His wife, our grandmother Fern, was raised on a rice farm in Evangeline Parish, and when she first saw young Elmer Lowe, Scots-Irish handsome and driving the first automobile she'd ever seen, she knew she was going to marry that man, and they went on to have one daughter and then eight years later another, my future mother, two girls raised largely in trailer homes or rented houses not far from whatever power plant their father was working to erect.

Bits of this family history came to me sporadically and out of order, the way it tends to for the following generations, usually over coffee or beer or whiskey, early in the morning or late at night. Maybe some of it scribbled somewhere and found late, if at all.

All I knew is that by the time I was in my teens and early twenties and on a visit south from Massachusetts, when my mother's father looked at me I wanted him to only see a man who could work: whether he felt like it or not, whether it was too hot or too cold, whether his back was hurting, or even if he had a fever and thought he might pass out, he was going to do the damn job.

That July or August afternoon cutting all that wood for Pappy, he was already deep into his seventies but would have been working right along with us if not for the triple hernia he'd just gotten reroofing the main cabin of his and Fern's camp. And so while Deke and Micky and Eddie and I put on a show for him, Pappy stood off to the side in his zip-up coveralls, his back hunched slightly, a wad of chew in his cheek, watching us and saying nothing.

On one of my trips rushing to Pappy's truck, an eighty-pound log digging into my shoulder, I could feel my grandfather's eyes on me, and I could also sense his quiet approval. It was something I'd yearned for for a very long time, and if I hadn't earned it he probably never would have told me what he did the following winter as we sat in his truck.

But it took years to get to that moment.

Because my parents left their Louisiana roots and eventually moved to New England, where my father got his first teaching job and where their young marriage ended, my siblings and I were raised there instead of in the South, where every one of our blood relatives lived. My father's two older sisters and their husbands lived in Baton Rouge, where they had thirteen children between them. They were raising them one street away from each other, too, but we barely knew any of our first cousins and they didn't know us.

My father's mother lived in Lake Charles, her first husband, my grandfather, having died when I was three. She was a lovely Irish woman with green eyes and an aristocratic air, her father a former state senator, but despite her warmth, the very few times I was around her I felt shy and poorly dressed and as if I did not know any manners and never would.

The truth is, I felt more comfortable around my mother's side of the family, people who came from rice farmers and mule skinners, men and women who worked with their hands. But in those early years after my parents' divorce, there just wasn't enough time or money to travel sixteen hundred miles south for a visit, and so we didn't. I did not see Fern or Pappy at all between about age three to age ten, though I still held images of them inside me: Fern's narrow back as she stood at the kitchen sink rinsing peas in a strainer. Pappy in a sweat-stained work shirt, smiling widely at us kids as we ran to his pickup truck for a ride to the swimming hole, the sun hot, the concrete patio under my bare feet, my grandfather's wide back and a foldable measuring stick in his rear pocket, then me tripping and stubbing my toe and crying because it was bleeding, and I had to stay home and my aunt Jeannie had me stand in warm soapy water in an iron washtub where she spoke soothing words and washed that bleeding toe.

Back in Massachusetts, not long after I turned ten and before my father moved out for good, he lived with us in a house that had a big backyard. Its grass was cut short when we moved in, though in the time we lived there it kept getting longer and longer until it was as high as my chest. There was a toolshed at the rear of that backyard, but our father never went into it for that lawn mower. In fact, I had never seen—nor would *ever* see—my father cut grass or hold a tool of any kind. What my father did was write and run and teach classes and read books.

There was another moment I held inside me from being with my mother's family in that camp in the heart of Louisiana. Her older sister Jeannie, who looked to me like Dorothy in *The Wizard of Oz* and whose smile at me seemed to be forever infused with love, asked me once in front of other grown-ups, "Andre, do you want to be a writer like your daddy?"

"I don't want to be a *writer*. I want to be a *working man* like Pappy."

As a boy, it was clear to me that what my father did—closing his den's door every day to smoke a pipe and write in notebooks and on his typewriter, sitting in his chair and reading books, driving to some college where he talked about those very books—did not seem like real work. What Pappy did, though, and what my friends' fathers did, most of whom were plumbers or roofers or housepainters or electricians, well they *worked*.

Maybe Fern and Pappy missed us. Or maybe they were concerned about their newly single daughter living alone with her four kids. Or maybe they just needed a trip, or all three, but for a week or more they visited us in that fatherless house with the uncut grass not far from the river. Because I had seen very little of them in our young lives, I was shy around these two old people, though they were probably only in their sixties at the time. It was strange, too, to see in our driveway Pappy's pickup truck with Louisiana license plates and a camper fastened in the bed. I'm sure we must have shared meals. I'm sure we must have had some fun. But the only memory that's left its teeth in me all these years later is seeing Pappy cut that tall, tall grass in our backyard.

His broad back, a V of sweat down his shirt, a wad of chew in one clean-shaven cheek, his lined face glistening under the sun. And the way he tilted that loud sputtering mower back on its rear wheels so the spinning blade could hack into the grass that was as high as his waist, and then he'd drop that machine and let it cut into what he'd sheared away, and then he'd do it again and again.

I was a boy who wore glasses and liked riding my bike. Those days my mother cried a lot in her room and this weighed on me, but what weighed on me more as I watched this man who was my grandfather cut our grass is that I, the oldest son, had not done it, that I had no idea *how* to do it.

A year later, my mother and sisters and brother and I were living in another town, this one at the mouth of the Merrimack River two miles from the ocean. It was a cluster of abandoned mill buildings and narrow streets of curling clapboard box houses, a lot of yelling coming through the screen windows of our neighbors' houses only feet away, my mother working her first real job as the director of a program for poor kids. And perhaps to save us from a summer of doing nothing, Fern and Pappy bought the four of us plane tickets they mailed to our mother, who drove us to the airport and hugged us goodbye.

My older sister Suzanne was twelve, I was eleven, Jeb ten, and our baby sister Nicole was eight. None of us had ever been on a plane before, and to see clouds below us instead of above made me feel wonder and a kind of joyful terror at just how much I did not know about this world and seemingly never would. Then we were in a massive airport in some place called Houston where we had to change planes and had no idea how.

In a loud and rushing crowd of grown-ups in this high-ceilinged and air-conditioned building the size of a city, I remember following my sister Suzanne, her long brown hair and blue jeans. Maybe we four held hands or maybe we didn't, but we seemed to be completely lost. Suzanne was angry and then she looked scared. Jeb, cool in his long frizzy hair and languid walk, seemed to be having fun. Nicole, ever quiet, with her thick red hair and pale face, had her head down and was putting her faith in her big sister. But it'd been over an hour and we were hungry and thirsty and it began to seem like we'd never get out of that place.

Then somehow we four were sitting in foldout chairs in the office of airport security, drinking cold Cokes out of bottles. A woman in a uniform kept shaking her head and saying, "Can you believe these kids are flying all *alone*."

When we landed in Alexandria—the largest city in the middle of Louisiana—it was night and we left the plane by walking down a movable staircase, the air smelling of jet fuel and the cooling concrete tarmac and some kind of moist vegetation that did not grow in New England. The air was so humid my glasses steamed up and I had to take them off and wipe them on my shirt, and when I could see again, there, under the lights behind a wooden barricade, stood Fern and Pappy. Our grandmother wore a yellow blouse, and my grandfather's shoulders were slumped a bit, his hair thin and gray, and even from fifty yards away I could see that he was chewing tobacco.

The next three weeks were unlike any other that I or my sisters and brother had lived so far. We were kids who'd moved a lot and had few friends and so we watched TV, hours and hours of it every day. Our mother tried to get us to do chores around the house, but we rarely did and she'd be too tired at the end of a long workday to put up much of a fight about it. But here in Fishville, Louisiana, where our grandparents had a ten-acre summer camp in the piney hills, there would be no lying around watching TV all day.

Fern and Pappy rose with the sun, our grandmother making strong coffee and baking powder biscuits while Pappy got in an hour or two of work out in his vegetable garden before he even sat down to eat. When they'd first bought this camp years earlier, there was only a single-story cabin with screened windows and linoleum floors. It had a small bathroom and three or four bedrooms, and that summer Jeb and I took the one with the bunk beds. For years the kitchen had been outside on a concrete slab Pappy had poured, but over time he added a roof and walls, and then later, after he'd retired and they moved to Fishville for good, he built an addition onto that kitchen that would have air-conditioning and wall-to-wall shag carpet. That hadn't happened yet, but the outdoor kitchen was now indoors, its casement windows cranked wide open, its exterior walls made of sheet metal because, I'd discover later, Pappy was no carpenter, he was a pipe fitter.

That first morning of that long-overdue visit south, we woke to the smells of chicory coffee and smoked sausage and biscuits and grits. We left the cabin and walked barefoot over the concrete patio that was already warm under the sun, a green lizard, of all things, skittering by, and we stepped into those wonderful smells and sat at the long, varnished picnic table, the first one I'd ever seen inside a house. Pappy was already bent over his plate, his thinning hair matted with sweat, nodding and smiling at us as he chewed. Fern, who was a quiet woman, wished us good morning, and her smile at the four of us seemed to extend into the very plates of food she lay before us.

Nestled in between my sausage and buttered grits were two fried eggs and then those steaming biscuits. In the center of the table was a yellow can of Steen's cane syrup, and when I saw Pappy pour some of it onto his biscuits, I did the same, then stuck my fork into my sausage and rubbed it into my eggs and grits and syrup, and when I bit into those sweet, spicy, and savory flavors, it felt as if I was doing more than just eating; it was as if those tastes opening up in my mouth were turning me toward all the people who had come before me and to all I would be called to do, beginning with letting Fern fill my plate for a second time, Jeb's too.

We were kids whose mother could not cook like this until holidays when she wasn't working and had set aside just a bit more money for this kind of early morning extravagance. Back home, we might eat a bowl of cereal if there was milk. Surely this breakfast Fern had made us was a special-occasion kind of feast. Surely they didn't eat like this all the time. But they did, we soon discovered, and we also quickly learned that a meal like this was meant to provide not so much pleasure as *fuel*, fuel for a day of work.

For Jeb and me, this meant following Pappy after breakfast, our stomachs too full, back down to his garden where he grew okra, peas, snap beans, and tomatoes, all of which—except for the okra—I'd only seen in the produce section of the grocery store those rare times I'd go shopping with my mother back north. My younger brother and I were sedentary kids, though he was skinny and I was pudgy, and it was clear in the way our grandfather looked at us that he knew this. He knew this and he didn't like it.

Our first task may have been kneeling in those narrow rows of sun-warmed plants to pick beans, the ancient scents of leaf and root and dirt, sweat already stinging our eyes. Or it may have been pulling weeds away from Pappy's plantings, the palms of our hands raw in no time. Or it could have been having to clear and rake the untilled section of Pappy's garden, which was long and wide and seemed less like a garden to me and more like a farm. Or it could have been the hardest job that we did first, which was running the rototiller to carve up Pappy's ground to seed even more vegetables than he already had.

There were the smells of gasoline and motor oil, of Pappy's chewing tobacco as he got the machine ready for us, then yanked on the cord till it started up. He squeezed the throttle and revved the engine, blue smoke rising into the hot sky above us, and Jeb and I just stood there in our shorts and T-shirts and sandals. Maybe we thought we'd be spending our days at the swimming hole, its image of cool brown water in the shade of cypress trees still inside me from when we were little. Maybe we thought we'd be playing some kind of games or climbing into Pappy's pickup with him to explore the backwoods. But our grandfather just squinted down at us like we were a project he had no real time for, and then he showed us how to put that loud tiller into gear, which dropped its spinning teeth into the dirt, our grandfather gripping the machine handles and guiding it straight ahead while it did its violence to the earth.

There again was that dark V of sweat down Pappy's back. There was that foldable measuring stick in the rear pocket of his jeans, in the other a round tin of Skoal. I did not want to work in this hot garden all day. But it would be worse to have this old man who was my grandfather keep looking at me the way he did, his eyes passing over my shoulder-length hair and narrow shoulders and flabby belly. Over my thin arms and legs. Like he'd just gone to the trouble to bring me and Jeb down south and look at what he'd been given: two weaklings who had no idea how to work.

I took the tiller first. Its handles were hot and vibrated up into my forearms, and when I put it into gear and the spinning teeth sank into the ground, the machine yanked me forward and I nearly fell over, its clattering engine the ageless sound of men driving nails and hauling steel and pouring concrete and punching each other in the face, something that happened to me regularly back home at the hands of one of the many boys in many neighborhoods who saw the same weak boy Pappy did. And as I kept yanking back on that machine that was tugging me forward too fast, that was pulling me off a straight path unless I jerked on those handles till my back hurt and my arms became liquid, it felt as if I was doing far more than just tilling Pappy's garden that day.

After a few minutes of this it was Jeb's turn, and I sat on a pine stump, my T-shirt sticking to my skin, my throat a dry gulley. I took off my glasses and wiped them with the hem of my shirt. I looked around for Pappy but there were just the shafts of late morning sun shining down through the tall pines, behind me my skinny, wild-haired little brother under that cruel sun handling that rototiller better than I had, for he'd always been stronger than I was. But what became clear over those three weeks and the years that would follow is that Jeb didn't seem to need our grandfather to respect him as much as I needed him to. My brother was a boy who liked to draw and to take things apart—a fan's engine, the guts of a record player or TV—and he was only two or three years from discovering his passion for classical guitar, which he would go on to practice for hours and hours every day of the week. Even on this first day of chores on that first visit down to Fern and Pappy's, Jeb would only work a few hours before disappearing somewhere with a pad of paper and something with which to draw. Pappy said little about this, but the way he looked at my brother across the picnic table that night over black-eyed peas and dirty rice and cornbread is not how I wanted him to look at me; he was looking at his youngest grandson as if Jeb was already failing a very important test, one that would decide my brother's fate for the rest of his life.

(But Jeb would go on to be the hardest-working man I have ever seen. Because he became a father just a few years later at age nineteen, he dropped out of college and started working construction. He found a union job as a carpenter's apprentice, and he discovered that he had a natural gift for the geometry of it all, for using those hands that could draw human faces and play Bach preludes on his guitar to cut and fasten wood into structures that were plumb, level, and square. And that was the name of the business he and I ran together in our twenties, *Plumb, Level, and Square Builders.* Jeb would bid the jobs and do all the design work, and he consistently worked ten to fourteen hours a day, a smoking cigarette between his lips, skipping breakfast and lunch and coffee breaks, as driven in this work as he'd been at mastering classical guitar, his instrument getting dusty on its stand back in his many apartments, while all he wanted to do all those years was to get back to it.)

Our sisters were being put through their own kind of tests with Fern that summer, ones that had to do with dishes and laundry and sweeping and vacuuming and shelling peas and baking biscuits and cobbler. Writing all this now, I don't believe our grandparents would look on our time with them in this way. (And I hope that they wouldn't be hurt at how I'm writing about it now.) I believe, instead, that except for occasional visits to the swimming hole, that cool water deep and brown, its rutted clay banks dripping tree roots that looked to me like hanging cottonmouths, Fern and Pappy just didn't know what to do with us.

But during those three weeks, Pappy taught me how to use a chain saw, its jagged spinning teeth scaring the hell out of me as I lowered it to the trunk of a fallen pine. He taught me how to swing a heavy splitting maul over my head down into the center of a hickory log, keeping my eye on where a natural crack in the wood was already showing itself and aiming my ax blade for that very crack.

I'd often miss, though, sometimes whacking the ax handle against the log and bouncing it back toward my bare shins.

Pappy'd shake his head and spit tobacco juice out the side of his mouth. "Don't break that handle." But he wouldn't walk away till I did it right once, the blade finally hitting that thin crack and the log cleaving in half, which felt like a kind of miracle to me: the deep grain of the wood, its smell from a world I'd always lived in yet had never truly considered, but especially that *I* was the boy who'd split that log.

Behind the outdoor kitchen was a pile of red bricks Pappy was going to use to rebuild some exterior steps on the other side of the building, and he needed that brick pile moved to about fifty yards down the sloping gravel driveway to where the steps would go. He could see that I wasn't strong enough to use the wheelbarrow for this, so he went to his workshop for a pair of steel tongs designed to carry six to ten bricks at a time.

He showed me how to load ten between the grips of the tongs, and then he lifted and carried them with one hand down the pine-needle-covered driveway and around the corner of the outdoor kitchen, where he wanted them stacked. I followed him. I was in shorts and flip-flops and I tripped a few times on loose stones while my grandfather walked ahead of me, his right hand gripping the handle of those tongs that held ten bricks as if he were carrying nothing heavier than that foldable measuring stick in his back pocket.

After he set down the ten bricks and released them from the tongs, he handed them to me and said, "Do what you can, Andre." Again his eyes passed over my narrow shoulders and soft belly, my skinny legs and nearly bare feet. And even though he'd been seeing me work for days now, my fingers and hands blistered, my small muscles so sore it felt like the flu, he looked doubtful as I took those tongs, which were heavier than they looked, and I turned and walked back up the slope of that gravel driveway to that pile of bricks.

It was just after noon on a cloudless summer day in Louisiana, the wet heat like some invisible enemy you didn't know you had, and it brought out all the smells of the camp: the magnolias and pine sap, the tar roof of the main camp house and the baking concrete slab of the patio. I could smell the kitchen's siding and corrugated steel, the diesel exhaust from logging trucks rattling up Highway 8 through the pines. And I could smell that pile of red bricks, like rust and blood and somehow my own fate.

There were dozens and dozens of them and I squatted and set down those tongs and grabbed the first brick. It was warm and heavy and I laid it down and lined nine more up against it. But when I clamped those tongs to them and lifted, I couldn't hold it all, the bricks landing with a thump near my bare toes. I got rid of two bricks and tried to lift eight and then I got a few steps with those, but it was like someone had shoved burning needles into my forearm and I had to lower them back to the ground.

I was thirsty and my cheeks were hot. I glanced over my shoulder, hoping not to see Pappy, and was relieved when I didn't. Finally, I was able to squeeze six bricks together and grip the tong handles and carry them down the slope and around the corner of the outdoor kitchen, where I released them onto my grandfather's ten. I was already sweating, my eyes stinging with it. I took off my glasses and wiped them on my shirt, then I turned and headed back up the slope.

I don't remember how many trips it took or how long I worked—two hours? three?—but the palm of my right hand seemed to have peeled away and the side of my right calf was bleeding from where each tongful of bricks kept tapping and rubbing against it, the muscles of my right shoulder burning.

If I drank any water, I have no memory of going inside the kitchen for some, though I do remember having to squat down a few times because the top of my head had become air and the pines shifted and swayed though there was no wind.

The last few bricks were coated in dirt, a few of them chipped at the corners, and it became clear to me that this brick pile had been there a long time. But it was there no longer. And I was the one who had moved it.

Maybe Pappy had been working in his shop or the garden. Or maybe he'd taken his truck into town, but when he came back from wherever he'd been, he just stood and stared down at that new pile of bricks. He had his hands on his hips and he kept shaking his head. I was standing on the patio in the shade watching, and then Pappy glanced over at me and squinted like he wasn't quite sure who he was looking at. Then he smiled, shook his head once more, turned and walked away.

As much as I'd needed that smile, as much as I'd needed any man to take notice of me in any way whatsoever, my own father living elsewhere, my uncles strangers to me, my mother's boyfriends transient figures, the fathers of friends nonexistent, male teachers few and far between, that afternoon I was beginning to learn that there was somebody else's approval I needed far more than theirs—my own.

———

IT WASN'T LONG AFTER THIS SUMMER VISIT SOUTH THAT I STOPPED allowing myself to be anybody's victim up north in those mill town streets. I began to lift weights and box and run and fight, a significant part of my life I wrote about in *Townie*. But the memoirist cannot drag a reader through every single aspect of his or her life, and what I left out of that book was how important it became to me and my sisters and brother to keep going back to Fishville, Louisiana, and how difficult it was for our mother to get us there.

It was hard for her to get enough time off from work, and even if she could, she rarely owned a car that could make the trip. For a few summers she'd be paid to deliver repo cars down to New Orleans and we went along with her, taking a bus up to Fishville, where Fern or Pappy would pick us up. Other summers our mother took a chance and drove us all down in her old Toyota, which she often tried to do without stopping at a motel she couldn't afford, and she drank a lot of coffee and smoked cigarettes and we'd count cars or turn up the rock and roll on the radio, greasy fast-food wrappers on the floor at our feet.

When we finally got to Fishville, it'd usually be late at night, and there'd be the crunch of gravel under our tires, our windows open to the hot air that smelled of jack pine and cooling asphalt and sheet metal, the crickets so loud it felt like either a warning or applause.

During these years I worked out six days a week for hours at a time, and even though I knew I'd be doing physical work with Pappy, the thought of missing even one workout was terrifying to me. Because by now I had chest and shoulder and back muscles, my upper arms thickened enough to almost strain the sleeves of my T-shirts, and I just could not risk losing any of these gains that had begun to change my life for the better up north, a place where, in my neighborhoods anyway, I was beginning to be seen as someone not to cross. And so wedged into the back of my mother's car were my weight plates and adjustable dumbbells and my leather jump rope. If I could have carried down my barbells and bench somehow as well, I would have.

My sisters weren't happy about having to shove their clothes in and around all this, nor were they happy about our brother Jeb bringing his guitar and sheet music stand and a metronome that he set ticking near his bunk the very next morning. He sat straight in a chair in front of it and played something called scales, his wild hair pulled back in a ponytail.

Our grandfather seemed a bit mystified by Jeb, the way I suspected he was also mystified by our writer father, a man Pappy never asked me about or talked to me about. My grandfather and I spoke little about anything anyway, though we did communicate with each other in an ongoing conversation that happened without words: that summer and the one that followed were a sweat-drenched blur of sun-beaten days rototilling and chainsawing and digging and planting, of hauling brush and fallen limbs away from the pines and setting them on fire, white smoke rising into the southern sky.

In the late afternoons I'd do hundreds of push-ups out on the concrete patio between the kitchen and the camp. I'd do dumbbell presses and rows and curls, and then I'd skip rope, ending it all with a hot sauna Pappy had built near the old camp house.

At night, when my mother and her two parents and my siblings played a card game called Rook at the picnic table, I would often feel Pappy looking over at me and Jeb with a kind of dumbfounded scrutiny, which made me feel relieved, but also protective of my brother, whose unrelenting discipline I could only admire, for I knew that if he hadn't been trying to protect his hands and achieve greatness with that guitar, then he would have been right out there with us. But I would never say any of this to Pappy. Instead, I quietly reached for my cards and found myself taking the passive, cowardly route of the newly privileged.

Then it was another summer and I was nineteen and had badly injured my back during one of those long workouts up north. I'd gone to doctors who put me in a lumbar brace, but once we got to Fishville I still planned to do whatever Pappy asked me to, even in a brace whose bars and straps made me feel encased in armor. It was a short visit, less than a week, and early in the afternoon of that first day, the morning of which I'd spent drinking coffee with my mother and grandmother and maybe my older sister Suzanne, girding myself to get ready to do chores for my grandfather, Pappy called me out under the hot sun on the concrete patio and said, "C'mon, Andre, we're going somewhere."

I climbed into Pappy's old pickup truck and he drove us through the pines down Highway 8, our windows open and hot air blowing into the cab. He was hunched behind the wheel in faded jeans and a loose denim shirt, his right cheek full of the wintergreen chewing tobacco I could smell, and we drove by the gas station and skating rink and the swimming hole across from it, then accelerated up a rise through more pines, the sun glinting off the hood of his truck.

It had no radio, and when I asked where we were going Pappy just shrugged and spat tobacco out his window, and then soon we pulled into the gravel lot of a liquor store. Its flat roof sagged over the entrance, and Pappy said he wouldn't be long. A few minutes later he came back carrying a case of Falstaff beer. There was the creak and slam of the tailgate, then Pappy climbing behind the wheel with a six-pack he set between us, pulling one can out for me and another for him.

"We're not gonna do some work?"

Pappy took a long pull off his beer and so I did the same. It was cold and delicious and it was the first time I'd ever sat beside my grandfather drinking a beer. He nodded at the brace he couldn't see under my shirt. "You need to rest that back. No work today."

Then we were driving down a narrow road through thick stands of pines, the sun filtering down through them, and there were the smells of pitch and red clay and the nestings of birds and small animals I couldn't name. Pappy finished his beer, tossed his empty out the window, and opened another. I finished mine too, though I dropped the can at my feet before pulling another free.

Until the beer, I had been feeling shy around my grandfather. It was rare that we'd ever been together without doing some kind of work, and what was there to talk about? Especially with a man who did not talk much at all? But the beer was already pushing a calming warmth through my veins and there was the road wind and wherever we were going, and that was enough.

Then we were pulling up to a shack on a river and at first I didn't quite know what I was seeing. All around this place were low mounds of something white, something I thought had to be mushrooms or white stones, two things there didn't seem to be too much of in Louisiana. But as I followed Pappy, who was carrying the case of beer, we had to walk through all that white and now I knew what I was seeing—hundreds and hundreds of empty beer cans, mainly Falstaff.

"Who drank all these?"

Pappy didn't answer me and I followed him around the shack, my feet shuffling through those empty beer cans. Around the side of the structure was a small covered porch, its floor made of weathered boards with knotholes that went all the way through. Gnarled tree posts held up the roof, and sitting on that porch was an old man who nodded and smiled at Pappy like they'd been having a long conversation and my grandfather had interrupted it just long enough to take a leak and come right back.

The porch had no railings and Pappy set the case on it, climbed two wobbly treads, and sat in a ripped cane chair beside this friend of his I'd never known existed. Pappy nodded in my direction and said, "This is my grandson. Pat's oldest boy."

The old man nodded and smiled at me too. He took a long pull off his own can of beer and he and Pappy looked down a slope overgrown with young pines and brush to a narrow muddy river, its receding banks showing tree roots, tendrils of Spanish moss hanging over the water. I stepped up under the covered porch and sat on a stack of tires and drank more of my beer.

My grandfather and his friend were talking about hunting on that river for loggerhead turtles, which is what I found out later the old man partially lived on. Like Pappy, he was clean-shaven and in worn denims, and it was clear that at one time he would have been considered handsome. Behind him, his back door was wide open and there came the voice of a DJ or news announcer on what sounded like a transistor radio. I hadn't eaten lunch and this second beer was doing the good work of the first, and when I got myself a third Pappy asked me to pass him and his friend one too.

I did this, but it was hard to move well in my brace, and when I sat back on that crate I was sweating. Pappy and his friend were talking about nets and bait and turtle meat, and I was trying to fight the feeling that I was wasting away in that brace, that whatever muscles I'd built were now gone for good, even though back home (off weight training until the doctors said I could do it again) I was swimming a mile every day, and Pappy's voice kept echoing through my head. *My grandson.*

I couldn't remember ever hearing him say that word in front of me before, and it felt good to hear it.

That afternoon we drank every one of those beers, and when Pappy drove us home he concentrated on the road and took it slow, the late sun over the pines a warm golden light that I stumbled under on my way to my bunk, where I slept till supper.

The entire week seemed to go this way. If we weren't going to do any work, well then it must be a holiday. Pappy had built his own meat smoker out of a 55-gallon oil drum he'd welded on its side on wheels, one that he and Fern had hauled up from where they were living in Texas before they retired here. He'd cut a square opening in the side and used what he'd cut away to make a hinged door with a handle. On the top of the smoker he'd installed a galvanized smokestack, and there were steel trays on either side of the grill to hold trays of chicken and sausage, brisket and ribs, all of which Pappy would cook slowly for hours on the grill over glowing hickory coals inside that smoker.

That week another friend of Pappy's I'd never heard of came around. His name was Eddie Wayne, and he was a tall, big-handed man whose face had the rosy gray color of one who'd been drinking heavily for years. He had thick brown hair and a crooked nose and his backwoods Louisiana accent was so strong I often did not know what he'd just said. He also spoke loudly and continuously and held the nervous energy of a man who had been locked up for years and was finally outside under the sun.

I came to learn that he lived with his mother after his wife left him for selling their rented furniture to pay a poker debt. I learned that Eddie Wayne had lost his license again for driving drunk and he would get to Pappy's place either by walking down Highway 8 or by riding his tractor mower on the shoulder, a case of beer tied to the back. And I learned that Eddie Wayne had worked for Pappy years earlier on power plant jobs and called him Cap, short for Captain.

I knew Pappy had been a foreman, but now I could see and hear the deep respect this man Eddie Wayne still had for his former boss. Eddie Wayne was into reminiscing, and so while the three of us stood at the smoker, Pappy's hands in oven mitts when he pulled open the smoker's door and blue hickory smoke billowed out of it and he basted whole chickens with his homemade barbecue sauce, Eddie Wayne told me how the first thing my grandfather would do when he got on a job was to fire everybody. "In't that right, Cap? Every damn swinging dick."

Pappy nodded and looked like he was only half listening, though he seemed to like having Eddie Wayne around.

"Cuz he brung his own crew, see? Boys who knew what the hell we was doing, right, Cap? And Andre, men *respected* your grand-daddy." Eddie Wayne glanced over his shoulder in the direction of the kitchen door. "Them boys knew not to mess with Elmer Lowe. Right, Cap?"

This was that time in my life when I was learning how to step into my fears, how to face a fight in the street instead of running from it, and so I looked at my grandfather to hear what might be coming next, but he was busy holding the smoker door open again and squinting into the smoke as he turned over sausages and chickens with tongs.

"You mean he'd beat 'em up?"

"You damn straight." Eddie Wayne smiled, his eyes glassy but his face lit with an admiration for Pappy that had clearly never waned over time. "Right, Cap?"

Pappy didn't say anything to this. Just closed the smoker door and took a drink of his beer, his lined face glistening with a sheen of sweat, his eyes on the camp and maybe on whatever Eddie Wayne was talking about.

Another afternoon that week Pappy had taken Fern's Toyota wagon so I could sit in the back and he and Eddie Wayne could sit in front. Eddie Wayne also hunted loggerhead turtles and he did a lot of that with Pappy's friend in that narrow river down the slope from his shack. It was an afternoon of many cans of beer we added to the piles around the old man's cabin, and after the sun went down Pappy and I held flashlights on his old friend and Eddie Wayne as they waded into that dark water, Eddie Wayne gripping a long pole on the end of which was a silver hook. Then they were dragging a massive turtle, decades old, out of a net in that water, and minutes later I watched them butcher it in the light of a fire we sat around among those mounds of empty cans.

The old man slid the meat into a large plastic bag, and then the four of us sat there watching that ancient turtle's heart torn from its body and lying in a pile of its own organs, beating and beating long after that turtle had been killed.

On the slow drive home, Pappy was talking about the gumbo Fern would make with the meat we were given by the old man, and Eddie Wayne began to praise Fern's cooking. How her chicken and squirrel gumbo was the best he'd ever had. He'd probably drunk over thirty beers over the course of the day and night, but there was hardly any sign of that. "I'm telling you true, Cap. That wife of yours can *cook*." Then Eddie Wayne turned his head toward me in the backseat. "Whatever you do, Andre, get yourself a good woman."

I don't know if I said anything to that, though it was rare for me to get advice from a grown man, and even if this man was newly womanless himself and didn't have a job and was slowly drinking himself to death, I thanked him. I suspected, too, that his idea of a "good" woman was one who would cook for her man and not make such a big deal out of poker debts. But I said nothing and looked straight out the windshield at our headlight path sweeping past the dark swimming hole, the closed skating rink and gas station, Pappy aiming Fern's car up the narrow asphalt of Highway 8, a flattened armadillo carcass on the side of the road.

———

THE NEXT TIME I SAW PAPPY I WAS STOPPING OFF AT FISHVILLE ON my way to the University of Texas at Austin. I'd been accepted there as a transfer student from the small liberal arts college where my father had taught for years, and a day or so before I boarded the Greyhound bus in that fallen mill town I could not wait to get away from, my father gave me his wooden trunk from the Marine Corps. It had held all his gear aboard ship off the coast of Japan, and it was painted red with yellow lettering on the lid: *1st Lt. A.J. Dubus, USS Ranger.*

A duffel bag might've been easier to carry onto a bus, but I was grateful for the gesture and packed it with all my clothes and a dictionary and a few issues of *Muscle Builder* magazine.

When I got to Alexandria, Louisiana, two days later, it was night and Pappy met me under the flickering fluorescent light of the Greyhound station. Over the years I had gotten bigger and my grandfather had gotten smaller. His shoulders seemed narrower and slumped more, and his hair was now wispy and nearly all white. But he was dressed in loose khakis and a short-sleeved button-down shirt, and his bare forearms still looked muscular with thick veins running down to his cupped hands and those thick fingers, ones that when I was young and small would reach over and squeeze my knee hard. "Horse bite," Pappy would say.

Now he was smiling widely as I carried that trunk over to him, and he insisted on grabbing one of its handles, the two of us walking with it out of that dim light and into a dark lot that smelled like Louisiana to me, like pine and fetid water and leaking gasoline and something dead on the road. He probably asked me about my long bus trip, but what I remember more clearly is how we said little as we carried that trunk together and he lowered the tailgate of his pickup and we slid that trunk in and slammed the tailgate back into place, both of us walking toward the cab of his truck to go do something that needed doing.

I stayed in Fishville only one night. After a meal of crawfish étouffée Fern had heated up, my grandparents sitting across from me at the picnic table, these two old people from the Deep South who were my mother's parents and who I often sensed were from a foreign land, as I was to them, I felt such a deep and abiding love for them both that I became shy and ate too quickly.

After, Pappy stood and told me to empty my trunk and bring it down to the shop. I asked him how come, and he said, "I need to fix it."

Pappy's shop was as large as the hangar of a small airplane, its sheet metal walls lined with large stationary power tools that at this time in my life I knew absolutely nothing about. I didn't even know what they were called, though I'd seen Pappy drill holes with them and cut wood—one saw for across the grain, one for ripping the length of it. There was a machine for making thick boards thinner, and another for turning long blocks of wood into fancy chair legs. I knew the name of that one, a lathe, a lovely word, I thought, and now under the light of the naked bulb hanging above us, Pappy studied my father's empty Marine Corps trunk resting on two sawhorses.

Pappy showed me how cheaply that trunk was made, how the plywood sides were nailed together at the corners and were beginning to come apart. I had not noticed this. I also thought how little I had carried down from Massachusetts in that trunk and how it would probably last till I got to Texas the next day anyway, but this is what Pappy and I did together. We worked on things.

He began to show me how to cut strips of sheet metal with shears, how to bend those strips into hard ninety-degree angles, and then how to use a rivet gun to fasten them to the outside corners of my father's trunk. Pappy did the same with the bottom corners, and as I watched my grandfather work, his eyes narrowed under bushy white eyebrows, his focus complete on the task before him, I felt the way I sometimes did when our father would still take us four kids to church, like I was in the presence of something far older and larger than myself, that by Pappy shoring up this gift from his former son-in-law to his oldest son, my grandfather was perhaps taking part in some quiet and overdue act of forgiveness.

Then Pappy turned that trunk over, and its side and bottom corners glinted under the light.

———

TWO YEARS LATER, MY BACHELOR'S DEGREE WRAPPED IN ONE OF my T-shirts, I carried that trunk back to Fishville, where I would stay for two months. The trunk was stuffed with all my clothes and many books, primarily what I'd studied in Austin: sociology and economics, history and political science. I was the boy whose hatred for bullies had become a hatred for injustice of all kinds—for imperialism and colonialism, for racism and poverty, for a world where cruelty and violence and oppression were rewarded with power and vast sums of money for the brutal few at the expense of the many.

I wanted to keep reading all I could about this, and I planned to get a PhD in the study of it, then maybe law school, politics. But I also wanted to go back north to see my family, something I probably would have done right away—I'd seen little of them since I'd boarded that Greyhound bus two years earlier—had Fern not broken her hip in Austin the afternoon of my commencement.

It happened on the three-block walk from campus to the house I'd been sharing with eleven other students. The sidewalks were buckled and in the shade of pecan trees, and maybe my grandmother tripped on the sidewalk or slipped on some pecan shells. Walking with her were her two daughters, my aunt Jeannie and my mother, whom I had not seen in over two years. She was living with her boyfriend in St. Maarten then, helping him to run his brother-in-law's business transporting restaurant supplies from

Miami to the island, and she was lean and tanned and beautiful, only forty-two years old, and if I'd ever seen her look happier, I did not know when.

I don't remember why my father didn't fly down to see me graduate from college. Maybe he was busy with the many duties of a professor at the end of his semester. As I write this, though, my three children having graduated from their own universities, I can no more imagine missing that important moment in their lives than I can imagine pulling my own heart out of my chest. But my father, who had lived away from us since I was ten years old, had already missed so much, as I had missed him, and so when he told me on the phone that he'd sent me something instead, that he'd see me when I got home, my disappointment was sharp but brief, and then a day or two later I got what he'd sent, a check for three thousand dollars, which was more money than I'd ever heard of anyone having at one time, and more money than I would see again for many years.

But my mother was at my commencement, and my lovely aunt and my quiet but steadfastly loving grandmother. She told me that Pappy wanted to come too, but he had shingles so bad he couldn't leave his bed. It was something I had a hard time picturing, my grandfather in bed during the day when there was so much daily work to be done.

And now Fern's hip was broken and somebody needed to take care of them both and that person was me.

By now Pappy had built that addition onto the outdoor kitchen. There were no walls separating the two, so the kitchen opened onto a carpeted and air-conditioned living room with deep chairs that faced a big TV, and in the back were two bedrooms and a small bathroom and sliding glass doors to a deck looking out over all those pine trees.

Fern slept in the bedroom closest to the living room, her crutches leaning against her lamp table, and Pappy had the one built over the spot where I'd made that pile of bricks years earlier and where he spent his days lying in bed reading westerns, mainly the novels of Louis L'Amour.

I did not know that my grandfather even read books. All I'd seen him sometimes read was the local newspaper or *The Farmer's Almanac*, usually after dinner and before we all might play a game of Rook. But that summer, living with Fern and Pappy and helping them in any way I could, my grandfather read dozens of paperback books. And despite my plans for graduate school and further study in the social sciences, I was also beginning to feel the subtle pull toward doing something other than all that. Maybe something more creative. Maybe something with words. Though none of this was in my conscious mind. When I'd knock on the casing of Pappy's open bedroom door and stick my head in to tell him that breakfast or lunch or supper was ready, I'd see this old man in pajamas who had always been nothing but a worker to me, one of the very best, holding yet another book in his hands. He'd nod but keep his eyes on the page, and as I walked back to the kitchen it was hard not to feel that my grandfather's life and my father's had finally merged beyond marriage and children and grandchildren, that all of Pappy's reading was giving him a respite from his pain, yes, but it was also honoring what my father had given his life to: sentences and characters and stories and books.

———

THE HELP I WAS THERE TO GIVE WAS MAINLY TO COOK AND TO clean, though for the first few days I was worried about how my grandfather would look at me doing that. It is forty years later as I write this, and I'm a bit stunned to uncover that I really felt that way then. I had been one of the happy cooks and housecleaners in the house where I'd lived in Austin. And I suspect that long after I'm gone, one of the lingering memories of me for my three children will be of their father in an apron cooking in the kitchen. It has been my main domestic job, Fontaine's the laundry, for all of their growing up, and I of course have never once felt emasculated doing it.

But by the second day, this silly fear ended. It was lunchtime and I was making egg salad sandwiches, sliced tomatoes from the garden, and a pitcher of iced tea when Pappy shuffled in from his bedroom. His back was hunched from the pain of the shingles along his ribs, his face covered with a bushy white beard, and he glanced at Fern sitting in her chair reading a magazine, her crutches propped beside her, and then he sat heavily in his own chair, looked over at me in the kitchen, and said, "What we eatin' today, Cookie?"

Cookie. The grizzled man in the wagon train with a bloody apron around his waist, one who covered up his own gun as he stirred a buffalo stew over an open fire. I am embarrassed now that I needed to hear Pappy call me that, but after he did I felt immensely better about my domestic duties that summer.

Fern and Pappy and I got into a rhythm, a daily and nightly ritual that rarely varied. After lunch, I was shocked to learn that my grandparents sat in front of the TV and watched soap operas, two or three of them in a row. I had never watched them and felt above them in every way, but by the third afternoon overhearing them while making lunch in the kitchen, I found myself asking Fern and Pappy what Billy Joe did to be going to trial and why his mother also seemed to be his aunt, and it was not long at all before I too was sitting there with my grandparents watching our daily soap operas, each of us sipping a cup of hot black coffee.

In the afternoons Pappy read and napped, and Fern would do laps with her crutches on the shaded deck before her own nap. One particularly hot afternoon I brought her a glass of water with lemon and she thanked me and paused to sip from it. Her small face was lightly beaded with sweat, but she smelled like talcum powder and cotton, and when I asked how she was doing she smiled. "Oh, I'm doing great."

"Really?"

She nodded and sipped more water. "I feel like this is a special time in my life."

It was rare to hear Fern speak so openly about herself, and I wanted to ask her why she felt that way, given her injury and Pappy's condition. But it seemed that she meant having me there with them, and maybe, too, having a halt come to the long list of daily chores that had always been her lot. But it seemed to be something else, and as she thanked me for the water, then gripped her crutch handles and continued on with her laps, I walked back to the kitchen feeling that the three of us were somehow suspended that summer in some sort of state of grace, though I had no words for any of this.

While Fern and Pappy napped, I'd run along Highway 8 and do push-ups out on the concrete patio, pull-ups from the low roof of the main cabin. I'd read history and political science—Karl Marx mainly—and I'd shop for groceries and cook supper, which turned out to be a lot of black-eyed peas and rice and tomatoes and cucumbers from the garden. I learned that Fern and Pappy liked a cocktail before dinner, a glass of red wine for Fern and a Jack Daniel's and Coke for Pappy, which he'd take from me sitting in his chair, reading one of his westerns, Fern in her own chair watching the news on TV.

After supper I'd wash the dishes, and we'd watch a TV movie together. But Pappy would soon doze off in the lamplight beside his chair, his chin dropping to his chest, his once broad shoulders now narrow and bony, his gnarled working hands cupped in his lap.

Four more years, and he'd be gone.

Time has washed out chronology for me. What comes instead is a stream of images in no natural order: Winter. It was Fern and Pappy's fiftieth wedding anniversary and we'd all come to Fishville to celebrate it. Jeannie and Eddie and Micky and their families. My mother and us four grown kids. And dozens of old men and women, many of them relatives I'd never met, who drove to Fishville from southern Louisiana and East Texas, from Arkansas and Oklahoma, to toast Fern and Elmer Lowe around a three-tier cake set on that picnic table in that once outdoor kitchen. Fern wore a dress and Pappy a dark V-neck sweater with his shirt collars sticking out, his face clean-shaven, his shoulders slumped as if they were heavy iron and there was a magnet deep in the earth.

There was Micky and Eddie and Jeb and me watching our old grandfather take his chain saw to a tall pine and the tree coming down right where Pappy stood, Pappy dropping that chain saw and running backwards through the dead pine needles, tripping and falling on his back, the pine landing with a branch-snapping whoosh at his feet. We four hurried over to him, but Pappy just stood and wiped the pine needles off his pants, smiling at the four of us and saying, "Hoo-wee, I was hotdogging it that time."

There was Fern having just read my first published short story, one full of sex and violence and profanity, and I was worried what her reaction would be. A few years earlier she and Pappy had the camp building moved to the other side of the kitchen so they could build a greenhouse for herbs, and now I waited on the new porch of that camp. It was summer again, the heat cruel but also sweetly familiar, and then Fern was walking out the kitchen's side door, her eyes on me. She was in her seventies and wore a blouse and jeans, her white hair cut short, and when she stepped close her small face looked stricken in some way. But then she reached up and held my face in both her hands. "You're a writer, Andre. You're a *writer*."

She kept her hands there a few seconds longer, and I felt moved by her loving belief in me. I thanked her for reading my story, and I stood there feeling deeply encouraged but also guilty, guilty for stepping onto the same road as the man who'd left her daughter. That, and strangely disloyal to the way of life my grandparents had come from and lived.

If Pappy ever read that story, he never talked to me about it, nor would I have wanted him to; Jeb and I were in our twenties then, a decade when my brother and I started working together as self-employed carpenters. It had taken me years before I could call myself that, years of working as a laborer and then a carpenter's helper, and when there was no work I also tended bar and worked overnight shifts in halfway houses, night jobs I preferred because they freed up my mornings to write. But on any visit south, I never mentioned these other jobs to Pappy, or my writing, for I now knew what all those tools in Pappy's shop did, and I'd spend days in there clearing out his old scrap wood and sheet metal, oiling and organizing his hand and power tools, a chore he'd always thank me for, though I'd heard him tell my mother once, "That boy sure can work, but I can't find a damn thing after he's done."

One afternoon I was driving Pappy somewhere in his truck, the sky low and gray over the pines. Pappy put a fresh wad of chew between his cheek and gums and said, "My four grandsons aren't afraid to work."

"No, Pappy, we're not."

"I've been thinking about a family business."

"You have?"

"LOD. Lowe, Owens, Dubus."

"That sounds good."

"We could do something with that."

Though I knew we would not. Pappy was very old by then, and while Micky lived just down the road with his wife and two young kids, Eddie lived with his wife in East Texas and Jeb and I were rooted in New England, where we saw ourselves as enduring this construction-working period of our lives until we were free to live more artistically fulfilling ones—Jeb with his classical guitar and me with my writing, again two things we just didn't talk to Pappy about.

And now it was winter again and probably the week when Pappy and I were sitting in the cab of his pickup truck on a cold December afternoon, the oak cistern up against the cabin filled with ice, Pappy spitting his wintergreen chewing tobacco out his passenger-side window. Because we'd all enjoyed being in Fishville that time of year for Fern and Pappy's fiftieth, we were back to celebrate Christmas. My mother, my sister and her new husband—a man she would soon leave for good reason—Jeb and Nicole, and my lovely and loving aunt Jeannie, who, along with Fern, was beginning to go blind from macular degeneration.

I don't remember where we were getting ready to go or why, nor do I remember how the subject of violence came up, only that during those years up north I was still trying to exorcise from my body the physical coward I'd been as a boy.

Pappy turned to me in his truck that afternoon and said, "I've been in some fights."

There was Eddie Wayne, who would soon die of cirrhosis of the liver, that pride in his eyes as he told me how men *respected* my grandfather. "At work?"

"Yeah. And one time these two ol' boys come up on me on Lake Pontchartrain." Pappy spat out the window, then rolled it all the way up, and he began to tell me how it was three in the morning and he'd just finished a job outside New Orleans and now he was driving home on the Causeway, a low bridge across the water over twenty miles long. He was tired and driving his pickup slowly. "Not too slow, but I was taking my time. Then these headlights come up on me." It was some kind of sedan, its brights on, and Pappy told me how that car pulled up fast to within a foot of Pappy's rear bumper, "and that pissed me off." So when the sedan tried to pass Pappy he pulled to the left to box it in, the sedan's horn going off and the driver stepping on it so that his front bumper was nearly touching the tailgate of Pappy's truck. This went on for a few miles till Pappy had had it and he cut his wheel and stomped his brakes, his pickup blocking the road. Then he was stepping out onto the asphalt and reaching into the bed of his truck. "I had a length of chain and I grabbed that and then I whipped those two sonsabitches with it and threw 'em both into Lake Pontchartrain."

"The *men*?"

Pappy nodded. He was staring out his windshield at the pines. He rolled the window down again and spat outside, cold air moving into the cab that felt too warm now. "You think you killed 'em, Pappy?"

"I could have."

"What'd you do?"

"I threw my chain back in the truck and drove home." He kept his eyes on the pines, at the narrow shafts of winter sun shining down from above. "I never told anybody that before."

I don't know if I said much after that. Part of me wondered if it was a tall tale of some kind, for I'd heard Fern and Jeannie and my mother over the years say that Pappy was good at exaggerating things. But he'd told me that story with none of the fervent enthusiasm of the storyteller who's got a good story; instead, it sounded more like the quiet admission of a man who knew he was nearing the very end of his life.

There's a story my aunt Jeannie used to tell about her father just two or three years before he died. A power plant on the West Coast, one that Pappy had helped to build, needed him to come show them the inner workings of whatever it was that he and his probably long-dead crew had fabricated there decades earlier. The company offered him thousands of dollars to do this, and they sent a Concord jet to the small airport in Alexandria to pick him up. They even sent a black Town Car, its driver going slowly over the rutted gravel road of Fern and Pappy's camp in Fishville. And Jeannie, who was there and could still see then, said that for the first time in years Pappy stood straight as a young man, no slouch in his shoulders whatsoever, as he carried his overnight bag to that Lincoln, its driver holding the rear door open for him and calling him sir.

———

THE BEGINNING OF THE END CAME WITH A FALL. PAPPY WAS LEANing back in his chair out on the concrete patio and he fell backward and hit his head hard. I don't know if he was knocked out or not, but I do know that after that he was often confused. On one of my short visits south, he'd look up at me from his chair, his face now completely covered with a white beard, and say, "But where are we *located*?"

"Fishville, Pappy. This is your house."

"But, who *built* this house?"

"You did, Pappy. With your own hands."

He'd take this in, then look down at his knees or the carpet, his thick fingers tapping the arms of his chair.

Other times, he'd be his regular self and it was clear he knew where he was and who he was talking to. It was summer again but Pappy no longer spent much time working in the garden. One morning after a breakfast of baking powder biscuits and smoked sausage and Steen's cane syrup, I sat with Pappy on the back deck overlooking the pines. There were the smells of pine needles and dried bark and the hot chicory coffee I was sipping. Pappy was wearing a short-sleeved shirt and faded jeans. His legs were crossed at the knees, and I tried not to stare at how thin his thighs had become. He turned to me and said, "Andre, don't get old."

"Why, Pappy?"

"Your damn knees go, your back, your eyes—you can't *do* anything."

"That must be hard."

"I always thought I'd get killed on a job. I never thought I'd get *old*."

———

ANOTHER TIME, MAYBE LATER THAT SAME DAY AS WE SAT SIDE BY side on that deck, Pappy drifted off somewhere and when he looked at me he didn't seem to see me at all. But he said, "Too bad, so sad, no dad."

"What's that, Pappy?"

He just shook his head and said again. "Too bad, so sad, no dad."

I didn't know if he was talking about me or someone else or maybe even himself. But I just nodded and looked out at the pines, two squirrels chasing each other up one trunk and down another.

———

THAT MAY HAVE BEEN THE LAST AFTERNOON I SPENT WITH MY grandfather. The following January, Fern drove him to his doctor for a checkup, and after the nurse led Pappy to the examination room, after she took his pulse and blood pressure and said the doctor would be in shortly, Pappy lay back on that paper-covered table and he closed his eyes, then breathed deeply into the slowing of his own heart, that valiant heart whose beats grew farther and farther apart until they came no more.

We were all there for the funeral: Fern, my mother and her family, Jeannie and hers. And many of the same men and women who'd celebrated Fern and Elmer Lowe's fiftieth not long before. It was a cold afternoon, thin ice along the clay and gravel shoulder of Highway 8. At the grave, some sort of clergyman in a suit read a prayer over Pappy's casket, and Fern sat straight in her foldout chair, black gloves on her hands in her lap, one grown daughter on each side of her.

They hosted a reception back at Fern and Pappy's place in Fishville. And that kitchen and living room were soon filled with old, well-dressed women and men, with polite conversation and occasional laughter, with the smells of cigarette smoke and brewing coffee and various colognes and perfumes. My cousins had skipped all this, taking a big bottle of Jack Daniel's to that half-acre that Micky, Eddie, and his friend Deke and I had cleared summers before. They built a fire there to sit around and I would join them later, but I didn't want to leave Pappy's house so soon. I also hadn't slept much and so stretched out on the floor not far from my grandfather's reading chair, and I fell asleep to the soft southern vowels of my mother's people, who were my people, even though I'd lived away from them all my life.

———

DOWN THE STAIRS FROM THE SMALL ROOM WHERE I WRITE THIS sits my father's Marine Corps trunk, its side and bottom corners still wrapped in strips of sheet metal more than forty years after

Pappy and I riveted them there. That trunk now holds my handwritten notebooks from years of daily writing. Fifty yards from my front door and just beyond some cedar trees sits my shed. Inside it are all my tools: my chop saw and table saw, my wet saw and circular saw and cordless drills, my planer and hand tools, for I am forever finishing up projects around my homemade home—building more bookshelves, building our dining room table, repairing decking that New England's unrelenting four seasons have already begun to rot. It is a home that my writing gave us, my father's trade passed down to me, but each time I carry a tool outside I pass one of Pappy's old hard hats hanging on a nail. Printed above the visor, in fading letters, is: *E.L. Lowe*. I always look at that as I pass. Always.

Then I carry my tools and electric cords out into the sun. I lower the tailgate of my own pickup, and I feel my grandfather's eyes on me, my father's too, the working man and the writer. Then I pull on my carpenter's belt, and I get to work.

RELAPSE

At the bar, a face appears just inches from the side of my own. I can see that it is a man's face. Dark whiskers and crooked teeth. Narrow eyes and waxy skin, though in the dim neon of this roadhouse it's hard to see clearly. He looks to be in his twenties, a good thirty years younger than I, and he's staring at what I'm wearing, which is a cheap Bermuda shirt, black with bright tiny padlocks printed all over it. I've been on a motorboat all day out on the lake and so I am sunburned and windblown. I am also over fifty and wearing eyeglasses.

Maybe I look to him like some lawyer on vacation, or an accountant, or some other man whose profession allows him to rent boats, then come to this bar in a clearing up the hill from town where the tourists are not supposed to go; we're supposed to stay in the restaurants along the southern tip of Moosehead Lake, a thirty-two-mile-long stretch of water so far up in the Maine woods that we are north of Toronto and Montreal. It is my family's last day at the cabin we rent here every year, and after a long day on the water and then grilled burgers and s'mores by the fire, my wife and kids back at our camp, I'm having a nightcap with my best friend and his grown children up here in Woody's.

It's a cavernous barn of a place with a long pine-top bar and pool tables under lamps hanging from the rafters. Over the sound system Bachman-Turner Overdrive is singing about taking care of business, and there are the smells of beer foam and French fries and the cigarette smoke that drifts in through the open windows, the smoking area a few plastic chairs surrounded by chicken wire.

My friend's two grown kids are in their twenties, and they both call me Uncle. My niece is a lovely young woman who was also one of my writing students at the university where I teach, and with her is her boyfriend, Bobby. He's muscular and tattooed, and like so many of the people I grew up with in the mill towns north of Boston, he's part Italian, part something else—French or Irish probably. Just two generations or so removed from the men and women who migrated from Europe to work in the mills making textiles and shoes.

He's still in his twenties but looks ten years older. His head is shaved and he has lines in his forehead and around his eyes, his skin like suede, not from the week we've shared up here under the sun, but from the job he does working for a cable company climbing utility poles all four seasons of the year. Bobby lifts weights after his shifts and on weekends he goes out drinking. He's got thick, rounded shoulders and a deep chest padded with muscle, and his tattoos are wrapped around his forearms and biceps and triceps. He looks like someone not to mess with, yet he gets into fights regularly down in the bars along the Merrimack River where I too used to fight thirty years ago.

But before this moment with this man's face leaning in too

close to my own in this roadhouse in the North Woods of Maine, a place that is the home of loggers and truckers and men and women who live here year-round, my last fight was when I was twenty-nine years old, when I went after a man who was beating up his wife or girlfriend in the street. In the nearly three decades since, I have been able to stay away from violence; I stopped seeking out places where this kind of trouble was easy to find—bars like this one, for example—or loud house parties in trash-strewn neighborhoods where I no longer had to live.

Miraculously, my daily writing ritual, one I began when I was just a little younger than Bobby, has given me a life of peace and stability and deep fulfillment, has led me to my wife and our three children, to the publishing of books and to the teaching of young people in classrooms on a campus very close to that same river along which there were bars where I used to go looking for trouble, the kind I seemed to find myself in now while waiting for the four beers I've just ordered for me and my best friend and his wife and mother-in-law.

The man's face is in a sneer and I can smell him—cigarette smoke and motor oil and jeans that haven't been washed in a long time. He's leaning so close to me that his shoulder is just beginning to touch mine. He says, "Nice fuckin' shirt."

He is calling me on, of course, and it is not the first time I have been tempted to forget my deep desire to live a peace-loving life.

———

IT WAS 2001, AND I'D JUST BEEN AWARDED A GUGGENHEIM FELLOW-ship. To celebrate, I and my wife Fontaine, a dancer and choreographer, went to dinner in Cambridge with some friends, all of us in our forties then and all of us working in the arts in some way: there was a writer, an actor and his director wife, a dancer and a poet.

It was spring in New England and there were still low mounds of dirty snow plowed along the sidewalks, the air cold and smelling like the parking garage we were in, like concrete and congealed spots of engine oil, like the perfume of our director friend as she leaned into our minivan to climb inside. We'd had a good night in a place that served a fusion of Caribbean and Mediterranean food, and now we were heading home. I was already in the far backseat, Fontaine at the wheel, our other friends already seated too, when a man's voice rang through the parking garage, "Hey! I've got a hard penis for that ass!"

My director friend, who was still bending over to climb inside our minivan, looked right at me. *"Andre."*

But she didn't have to call my name because I was already scrambling to get outside, my blood thinning out in my veins, whatever I drank in the restaurant seeming to evaporate instantly. She stepped aside, and as I climbed out as fast as I could I was aware that she hadn't called her husband's name, not because he wouldn't also look out for her safety, but maybe because, like many men, he had never before been in a fight and my friend knew that my youth and early adulthood were so full of fights that I still could not remember them all.

Fontaine and I had been friends with this actor-director couple for a long time and so we had shared many dinners and talked about our childhoods the way people do. When it had been my turn to talk, I could not leave out all the street violence of my youth—not the lethal gun violence that so many today have to face, especially young brown and black men in blighted neighborhoods, but fistfights that were nonetheless ugly and bloody and often people got seriously hurt.

In my telling of these stories I was always aware of how alive I felt when I stood in one of our living rooms to reenact a particular punch or kick to the head, and I could sense that my wife and friends could see this too, how in the telling of these stories the years fell away and with a dark recklessness that felt nearly euphoric I was facing off again with another human being, one who may have just slapped his wife or punched his girlfriend in the face, or pulled a knife on my best friend after breaking a beer bottle across his face.

As truly happy and relieved as I was to have those years long behind me, I was inadvertently mythologizing myself with every story I told of these fights where I was the hero, and so why wouldn't my friend call my name now?

The man who'd just yelled that ugliness was leaning against a pickup truck in a wool cap. His arms were crossed and he had a scraggly beard and there was something off about his face. It might have been his eyes, which he seemed to be trying to put into some kind of focus, as if he was either drunk or deeply unbalanced in some way. But his eyes were also still on my friend near the open door of the van, and I took two steps in his direction and said, "Watch your fuckin' mouth."

From around the corner of the pickup came another man walking fast right to me. He was short and in a denim jacket and I could see that he was thick in the shoulders and had big hands, and now he was standing inches from me, his chin up and his eyes on mine. "Yeah? What're *you* gonna do about it?"

It had been many years since I'd been in a moment like this, but my weight shifted immediately to my right foot and my hands hung loose at my sides. It was the stance for throwing a right cross up from the hip, one I'd used in the past to undeniable effect, and I felt like the man who thought he'd put away his gun years ago only to find it firmly in his back pocket, oiled and ready to fire.

I said, "Your friend needs to watch his manners." I could feel my pulse in the back of my tongue, but my limbs felt like warm water, and now this man was spewing words into my face, his eyes narrowed. I took one step backward to set my range so that if he swung at me, then the right I was ready to throw would be at the precise distance to drop him.

And what you should know, what I'm not proud of writing now, is that I *wanted* to drop this man. But why? Because what he'd been yelling at me, droplets of his spittle on my cheek, was something like this: "Maybe my friend isn't right in the *head*. Ever think of that? Maybe he needs some fuckin' *help*. And what the fuck're *you* gonna do about in your suit jacket and your little fuckin' *minivan*?"

I could feel the quiet presence of my wife and friends somewhere behind me, and the truth is, if I had been alone that night I think I would have tried to lower the heat right away. I think I might have said something like, "I get it. You're just looking out for your friend."

But I was not alone, and now all those stories I'd told felt like some mirror that my friends were holding to my face: *Here you are. Were those just stories you told? Or do you actually know how to handle yourself in times like these?*

And there was this man's expression when he asked what *I* was going to do about his friend's behavior? Me with the suit jacket and minivan? Because when he said that, I could see that he truly saw me as no threat whatsoever, as someone he believed he could have dispensed with easily. And maybe he could have, though standing there I didn't think so, and now it was clear that he would only throw a punch if I did, and could I justify doing that? Just because this man was verbally putting me in my place? For that's what it must have looked like to my wife and friends, that if I was letting this guy threaten me, then I was backing down. And I am ashamed to write that I actually *cared* if they saw it this way.

The man who'd yelled his assault at my friend was staring at the concrete and laughing to himself. He seemed afflicted in some way, and his friend in my face was clearly his caretaker, at least for the night.

It was time to walk away, to tell the man's protector that I could now see the situation and let's all just move on. I had not yet begun to write *Townie*, but one of the many things it showed me was just how narcissistic the roots of my own violence were. How clear it became to me that I would rather die a violent death than see a coward in the mirror ever again. And standing in that cold parking garage in the light of its security lamps, the man inches from me clearly no stranger to street violence either, I was ready to walk away, but it was far too important to me that this man know I was backing down not because I was afraid of him, but because his larger situation had revealed itself. There was something else, too: I feared that if I were to throw that punch, then it would be like a recovering alcoholic, after years and years of sobriety, tilting a glass full of vodka down his throat.

I said something like, "He needs to watch his manners." Which brought another string of threats from the man I was now walking away from, my director friend climbing into my minivan ahead of me, everyone quiet as we drove out of that parking garage and into the night.

Later, lying in bed with my wife, I turned to her and said, "You do know I wasn't afraid of that guy, right?"

I don't remember what she said back to me, but it was something warmly dismissive of the whole incident. She also sounded distracted because she was reading a book in the lamplight of her bedside table, and I lay there, our kids asleep in their rooms, feeling so very immature and insecure and wrong to care so much about how I had appeared to my wife and friends earlier that night. I was nearly forty-two years old and my life was blossoming in such a lovely way, blossoming precisely because I no longer went around getting into fistfights.

Soon Fontaine turned out her lamp and we kissed good night. I lay there awake in the dark a long time, for what I feared, even more than my wife perhaps thinking all those stories of my youth were lies, was how dangerously close I'd come to throwing that punch which part of me was aching to throw, a weak part of me.

I've gotten many letters about that memoir I wrote a few years later about my violent youth, most of them from men who seemed grateful for my having written about the kinds of childhoods that they too had experienced: having been bullied, having to learn to fight back or never having learned to fight back. They wrote to me about their relationships with their fathers, about also having grown up in poverty. Some of them had done time, others were cops. Others were men with office jobs and families to support. But what became clear to me reading these letters is how much of the layered texture of our lives is shared by others. And how the reading of one person's story can bring us more fully back to our own.

I don't know if Bobby read that book, but I do know that by the time I met him he'd heard stories about the youth I share with his girlfriend's father. He'd heard about the fights we'd been in in the same bars he went to now, one of which had a long stairwell where a local bully pushed my younger brother down the stairs right before I went after him and threw the first real punch of my life.

But something had happened here that I had not foreseen. By writing directly about all of that, even though I tried to do so as honestly and nakedly as I could, trying to capture my terror and my self-loathing, trying to capture the strange intimacy of punching a fellow human being in the face, I also ended up shining a light on myself as a former fighter when I was trying to go far deeper than the word *fighter*: I wanted to capture the vulnerable boy still living inside the body of the man. I wanted to do the opposite of romanti-cizing a street fight; I wanted to show what a colossal human failure it always was, no matter what caused it.

And yet, there was—and still is—that small boy living inside me who is a bit shocked and proud of how he was able to change his life, how he was able to stop being anyone's victim, and, to be as honest here as possible, how a piece of him *enjoyed* fighting.

But *why*?

I don't think I'd have the answer to this if I had not been sitting with Bobby in front of a campfire one night during that week up in the North Woods. This was at my friends' place on the big lake. It was a cool August night, the stars above bright and so very close, a light wind raising whitecaps out in the darkness on the water, my friends' rented boat knocking lightly against the dock. My niece was playing low music on a small speaker set on the picnic table, a rapper's rasp cut into by a woman's voice singing of lost love. It was street music, my friends and wife and our kids all engaged in sepa-rate conversations in the flickering light of the flames, and Bobby was leaning in close to me telling me how he was trying to stay out of trouble, how he was trying to leave it all behind. "But—" He was looking right at me and he was smiling almost shyly. The tiny bristles on his head caught the firelight. "I miss it."

"What, fighting?"

"Yeah, you know."

"Which part?"

"When it's just you and some other dude and you're squaring off and—I don't know—the adrenaline."

I found myself nodding. "The unknown."

"Yeah, you don't know what's gonna happen. I mean you might get *killed*. It's a fuckin' rush, man. I miss it." And he clapped his big hand on my knee, drained his beer, then got up to get another.

I sat there staring into the embers. I was thinking of someone I knew long ago, and while I do not intend to even remotely compare a fistfight to the horror of armed combat, the person I was thinking of had been a soldier in Vietnam. One day on Fred's deck under the sun, he had his shirt off while reading the paper and all along his ribs and across his back were coin-sized welts of raised flesh, scars from the nine shards of shrapnel that tore through him from a land mine that killed his friend a few feet ahead of him.

Fred taught at the same college my father did, and more than a few times, the three of us drinking together, Fred would talk about how alive he felt back there. "I mean, whenever we got shot at. Isn't that *fucked*?"

Maybe all I'm talking about here is merely chemical, a rush of hormones a man or woman needs to fight or to flee. But I think it goes deeper than that. Or it at least *feels* deeper than that. And sitting there in front of that fire in the North Woods with my family and close friends, their talk and laughter rising over the music and the tapping of the boat against the dock, the smell of woodsmoke in the air, I felt like someone who for years had hacked his way up a steep mountain only to find himself on a dry plateau overlooking the dark valley he'd never have to return to; but as wonderfully safe and secure as that stone shelf in the side of the mountain was, as grateful as I was to be able to raise our children on it, I sometimes missed the danger of that valley. Like Bobby, I too missed that moment when it was just you and another man, a man who had every intention of hurting you or worse. That flash of breath before one of you made the first move.

It is a moment between heartbeats and it is still and without sound, even if the air is loud with screaming voices or live music or cars whizzing by in the street. And while everything is muffled, it is also as clear as a blade and in it is the hovering presence of ancestors: there's cannon smoke drifting through the trees and there's the morning sun glinting off a sword, there are the mournful eyes of horses, the rising mists above a canopy of trees near the lip of a steaming volcano where you flick your eyes to the left and to the right and then slither over the edge into the hollow drop and fall where you can only burn.

I rose out of my chair and went over and kissed each of my kids on the top of their heads. Then I went down to the dock and looked out at the dark water and black silhouettes of trees on a small island one hundred yards to the west, the vaulted stars above. The air had gotten colder and felt like fall, and maybe I thought then of football, a sport I'd never played or watched or cared about whatsoever until my two sons did. In my twenties I could only see this game as some imperialistic blood sport where a gang of men hurt other men to invade their territory. But watching it every Sunday afternoon with my young sons, I began to see it as something else too, a way for boys and men, especially those who watched from the stands or from their living room couches, to both safely sublimate and express their warring ways, one tribe squaring off with another and fighting until there emerged a victor. I have never been a sports fan and am not one now, but I fear that without sports, without this cultural valve to release pent-up pressure and aggression, primarily in men, there would be even more bloodshed in the streets than there already is.

———

"I SAID NICE FUCKIN' *SHIRT*."

Now in the bar the young man's face is even closer to the side of mine, his shoulder pressing into my shoulder. I can feel the bare skin of his forearm just beginning to touch my own. I can feel his body heat, and my better angels are sitting up and beginning to spread their wings, but then—I turn my back on them. I'm still not sure what makes me do this: maybe I don't like how this one is looking at me in my glasses and Bermuda shirt, like I'll be easy to beat, embodying all the bullies I encountered as a boy; or maybe it is my recent conversation with Bobby and my discovery that a fallen part of me also misses the pulsing heart of a fight; or it could be that I am neither drunk nor sober but floating somewhere in between, a fraught place where I have always tried to tread carefully. Or maybe it's all three of these, but I hear myself say, "You like this shirt? I got it in a gay bar." Then I wink at him like he might want to go shopping with me, and his face becomes a snarl and everything goes quiet, and I must have done something for he's down and rolling under a pool table and I'm moving toward it on the balls of my feet, my hands up, and it is as if my last fight was not nearly thirty years ago but just an hour earlier, like I've never stopped fighting at all, like it's something I still do all the time.

The man is crawling out from under the pool table and I'm waiting for him to stand, but then two hands grasp my upper arms and I'm being pushed past the other pool tables and out the open doorway into the gravel lot. The hands belong to my nephew and he's saying calmly but firmly, "We gotta go, Uncle. These people'll shoot us."

Now there's the darkly blooming feeling that we tourists are indeed in the wrong place. In the shadows of that smoking area behind the chicken wire comes sudden movement, two or three men rising from their plastic chairs, and the woman bartender from whom I'd ordered our beer is yelling, "Don't fucking come back here!" And my niece is laughing and calling me crazy, her parents and grandmother behind her, her younger brother no longer having to hold on to me because now I'm walking fast with Bobby to his Jeep, Bobby chuckling, "Just like old times, huh?"

I climb into the backseat of Bobby's Jeep, my nephew beside me, my still-laughing niece buckling up on the passenger side just as Bobby accelerates out of the lot. I feel an untethered euphoria tinged with disappointment at that fight having been interrupted, and even though my ebullient niece is turning in her seat to look back at me, describing the way that man was in the air, then rolling under the pool table, I begin to feel the shame that comes with willfully doing wrong. The words *beneath you* come to me. *This is beneath you.*

Bobby downshifts as we descend the hill, his headlight path jerking at the pines alongside us. His eyes are on his rearview mirror, looking out for our friends but also for a truckload of anyone who might be following us. Because my nephew was right. These people do have guns, and look at what I started.

But no one does follow us, and back at my friends' camp, as we drink beer on their porch under the stars, my niece keeps smiling over at me. "This is the best last night of vacation *ever*." And I can see that part of the thrill for her is seeing that these stories of her uncle's and father's youth are not just stories, that we really did do all those things she'd heard we'd done.

Bobby seems to be getting some vicarious joy from it, too. He hands me a beer. "I saw how you had your hands up. That kid was gonna go down."

That kid. Yes, he probably *was* a kid. And what did I teach him tonight? Nothing his life probably hadn't already shown him. Nothing about tolerance and human understanding. Nothing about peace.

Sitting on that rented porch overlooking that dark lake under those ancient stars, I can feel what I'd done already getting reduced to some black-and-white image to be framed and hung on some wall in an amber light that obfuscates all the fine details of larger truths. And the thing is, I can't even remember exactly what I did to that young man. My body simply took over with a kind of muscle memory from so long ago. Then my best friend, who's been quiet, walks over and puts his hand on my shoulder. "You see the size of that guy?"

"No, he was too close."

But I can hear the disappointment in my friend's voice, which means that that man was small, which means that my oldest, best friend is perhaps seeing me as the kind of person we have both hated all our lives: a bully. And now I feel defensive. "Buddy, his face was right in mine. I had no idea how big or small he was."

My friend nods, but as I drive back to my family's camp a little while later, going slowly down the narrow dirt road through a thick gauntlet of trees, my headlights on the rise and fall of one hill after another, I try to shrug off my friend's disappointment in me because I truly had no idea of the size of that man, if he was drunk or sober, if he was an experienced fighter or just had a big mouth. And as I get closer to my camp it becomes clear to me that it was these unknowns that pulled me to do what I did, the dark seduction of them, and then I feel a nearly giddy wonder at how instantly my body did what it did. As if there is no time and space and my younger self is still living side by side with me on some other plane.

I'm still in this state of wonder when I slip into bed next to my wife. She's just turned out her lantern. "Have fun?"

"I got in a fight."

"What?"

"The start of one anyway."

And as I give her the details that come to me, I cannot deny the pleasure I'm taking in it, for it's hard not to hear again the words of that man in the parking garage a few years earlier. *What're you gonna do about it?*

Maybe my wife can hear this in my voice, maybe she can't, but oh how *childish* I feel feeling this, for isn't this male vanity and insecurity the very kind that starts wars?

And what kind of example am I giving to our three kids, especially to my two sons, who hear the story from their mother the next day?

My sons were teenagers then and neither one of them had ever been in a physical fight. They were also already bigger than their father and in the coming years would get even more so, both of them over two hundred pounds and six feet tall.

"Dad, you got in a fight?"

I don't remember if I gave them any details, but in their voices and faces was a kind of dark glee, and it was as if I was taking out a loaded gun and letting them hold it, the safety off. Maybe I tried to downplay it all with a shrug, or maybe I blamed it on a day and night of too much beer. But I remember feeling that we'd arrived at a moment where I should teach my kids something important, but that no matter what I said, my actions of the night before had already done all the talking.

———

IT WAS A JANUARY NIGHT A FEW YEARS LATER WHEN MY DAUGHTER Ariadne, a college senior studying philosophy, got kicked out of a bar for fighting. Her older brother was living in LA, and her younger brother was in his last year of high school, and that night Elias had a few friends over. They were sitting around a fire in the hearth, listening to music and talking quietly. My wife Fontaine was in New York City, where she'd taken over fifty teenage girls to perform at Lincoln Center, and I had an early plane to catch down to Florida, where I'd be teaching at a writers' conference the following week. It was after eleven, and I'd just come downstairs for a glass of water when my daughter walked in with one of her best friends, who looked like she'd been crying.

Ariadne was smiling at me with a sort of guilty shrug. I asked them what happened, and her friend said, "Ariadne got in another fight." My daughter's friend looked like she might cry again, and standing there in my robe, my youngest son and his friends clearly listening in, I asked my daughter what happened, and this is what she told me.

They were at the Port Tavern, an Irish pub in our town that on Friday and Saturday nights fills with men and women in their twenties. The place was loud and crowded, and Ariadne was at the bar with her friend when a group of drinking young men began to move in too closely to them. The loudest one, his head still shaved from a recent tour in Afghanistan, wore a tight pink polo shirt that showed off his muscular torso, and Ariadne, wanting to send him on his way, said, "I like your *pink* shirt."

"Man, this chick wants to get fucked."

"What'd you say to me?" Ariadne put her drink down, and before the young man could open his mouth to say more she thrust her open hand into his Adam's apple, the kid coughing and choking, the bouncer rushing through the crowd to escort my daughter out of there.

Ariadne asked him why he was kicking *her* out. "Did you hear what he *said* to me?

"Sorry, hon, you put your hands on him first."

Listening to this story, the Rolling Stones playing softly in the living room, the smells of perfume and burning oak in the air, my beautiful, brilliant daughter standing before me, I thought of her other fights, for this wasn't the first time she'd gone after transgressive young men.

At a nightclub the previous New Year's Eve, she and this same friend were standing in line for the ladies' room in a hallway that also held a line of men waiting to get into their own bathroom. The hall was dimly lit and there was music blasting, and when my daughter's friend bent over to adjust the strap of her shoe, a young man crossed the hall and planted his hand on her rear and my daughter grabbed his ears and ran him into the wall, his head bouncing off it. The kid was very drunk and slumped to the floor, and now his friend stepped in and told Ariadne that he had a sister and respected her for what she just did, but that he'd take over from there.

A few months earlier at a frat party in Boston, a young man she'd never met grabbed my daughter's crotch and she punched him in the face and kicked him in the groin and was still punching him when some other frat boy pulled her off and led her to the front door.

Now, tonight's story finished, Ariadne's eyes were on mine. She was waiting to hear what her father, a man she knew was no stranger to violence such as this, would say about this latest fight. I loved this young woman more than any other on this earth, and I felt my spirit pulled in two opposing directions: I was proud of her for making that ex-Marine literally choke on his ugly words, for I was sure that the kind of man who talked that way about women lived on the same continuum as one capable of assault and rape. Part of me felt a dark joy ripple through me as I imagined the momentary suffering that that gagging misogynist had endured, and I wanted to hear again the details of my daughter's attack. But I was afraid that if I asked to hear more, then she would see only the pleasure I was taking in this, as fallen as that may be. She would not see my fear, for I knew the world was full of men who had no compunction about hitting women back, again and again, and so I stood there deeply worried for my daughter's safety.

I told her that one day she might do this to the wrong guy, that she should always try to have people around her. As I told her this, my daughter appeared reflective and vaguely chastened, but also a little proud, a fighter like I in my robe used to be, a man who wished his daughter and sons knew nothing whatsoever of his childhood.

But as I hugged her, then went to the kitchen sink for that glass of water, I knew that my daughter's hatred of violence against women was more than just an ethical stance in the world. It came from a place that was far more personal, and this truth is a hot knife in my heart.

In an earlier draft of what you're reading now, I left out what follows, something I did to protect my daughter's privacy. But after she read my descriptions of her physical fights, she came to the living room where I was reading and handed me the manuscript with her marked corrections. She sat in the chair near mine. She was in her bathrobe, her hair down, the sun from the skylight above shining off the floor near her bare feet.

I told her that I thought she was quick to violence, the way I used to be, because she and I had both been abused.

"Yeah," she said. "But we don't have to talk about that."

"I know, that's your business. That's why I didn't put it in."

"You can if you want to, Dad. It happens to so many people."

I did not want to, but an old grief and rage began to well up inside me then, Ariadne sitting Fontaine and me down a year or so earlier and telling us through tears about a former boyfriend who, when she was a teenager, had treated her firm no as a yes. As she told us this, our daughter was curled up in her chair weeping, and there was a razored stillness in the air, a stark flatness that comes when what is feared for so long finally shows itself. My breath was gone from my chest and then I was holding her, kissing her forehead and cheek, hugging her probably too hard. She took a breath and insisted we please do nothing; she just needed us to know.

I let go and sat back down. I looked over at Fontaine, who appeared stricken but strong, her eyes on our daughter as she spoke quietly to her, words between women that I felt rightly outside of, and then I said, "I want to kill him."

"*No.*" My daughter looked horrified and she pleaded with me not to do anything, that if I did, it would only make what she'd endured far worse. It had happened years ago, and she had to leave it behind her. I nodded, I took a breath, and then Fontaine and I told her how heartbroken we were to know that she'd gone through this, that she'd been suffering through it alone. We asked if she wanted to go talk to a counselor, but she said no, she really didn't. It had happened years earlier, and she just needed us to know.

It was hard not to think of my own father then, how when my older sister was raped at nineteen, my father began to buy and carry guns. I thought about how the crime committed against my sister somehow became a crime committed against *him*, and I did not want to make the same mistake; I did not want was inflicted against my daughter to be anything but what it was: an attack against *her*.

But how could I just do nothing about it? I needed her to know that I would do anything to keep her safe, and now that I'd failed at that, I'd—*what?*

Get revenge.

I hugged and kissed Ariadne one more time, then walked outside. I stood on our porch and stared into the dark woods just feet from our house. How could I have let this *happen* to her? I knew the boy. I knew it would be easy to find his address. I could be there in less than an hour, and I wanted him to see that it was me coming for him. But this desire for him to see my face, what was this but some blood-hungry expression of patriarchal narcissism? One man reclaiming from another what belongs to him? How could any of this help my daughter?

Still, I wanted that young man to be punished, to suffer, and I pictured a moonless night and a ski mask and the baseball bat I keep beside my bed. I could feel the splintering crack of his knees and then his ribs and then—

I shook my head and went back inside our home, the place where our daughter felt safe enough to show us her deepest wound. It was time to only help her heal, something I knew would not happen just because the perpetrator, too, had been wounded.

———

BUT THIS NEW AND DEEPLY PAINFUL KNOWLEDGE OF OUR DAUGH-ter's experience made other things clear: When that man who bragged about grabbing women's genitals, a man who was also accused of outright rape, was elected president, Ariadne cried for days. Her senior thesis paper was a feminist critique of existentialism that began this way: "Existentialism was created by men, for men, period." And the night before her college commencement, she decorated the top of her mortarboard with silver glitter and wrote in large calligraphic letters: *F*ck the Patriarchy.*

I write all of this, with her permission, because here, once again, is the reminder that moral outrage is all too often born from real suffering. But that is only part of my daughter's fighting stance for girls and women, for since she was a little girl she has consistently shown herself to be a deeply compassionate and intuitive being.

Just days after my father's sudden death at age sixty-two, his body lying in the coffin my brother and I built for him, I let the boys watch *Star Wars*, their plastic light sabers in their laps. I was lying on the floor, my head propped on a pillow, and Ariadne was behind me somewhere playing with her dolls. Then somehow I found myself watching the scene where Luke Skywalker is holding his dying father, and I couldn't bear it. Tears ran down into my lips and I tried to stay as quiet as possible for I didn't want to alarm my kids. Then a tiny hand touched my temple, and Ariadne—only three and a half years old—leaned close to my ear and whispered, "You're thinking of your daddy, aren't you?"

I nodded and held her hand and tried not to cry harder, but I didn't want her to have to bear the burden of comforting her father. I turned to her and whispered, "I'm okay. Daddy's okay."

A few days later, her younger brother Elias, barely two years old, stood in the open doorway to my and his mother's bedroom, where I sat at a desk I'd made at the foot of our bed. It was late morning, and my youngest son, who had been a large baby and was now a big toddler, stood there shirtless in a pair of shorts, his deep-set eyes a shocking blue. "Um, Dad?"

"Yeah?" I had my eyes on the screen.

"Um, since Pop died, well maybe now I can be your dad."

I turned to him, this little boy who'd just shot a deeply loving arrow right through my chest. "C'mere, buddy." And I held out my arms for him and held him close and told him that was so good of him to want to do that but he didn't have to take care of me like that. "I'm your daddy, okay? I'm here to take care of *you*."

———

THREE YEARS AFTER ARIADNE'S NIGHT AT THE TAVERN, SHE knocked on my and Fontaine's bedroom door. "You guys awake? Elias got in a fight."

We had not been awake, but we were now. I sat up, my heart somewhere behind my tongue, and flicked on my bedside lamp. "When? *Where?*"

"I don't know. Some party. He's on the way to the hospital."

"The *hospital?*" Fontaine turned on her own lamp and grabbed her phone, and now we were calling Elias and he picked up right away.

"Hey, I can't talk, I'm in the ambulance."

"Elias, what happened?"

It was clear that our youngest son was pretty drunk, his tone boozily cheerful yet wistful too, as if all of this was happening to someone else and why do you guys sound so upset? We got a few details from that brief conversation, mainly that Elias had a fat lip and at least one broken tooth, and then after he hung up we called his close friend and learned more.

It was one of those fall Saturdays when their university's football team was hosting a home game, and Elias and his friends had been tailgating all day in the stadium's parking lot. When night came, they moved to a huge party in a field behind a row of houses, the speakers of a sound system in the open window of one of them blasting rap and hip-hop. A few hundred young people were making loud joyous noise while drinking too much and blowing off academic steam, and our son was in the thick of it. He was now six foot three and lifted weights and his feet were so large he had to order his shoes online. He was also a smart, kind, and affable young man who at age twenty had never been in a fistfight. Then one broke out in the crowd a few feet behind him. At first he could only sense a change in the air, but then he turned and there on the ground, some young man was straddling the chest of another, punching his face and head again and again. No one was trying to break it up. No one was screaming for it all to stop. Instead, there were perhaps two dozen iPhones pointed at that beating, nearly two dozen young people recording it to post later.

All of this happened in seconds, and now Elias rushed over and grabbed the assailant's shoulders and jerked him up and off the bleeding boy, pulling so hard that my son fell backwards into the dirt, and now another young man was on *his* chest, punching my son over and over in the face before one of Elias's friends pulled him off.

Both of our son's two front teeth were broken at their roots. The emergency room doctor did what he could, but Elias needed to come home for dental surgery, so early the next morning I drove the two hours to his campus in western Massachusetts to pick him up. I hadn't slept much. I hadn't slept because I kept picturing our big son doing the right thing only to get punished for it. I kept picturing that young punk punching Elias over and over again in the face, and I could feel my hands pull this kid off him, could feel myself set my feet and start throwing punches into the face of some other father's son.

This was wrong, of course, and I knew it, but just as soon as I got Elias taken care of physically, we would call the campus police to see what they could do.

The drive home was a long one for him. His cheek was bruised and his lips were dark and twice their normal size, but it was his broken front teeth that were causing him such pain. Normally a joyfully talkative young man, who would hold forth on music and movies and books and baseball, he was now quiet and kept lowering his head to his hands. "Dad, it really hurts."

It was heartbreaking to see him this way, yet I knew it could have been so much worse. The fight had been stopped just in time, and there were no knives or guns, and I was proud of my son for stepping in to help another. I told him this. But I was also haunted by his innocence, one that I had helped to maintain all his life: the big house I built for him and his sister and brother in the woods, our neighbors an architect and a dentist. Cars that started right up all year long. More than enough food in the house at all times. The private high school we sent them to because our local regional one was too much like the one I'd gone to in the seventies, its teachers underpaid and overwhelmed, many of their students falling through the cracks into drugs and occasional street violence I'd read about in the paper. But beyond the material security we'd been able to give our kids, there were the steadily creative, loving, and peaceful days and nights my wife and I were able to have together and with them for all of their growing up. How had we gotten so fortunate?

Our ability to make a good living in the arts was part of it, something for which I never stop feeling deeply grateful. But it was also the nearly cosmic good luck of Fontaine and me having clearly married the right person for the other, a compatible union that provided the most stable foundation of all. That is what truly carved that stone shelf into the side of that mountain, the one so far from the kind of dark valley where things like what happened to Elias the night before happened all the time. And I sometimes worried that I'd sheltered our kids too much, that my desire to keep them from violence and human ugliness of any kind kept me from teaching them a few things they might need to know.

We were an hour into our ride back home now, the sun high over the highway and the yellowing leaves of the maples along the shoulder. I turned to my son. He lay back with his eyes closed, and I asked him if I could ask him a question.

"Yeah."

"When you jumped in to help, how come you weren't ready to get jumped yourself?"

"I don't know. I didn't think anybody would get mad at someone for trying to stop a fight."

"Guys who fight aren't rational, Elias. If you jump into one— even to do the right thing like you did—you should always be ready to fight."

He nodded and turned his head toward the window, and I felt as if I'd failed him.

Over the years, there were brief moments when I had shown him and his brother and sister how to hold their fists up, how to jab, then throw a right cross from a pivoting hip. But again, I'd always feel as if I'd taken out a loaded gun and let them hold it and even aim it, an action that could only invite trouble. Like all parents, trouble of any kind is what I wanted them to avoid, and so I stayed away from these kinds of lessons, for if I had learned anything about physical violence, I had learned this: being overly prepared for trouble is another way of looking for it, and the spilling of blood leads to only more of the same.

Our family dentist was a good man who on his vacations would travel to Appalachia to work on the teeth of low-income families for free. After I told his receptionist that morning about Elias, our dentist moved another appointment to see him, and then he worked on Elias for over an hour, saving his two front teeth, though he told us that their nerve supply was forever gone. He also X-rayed Elias's face for any fractures, found none, and prescribed my son antibiotics and painkillers, apparently the same kind the rapper Eminem got hooked on, which is why Elias played some Eminem in my truck on the drive to the drugstore, my young son's humor trailing back from where the pain had taken him.

He missed a week of classes and spent most of that time resting on the couch in front of the TV. The morning I drove him back to his campus in western Massachusetts, he was cheerful and ready to get back to his life. His lips were no longer swollen, and his pain was largely gone too. But just before we got to his dorm at the Honors College, I parked in front of the local police station and we went in and filed a report with a young lieutenant behind a thick pane of glass. When he heard of all the students who'd filmed the fight on their phones, he said, "You might find it on social media, but don't get your hopes up." He looked up at Elias. "If you hear anything, call us." And he handed two of his cards through the slot to me and my son, his implication being, *Don't go looking for him yourself.*

But Elias did. At the gym, in the library or dining hall, or just walking across campus, my son scanned the hands of every young man he passed, looking for scabbed-over knuckles, the ones that had forever taken the nerve supply from his two front teeth.

Part of me wanted Elias to find that kid, but then what? Did I want my son to call this kid on and fight? No, but I did want this young man's name, for I wanted to go after him legally, and I wanted the parents of this predatory kid to bear the financial consequences of their son's brutality. It was hard not to think then of my own violence when I was this boy's age. I felt sure that the family who had created the young man who had hurt my son had a big hand in making him the way he was, and I wanted them to pay.

But Elias never did find the one who jumped him just for trying to stop violence, and eventually I was relieved that he never found him. Let trouble from the past stay in the past.

———

BY NOW, MY SONS AND MANY OF THEIR FRIENDS HAD READ MY memoir, *Townie*, a book where I tried to capture, among other things, the dark, thorny ugliness that is physical violence. But when Elias told me that he'd gone looking for the boy who'd hurt him, I worried that his new knowledge of all his father's fights so long ago had put him on a vindictive road that he might not have treaded otherwise. And I thought of the legacy of bloodshed, the son of the World War I veteran feeling duty-bound to march off to World War II, his son shipping off to Vietnam, and his son or daughter to Iraq and Afghanistan, blood spilled decades earlier triggering the spilling of new blood today.

A few years before Elias's fight, Austin read my memoir in our rented place in the North Woods of Maine. The cabin was small and had no electricity, and it sat at the base of a steep, wooded hill, on top of which was a cistern that provided running water for the kitchen and bathroom. For light we lit the propane sconces hanging from the walls, though we spent most of our time outside because the cabin was built only ten feet from the dock on a lake where there were few other camps or people, and on the other side of the water was a valley of hardwoods, then the rise of Elephant Mountain, so named because its profile looked like the head and trunk of an elephant, its eye an outcropping of rock.

Fontaine and I had been taking our kids here since they were very young, and members of my larger family would join us too. My mother and sister Suzanne and her husband and daughter. Sometimes my blind aunt Jeannie from Louisiana and Kentucky, or my brother Jeb and his kids. It was a week or two with no cell phones, no mail or emails, no TV or radio, just each other's company while we played card games or went swimming or did art projects out on the picnic table, or just went off to our beds in the afternoons to read and nap. At night, after a grilled supper, we'd sit around the fire and roast s'mores, the searching cry of a loon out on the water under the northern stars.

And because I could not go even a week or two without lifting weights, I would haul up to Maine in the bed of my pickup truck hundreds of pounds of dumbbells. For decades I have known that I have many of the psychological symptoms of post-traumatic stress disorder. I cannot sit in a public place unless I have my back to the wall so that I can see whoever might be coming for me or my family. Even though I live in a big house in the woods in a safe neighborhood, I sleep with a baseball bat beside my bed, and I've never been a sound sleeper, the low hum of adrenaline so often coursing through me, especially after our children were born, the world outside our walls feeling more dangerous to me than it's ever been.

After writing that memoir, after disturbing layers of emotional sediment by going back to where my memories took me, to the jolt of bone on bone, the searing light that flashes through the brain when punched or kicked in the skull, I could no longer close my eyes when I was at the gym or any other public place because when I did I'd see some man rushing at me with his fist up.

This irrational sense of constant danger is why I could never bear to miss workouts, and rarely did in the over forty years I had been doing them four to five times a week. The few times I had missed them—twice when I had pneumonia, and a few days after each of our three children were born while Fontaine recovered from surgery—I felt weak and exposed and as if I'd just stepped into a battleground half-naked, my sword and shield gone.

As I write this now, our three children deep into their twenties, each of them has a four-to-seven-day-a-week workout habit. This is not something I or their mother ever told them to do. It is the daily ritual they came into on their own, but maybe some of the seed of it was planted when they were little and watched their father regularly drive off to the gym, or saw me lift weights in the sun-dappled light under the pines of our camp in Maine before I would then run hills through the deep woods near our cabin. They also spent their childhoods watching their mother set aside time each day to change into her leotard and leggings and drive to the studio where she would dance. When she was five years old, Ariadne began to go with her too, becoming a performer like her mother. And by the time Austin and Elias were in high school, they were both lifting weights, at first doing the basic program I set up for them and then steadily moving beyond that and lifting more weight in some movements than I ever could. Fontaine and I are grateful that our children have this healthy habit in their lives, and watching it all unfold has been yet another lesson that children seem to be shaped not so much by what we parents tell them as by what they see us *do*.

Part of the joy, then, of going to that North Woods camp every summer was working out with my big sons under those pines and then running with them up and down those steep roads in woods so thick that we were in constant shade.

It was a workout day the morning Austin finished reading my memoir on the dock under the sun. He'd been reading it for a few days, but because he has never liked to discuss a book until he's finished with it, I kept quiet. Sometimes, though, I'd see him glancing over at me as he closed the book, his expression darkly reflective, and I worried about what reading my childhood story might be doing to him. Not the poverty we lived through after my parents' divorce, or even the sex and drugs and alcohol I took part in when I was far too young for any of that. No, it was the violence I worried about. And not those acts perpetrated against me, but those I eventually inflicted upon others; never mind if they were boys and men who I believed were predatory themselves and were asking for it. Never mind that.

My son, just graduated from high school, had never seen this in me, and I worried that after finishing the book he might now see the loving father and husband that I'd always aspired to be as some kind of performance, that the real me was dark and violent and for all of Austin's and his siblings' lives I had hidden this behind some sort of mask.

Elias and I were already in our workout clothes and we'd pulled the tarp off the weights and set up the bench in the clearing under the pines. But I knew Austin was nearing the very end of my book, so I waited until I saw him close it, lay it down on the dock, then lean back in his foldout chair and stare out at Elephant Mountain.

The final scene is the burial of his grandfather, which happened when Austin was six years old. Of our three kids, he's the only one with clear memories of my father, warm ones at that. And one I have is of four-year-old Austin gripping the back of Pop's wheelchair and pushing him up and down my father's long hallway, my dad smiling widely behind his gray beard as he called out encouraging words to his grandson.

I went down to the dock, the sun high over the lake, the damp-wood smell of its banks in the still air. I was about to tell Austin that we were getting started, but standing a bit behind him and to the side, I could see that he'd been crying.

"You okay?"

He nodded, and I knew it wasn't time to say anything about what he'd just read. "We're gonna start now."

He nodded again.

For over two hours we worked out together, and the only time Austin said anything was when he encouraged his younger brother to get another rep or two, or when he asked me if I was done with a pair of dumbbells he wanted to use next. Out on the dock, Fontaine and Ariadne did a dance warm-up under the sun, and my mother sat at the picnic table with a cup of coffee and watercolors, brushes, and paper.

To get to the road above our camp, my sons and I had to first run up a steep hill, forty-five degrees in places and over a hundred yards long. After we covered our bench and dumbbells with a tarp, we drank the last of our water, then walked to the foot of that hill. It rose sharply ahead of us under a canopy of maples and elms and oak and pine, its rutted surface littered with loose stones and an occasional bulging root, all of this covered with dead pine needles.

I glanced up at my sons. Their handsome faces were flushed and beaded with sweat, their T-shirts sticking in places to their chests and broad upper backs. We three glanced at each other, cracked half-smiles, and then put our heads down for the pain that was now coming, climbing, swinging our arms for momentum, our thighs aflame after only a few yards, the air being snatched from our lungs by some trickster god we'd somehow invited to join us.

The crest of the hill intersected the road, and by the time we finally reached it, Austin and Elias were well in front of me, and then in no time I could only see their backs in the distance and then there was just the shaded rise and descent of one hill after another. On that run, my sons far ahead, Austin still quiet about what he'd just finished reading, I could feel him again as a little boy, his cheek against my chest as I read him a children's book on his bed. He may have been three years old. Austin said, "Daddy?"

"Yeah?"

"Do you think Pop's leg is in heaven?"

I had never allowed myself to think about where my father's severed leg had gone. I wiped my eyes and kissed the top of Austin's head and said, "Yeah, it's probably waiting for him in heaven."

And now Austin was a young man running ahead of me, and I worried about what else he'd just read in that memoir of mine— about how absent my father became after my parents split up, about how gone he was. My sweat was burning my eyes and I wished then that I'd talked Austin out of reading that book, this little boy whose grandfather was *not* absent for him.

For the rest of the day and into the night, my oldest son said nothing—not when we swam in the lake, not after our showers, not when I grilled barbecued chickens and we drank cold beer, not when we all went out in our rented motorboat to watch the sun set in rose and purple strips over the black hills, a blanket of stars swelling to the east.

But an hour or so later, as we all sat around the fire talking and laughing and roasting marshmallows we then slathered onto squares of graham crackers and chocolate, Austin got up and went into the cabin to use the bathroom. A few minutes later, I followed. Maybe I did this to refresh my mother's bourbon or my sister's rum drink or my own. Or maybe I just couldn't bear the silence any longer, I don't know. But I was walking into the cabin just as Austin was leaving the bathroom, his broad shoulders silhouetted in the light of the gas lamp behind him.

He looked at me and I looked at him, and then he stepped toward me and wrapped his arms around me and I could hardly get my own arms around him, this grown man who had been a baby only months earlier, it seemed, one who had now lived through the dark struggles of my childhood and young manhood.

"Dad, you fractured a guy's *fore*head."

I had, a man who'd been beating up a much smaller man, one who'd been begging him to stop. This had happened thirty years earlier, but it was as if those two men were now in that small hot cabin with me and my son. "Is that okay, Austin? You don't think I'm crazy?"

"No, but Dad." We let go of one another, and I looked up into my son's shadowed face.

"Yeah?"

"I could never write a memoir."

"Yes you could. You're a wonderful writer. Of course you can."

"No, you don't understand. I have nothing to write about. You and Mom gave us too happy a childhood. We weren't raised with any conflicts."

I don't remember what I said to this, only that I felt deeply moved and grateful, and I hugged my son again before we went back outside to the burning fire and the warm circle of our family.

———

IT WAS A HOT DAY IN MID-AUGUST, THE SKY CLEAR AND BLUE. FOR the six-hour trip west, I drove the U-Haul while Fontaine and Austin followed close behind in Fontaine's packed Honda. Ariadne had gone ahead in her own car with her boyfriend of five years, Bruce, a warm and loving young man who is not threatened by her power and treats her with consistent respect.

For years now I have been listening to audiobooks whenever I drive anywhere. But because I read fiction every night and all morning long on Sundays, I only listen to history books, mainly the history of the United States, a country whose origin story is steeped in blood and hope, in cruelty and desire, in racism and genocide, in beauty and despair, its deeply flawed texture one I recognize as one of its many flawed citizens.

On that summer afternoon moving Ariadne to the rolling hills of upstate New York, I listened to a book on George Washington. For hours I heard descriptions of his rural childhood and his time serving in the British army throughout the French and Indian War, of how he became a planter unhappy with the profit-killing policies of the British, which began to draw him into political action. As I kept listening, it soon became clear that this was, in most ways, a human being no different from the rest of us, one hungry for experience and the chance to thrive, one capable of seeing rising injustice against others but through a lens of deep self-interest, one who sometimes and then more often, in Washington's case, could rise above his own narrow desires in service to the greater good. Though our first president would own slaves too.

Only an hour from my daughter's new life, I pulled into a gas station and drove the U-Haul to the pumps. Fontaine and Austin parked in front of the convenience store, and I could feel that the resonant power of the past had put me in a plaintive state of mind; it was hard not to feel that we human beings had evolved little in the past 240 years, that each generation born would have to truly fight to keep the democracy that Washington—as fallible a man as he was—had helped to found, and that that orange-haired man currently in the White House on that August afternoon had already done more to dismantle it than any foreign foe we'd ever had.

And so maybe it was these thoughts, combined with my being hungry and thirsty, that put me in a less than polite mood when I pulled on my mask and walked into the gas station's convenience store.

My wife and son had used the bathroom and were now buying bottles of water. Behind the register was a masked woman with a name tag pinned on her smock, and to the left of her was a Subway sandwich shop whose trays of sliced turkey and chopped lettuce and tomatoes called to me. There was no one behind the counter, so I waited. Austin walked over with his bottle of water. I asked him if he wanted anything and he said maybe.

We waited another minute or so and then a young man emerged from the back room. He was in a black mask, Subway shirt and apron. I said hello and was about to give him my order, but he didn't even glance up at us. He just grabbed an empty metal bin from its place beside chopped peppers, then disappeared. All through my twenties, I'd worked as a bartender, and I could see that this kid wanted to restock some of his food and that us being here in front of him now was not convenient. I remembered the frustration of moments like this, and I also remembered having to constantly put the customer first, no matter how I felt, to turn to him or her and smile.

He was gone another few minutes. I was shaking my head and Austin lost interest and walked over to where Fontaine was thumbing through a rack of mixed nuts. But I hadn't eaten in hours and so I waited, and when the kid finally came back with his bin full of sliced black olives, I said hi again and was about to place my order, but he still said nothing and gave me no eye contact as he put his olives where they belonged, then scanned his work area for other items to restock.

I said, "Are you guys open?"

His eyes were on a bin of sliced cheese. Without answering me, he reached for that bin, and I said, "Screw you. You don't deserve my business."

My anger was a hot tautness in my jaw, and I was surprised by how deeply its roots seemed to go. I felt instant remorse for that lapse, especially in front of my grown son. But a man standing at the register in front of my wife was already yelling and swearing at me. "Hey, fuck you! You don't talk to the fuckin' help like that! You give him some fuckin' respect, motherfucker. Who the fuck are you to talk to him like that, you piece of shit?!"

He was a white man, an inch or two taller than I was. Maybe he was in a tank top, maybe a T-shirt. Maybe he wore a mask or maybe he didn't. Maybe he was buying a Mountain Dew or cigarettes. I don't know, but my body had gone still and loose, and the thing is I agreed with him. Even though that kid was terrible at his job, I shouldn't have said that to him, not *screw you* anyway. But the man doing the calling out was far more angry than what I'd said should have triggered, and it was as if I'd been walking barefoot through the woods only to step on a hungry copperhead.

From behind my mask, I said something like I'd been respectful to that young man, though I knew I hadn't been, and now I was standing slightly in front of Fontaine in case this guy started swinging, for he seemed to be getting only angrier and louder, spewing one profanity after another. The Subway employee rushed over and said, "Chris, it's okay. Chris, don't worry about it." But Chris just shrugged him off and kept yelling in my face. I could feel my big son off to my left, Fontaine to my right, and the lady behind the counter seemed to go pale behind her mask.

Then a man was standing in line with what looked like his five- or six-year-old son. Chris's torso was leaning toward me, his chin pointed at me, and it was time for something else to happen to change what was happening. I said, "Why don't you watch your language in front of the kid?"

"Well if you don't like it you can suck my dick!"

It was beyond clear that this man wanted nothing more than for me to swing at him. How easy that would have been. How good it would have felt.

Over the cashier woman's shoulder was a camera screwed to the wall, and I could feel the weight of law enforcement and of impending lawsuits, of months or years of potentially one hardship after another. I had a home I could lose, children who still needed my help, a few relatives too.

The man was still yelling, still swearing, his friend in his Subway apron still trying to calm him down. I took a breath and stepped back. "That's it. I've had enough of you." Which made him swear louder, raising his hand and pointing at me as if I was everything wrong with this world. Fontaine and Austin left the store then, and I should have left then too, but I did not. Instead, I walked slowly down the aisle of snacks looking for a bag of nuts or some beef jerky, maybe a bottle of water.

Reaching for a package of peanut butter crackers, my hand was steady, very little adrenaline flaring through me. Since I was a young man I'd been daily and nightly waiting for moments like this one to appear, and when it came a certain calm descended on me, an aligning of what I expected the world to be with what it truly was.

But I was not proud of the time I was taking now. I did not feel good about needing that man to know that he had not scared me away, nor could he. Unless he had a gun, which he could very well have in his car out there in the parking lot. And hot shame began to rise up my cheeks that here I was, entering the sixth decade of my life, and I was still being influenced by a terrified fourteen-year-old boy living inside me, one who had my name and younger face.

The door slammed as Chris left. I carried my snack and bottle of water to the cashier. Her mask had slipped off her nose and I could see the gray roots of her hair. She said, "I'm so sorry about that, sir."

I did not feel as if I'd earned the respect she was giving me. My *screw you* had started this. Then my wife was beside me saying, "Honey, he's still out there. Don't do anything."

"I won't."

Fontaine went back outside, and I paid for my crackers and water and thanked the pale woman behind the register, thinking how out of proportion to my words Chris's rage had been. We were in the sixth month of the pandemic, people out of work, men and women losing their homes, thousands of us dying. As I stepped out onto the asphalt under the sun, Chris was sitting sideways behind the wheel of his beat-up sedan, his driver's-side door wide open, smoking a cigarette while talking loudly to his friend in the Subway apron.

"And then I gotta deal with this fuckin' asshole."

Me, of course, the man walking slowly with his crackers and water to his rented truck. I glanced back at Chris and saw a chubby little boy on the passenger side. He was standing on the seat eating from a bag of potato chips, and as I nodded at Fontaine and Austin watching me from the idling Honda, it was hard to imagine that that boy had not regularly witnessed his father's rage. Maybe experienced it firsthand. And as I took my time climbing back into the driver's seat of the U-Haul, I thought of these two fathers—me and this Chris—and what bad examples of manhood we were putting on display to our sons.

Yes, it was the other man who'd exploded, but it was I who'd said *screw you*, and it was I who'd told Chris to watch his language, because I was really hoping he would swing at me and the cameras could record who swung first, and then I could—*what?* I could justify to myself and the law what I would then have free rein to do.

Driving away from the gas pumps, I glanced back at the sedan. Both men were smoking and seemed to be in a conversation that had little to do with whatever had just happened inside that store. The little boy was standing in the backseat now, staring at me through the rear window, his hand deep in that bag of potato chips as he watched me and the big truck drive away.

I thought of my own kids at that age. How small their bodies were and how open their minds, how they took in everything and missed nothing. And as I accelerated behind Fontaine's car as we hit the highway, I put on George Washington's story again, but I wasn't listening because I was looking at the back of my oldest son's head as he sat there beside his mother. I was remembering the few stories he'd told me of stepping into fistfights when he was in college in Ohio. But only to break them up. I asked him how he did this, and he said he'd just hug them. He'd just grab whoever was swinging his fists, then hold him tight. Talking to him. Maybe even trying to get him to laugh.

Both my sons had become peacemakers. They had no terrified boys living inside them. They had no lingering need to show to themselves that they would never be made anyone's victim ever again. And so this made them truly peaceful men. Unlike their father, who had lived peacefully for decades yet still carried the embers of raging fires inside him. And as I listened to tales of Washington and Hamilton trying to outmaneuver one another, it was hard not to see the roots of so much human suffering throughout the ages as coming solely from men. This was not an original thought, of course, but never before had I included myself in this kind of company. But I did now. I sure as hell did.

———

AND THEN I WAS PARKING THE U-HAUL IN FRONT OF ARIADNE'S apartment building. It was brand new and five stories of steel, concrete, and glass. She and her boyfriend had gotten here an hour or two earlier, and as she propped open the front doors for us, her hair tied back, she looked flushed and happy. She hugged her brother and mother and me, and I said, "You like your new place? Is it nice?"

"Yeah, I'll show you. But Dad, c'mere."

I followed her into the air-conditioned lobby. Its floors were polished concrete, and brightly colored chairs were arranged around a low table, and there were hanging pendant lights and a mounted bookshelf full of hardcovers.

"Dad, look." Ariadne reached up to a shelf and pulled out my memoir, my story of that hurt, scared, and raging boy. It's a book she started but couldn't finish because it made her too sad; she said she could not bear to witness any suffering I might have gone through as a boy. "Isn't this weird, Dad?"

I may have said something about it being a sign that you're in the right place, or something like that, but as I hugged my daughter, then walked back to the U-Haul, it felt like another kind of sign altogether, that what we put out into this world always comes back to us in one form or another: All my life I've told myself that I hate cruelty and injustice and violence, and I do, that I want the world to be free of them, and I do, but how can we be free of anything if we're still sheltering old wounds inside us? The kind that keeps our hands up, our backs to the wall, our eyes scanning the room for danger at every turn? How can anything larger and better and more loving ever enter us unless we lower our hands?

I grip the sun-warmed handle of the U-Haul's rear door and yank upward. It's locked and does not move. I take a breath. So many simple things to be learned over and over again. I shake my head, unhook the latch, then pull. The door slides easily up its tracks, and Austin is beside me now. Part of me wants to say something to him about what happened back at that gas station, about my obvious role in it, about my secret desire for that man to swing at me. But my wanting to do this feels like a lifelong weakness whose time has long been up, and as my son grabs the end of the ramp and begins to pull it free, it is clear that *he* is free, free of so much of the ugliness that has shaped me and that I no longer wish to express in any way.

The sun is directly on us. There are the smells of soft asphalt and the cardboard boxes holding all my daughter's possessions inside this big truck. I'm thirsty but will drink later, for now my son and I are both lowering the ramp and climbing into the hot darkness where together we begin to lift and to carry, where we use our hands not to hurt but to help.

Please, forevermore, only to help.

ACKNOWLEDGMENTS

I would like to thank my literary agent, Anne-Lise Spitzer, as well as Lukas Ortiz and Kim Lombardini. And I am particularly grateful to my Norton family: my longtime editor, Alane Salierno Mason, and her assistant, Mo Crist; my publicist, Rachel Salzman, as well as Meredith McGinnis, Gina Savoy, Don Rifkin, Elisabeth Kerr, Steven Pace, and Amy Robbins.

CREDITS

"Fences and Fields," *Hope Magazine,* 1998. (Reprinted in *The Best Spiritual Writing of 1999,* Harpers/San Francisco.)

"The Golden Zone," *Vice,* September 2014.

"The Land of No," *New Republic,* February 2012. (Reprinted in *The Writer's Presence,* Bedford/St. Martin's Press.)

"Blood, Root, Knit, Purl," *Knitting Yarns: Writers on Knitting,* W. W. Norton & Co., Inc.

"Carver and Dubus, New York City, 1988," *Carve,* an online publication. (Reprinted in *Five Points: A Journal of Literature and Art,* Spring 2016; Honorable Mention, *Pushcart Prize XXXVIII: Best of the Small Presses, 2014,* Pushcart Press.)

"Falling," *Guernica,* 2016. (Reprinted in *The Kiss: Intimacies by Writers,* W. W. Norton & Co.)

"The Door," *When I First Held You: Great Writers Reflect on Fatherhood*, Berkley Books/Penguin. (Excerpt reprinted in *Parade Magazine*, February 2021, and in *Heart of a Man: Men's Stories for Women*, Vineyard Press.)

"Shelter," *Wall Street Journal*, January 2013.

"If I Owned a Gun," *Narrative*, online publication, Fall 2018. (Selected for "Notable Essays and Literary Non-fiction 2019," *The Best American Essays 2019*, Houghton Mifflin Harcourt.)

"Beneath," *Virginia Quarterly Review*, 2015.

"High Life" (published as "The Lows of the High Life"), *The New Yorker*, June 2023.

"Risk," written for the PEN/Faulkner Awards ceremony but unpublished.

"A Letter to My Two Sons on Love" (published as "How My Rage Surrendered to Love"), *Fatherly*, online publication, February 2019.

"Vigilance and Surrender," *Alone Together: Love, Grief, and Comfort During the Time of Covid-19*, Central Avenue Publishing.

"Mary," *UMass Lowell Alumni Magazine*, Spring 2021.

"Ghost Dogs," *The Sun*, Fall 2021. (Selected for "Notable Essays and Literary Non-fiction 2021," *The Best American Essays 2022*, Houghton Mifflin Harcourt; Pushcart Prize Special Mention, Fall 2022.)

"Pappy," *River Teeth: A Journal of Nonfiction Narrative*, Spring 2022. (Selected for "Notable Essays and Literary Non-fiction 2022," *The Best American Essays 2023*, Houghton Mifflin Harcourt; nomination for the Pushcart Prize, December 2022.)

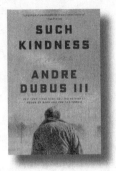 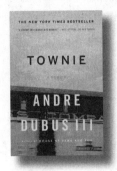
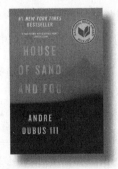